THE PSYCHOLOGY OF INNOVATION IN ORGANIZATIONS

In today's highly competitive market, organizations increasingly need to innovate in order to survive. Drawing on a wealth of psychological research in the field of creativity, David H. Cropley and Arthur J. Cropley illustrate practical methods for conceptualizing and managing organizational innovation. They present a dynamic model of the interactions among four key components of creativity – product, person, process, and press – that function as building blocks of innovation. This volume sheds new light on the nature of innovative products and the processes that generate them, the psychological characteristics of innovative people, and the environments that facilitate innovation. It also fills a significant gap in the current literature by addressing the paradoxical quality of organizational innovation, which may be both helped and hindered by the same factors. The authors demonstrate that, with proper measurement and management, organizations can effectively encourage individuals to produce and take advantage of novel ideas.

David H. Cropley is Associate Professor of Engineering Innovation at the University of South Australia. His publications include *Creativity and Crime: A Psychological Analysis* (with Arthur J. Cropley), *The Dark Side of Creativity* (with Arthur J. Cropley, James C. Kaufman, and Mark A. Runco), and *Creativity in Engineering: Novel Solutions to Complex Problems.*

Arthur J. Cropley is Emeritus Professor of Educational Psychology at the University of Hamburg. He was the founding editor of the *European Journal of High Ability* (currently known as *High Ability Studies*), and he is the author or editor of twenty-eight books that have been widely translated.

The Psychology of Innovation in Organizations

David H. Cropley
University of South Australia

Arthur J. Cropley
University of Hamburg

CAMBRIDGE
UNIVERSITY PRESS

CAMBRIDGE
UNIVERSITY PRESS

32 Avenue of the Americas, New York, NY 10013-2473, USA

Cambridge University Press is part of the University of Cambridge.

It furthers the University's mission by disseminating knowledge in the pursuit of education, learning, and research at the highest international levels of excellence.

www.cambridge.org
Information on this title: www.cambridge.org/9781107459175

First published 2015

Printed in the United States of America

A catalog record for this publication is available from the British Library.

Library of Congress Cataloging in Publication Data
Cropley, David.
The psychology of innovation in organizations / David H. Cropley, University of South Australia, Arthur J. Cropley, University of Hamburg.
pages cm
Includes bibliographical references and index.
ISBN 978-1-107-08839-9 (alk. paper)
1. Creative ability in business. 2. Organizational change. I. Cropley, A. J. II. Title.
HD53.C76 2015
658.4′063019–dc23 2015014017

ISBN 978-1-107-08839-9 Hardback
ISBN 978-1-107-45917-5 Paperback

Innovation is creativity with a job to do.

John Emmerling, Innovation Consultant

Everybody believes in innovation until they see it. Then they think, "Oh, no; that'll never work. It's too different."

Nolan Bushnell, Engineer and Founder of Atari

Innovation and best practices can be sown throughout an organization – but only when they fall on fertile ground.

Marcus Buckingham, Business Consultant and Author

CONTENTS

TABLES

FIGURES

PREFACE

"Innovate or die" is the catchphrase for commercial organizations today, but the necessary discussion about innovation is hampered by the absence of a comprehensive set of concepts for conceptualizing the issues and terms for a systematic discussion of it. This book offers a reorientation: on the one hand, a switch of attention away from properties and processes in organizations to a focus on human actors; on the other hand, a turn to psychological research on creativity to work out the necessary conceptual framework. The use of creativity research to cast light on organizational issues leads to some looseness in distinguishing between creativity and innovation, but tolerance of fuzzy boundaries is a core aspect of both domains.

The book deconstructs the traditional four Ps approach to creativity by dividing the P of person into three domains: personal motivation, personal feelings/attitudes, personal attributes. Each domain is characterized by various behavioral dispositions, such as a disposition to react to a problem by generating novelty versus a disposition to fix what already exists. These behavioral dispositions are seen in this book not as static properties that people either possess or do not, but as styles or even habits that provide favorable (or unfavorable) personal prerequisites for innovation and can be learned or developed with the help of, among other things, appropriate leadership from managers. Thus, this book provides highly differentiated insights into best leadership practice in guiding and developing the disposition to innovate in individual members of an organization. In addition, the traditional P of product is made more specific to innovation by applying the usefulness imperative: In the case of innovation, products must display commercial salience. The result is, in effect, a Six Ps model of innovation, although the six elements are referred to in this book as the building blocks of innovation.

The analysis deals with the paradoxes of innovation (such as simultaneous calls for innovation and rejection of innovation) in the society as a whole, in the organizational environment, and within individual people, as well as conflicting conclusions about what kinds of action promote innovation. This is done by dividing the process of generation and implementation of novelty into phases and working out the relationship between the building blocks and the phases. This approach shows, for example, that the effects of an aspect of the organizational environment, such as leadership style, or of a particular kind of thinking or motivation within the human actors differ at different points in the innovation process (that is, they are not static but dynamic); thus, they yield a proactive and dynamic model of the interactions among the various components of the overall system of innovation within the various environments in which it is embedded.

The book's closing chapters introduce the innovation phase model (IPM) of innovation and the innovation phase assessment instrument (IPAI) – both derived from the psychological analysis of innovation in organizations presented in earlier chapters. Taken together, these make it possible to work out tailor-made guidelines for promoting and managing innovation that fit the specific needs of particular organizations with their widely differing goals and vastly different areas of strength and weakness.

ACKNOWLEDGMENTS

I would like to thank my academic colleagues in creativity and innovation, spread around the world, for their enthusiasm and support. They make this a stimulating field in which to work. I would also like to thank business colleagues in Australia, Norway, and the United States who have begun collaborating on the implementation of the innovation phase assessment instrument (IPAI). I hope that we will all be able to look back, one day, and see what we contributed to an enduring instrument that is helping organizations to become truly innovative. I would also like to thank, as always, my family – Melissa, Matthew, Dana, and Daniel – for their active support and patience. Finally, to my co-author Arthur, thanks for waiting for me to catch up.

DHC

1

Understanding Innovation: A Reorientation

The acuteness of organizations' need for innovation was expressed by Buzan (2007, p. vii) when he concluded that "right now any individual, company or country wishing to *survive* in the twenty-first century *must* . . . *innovate*" (emphasis added). The purpose of this book is to present a broadened perspective on how organizations can become more potent in innovating. This will be achieved by (a) developing a more differentiated understanding of the nature of innovative products (Chapter 2); (b) analyzing the thinking processes through which such products are generated (Chapter 3); (c) identifying the key psychological resources (attitudes, values, motives, and the like) of individual people who carry out these processes (Chapter 4); (d) analyzing the external and internal environments within which the processes occur, the personal resources are applied, and the products are produced; and (e) working out the implications of this material for innovation management.

THE NEED FOR INNOVATION IN ORGANIZATIONS

Awareness of the need for organizations to innovate is by no means new, and the issue has been receiving substantial attention for many years. More than a quarter of a century ago, Van de Ven (e.g., 1986) was already reporting that managing innovation had become a central concern of CEOs. Early this century, Walton (2003) showed that 80 percent of managers he surveyed regarded creativity as vital for corporate success, and the 2010 IBM Report (IBM, 2010) concluded that creativity had become the chief concern of CEOs by then. Anderson, Potocnik, and Zhou (2014) confirmed that scholarly and professional discussions have experienced massive growth in interest in the topic in the last decade, both in the

English-speaking world and internationally. In fact, over the years, the call for innovation has reached life and death proportions, with Freeman and Soete (1997, p. 266) concluding that "not to innovate is to *die*" (emphasis added), and the slogan "innovate or die" has become an established catchphrase in the current literature (e.g., Collis, 2010; Kriekels, 2013).

An example of the failure to innovate leading to corporate death can be seen in the fate of Smith Corona, whose core product – the typewriter – was annihilated by the introduction of the word processor, not because of flaws in Smith Corona's typewriter technology (which had been improved constantly and effectively by the company over the preceding decades by means of incremental change) but because the technology itself had become irrelevant in a digital word-processing world. Hamel (1996, p. 69) came to the amusingly stated but nonetheless dramatic and easily understandable conclusion that "pursuing incremental improvement while rivals reinvent the industry is like fiddling while Rome burns."

Knapper and Cropley (2000) conceptualized the overarching problem societies are facing as the need to *deal with change*. Organizations are confronted by discontinuous change in many domains, including but going beyond the technological. Among other things, changes are affecting production, distribution, and marketing; are reducing the length of product lifecycles; are causing new and intensified demands from customers, increasing competition and the threat of becoming uncompetitive; expanding globalization; imposing unstable economic conditions; changing supply chains; increasing the urgency of calls for sustainable production; accelerating degradation of the environment; leading to diversification of the workforce; and raising pressure for fair and equitable working conditions. According to Barreto (2012, p. 356), organizations are now confronted with massive changes that cause shocks, either exogenous shocks imposed on the organization by powerful external forces such as market changes, technological advances, or regulatory pressures, or endogenous shocks arising from emerging awareness of inadequacies in the status quo in an organization and growing dissatisfaction with it. Organizations must cope by means of innovation.

The Benefits of Change

Nussbaum (2013, p. 38) argued that the bright side of change from the point of view of organizations is that it is causing "unmet needs" in society, and that innovative organizations can meet these needs to their own advantage. Cohen (2010) gave concrete, practical examples of highly beneficial innovations that have had such effects, including Citibank's introduction of ATMs, and Sony's introduction of the compact disc. Cohen went beyond conceptualizing innovation as a general life-saving force and listed some of the more specific benefits it brings, which in turn lead to the broad benefits of growth and increased profits just mentioned: for example, *obtaining competitive advantage* and *increasing revenue*. Kleinknecht and Mohnen (2001) mentioned improved *export performance*; Yamin, Gunasekaran, and Mavondo (1999) put the emphasis squarely on concrete bottom-line outcomes by concluding that innovation leads to *greater profitability*. Adopting a more process-oriented approach, Miller (1983) argued that an innovative organization is good at "*beating competitors to the punch*"; and Chan and Thomas (2013, p. 1) concluded that innovation adds to "commercial *competitiveness*" and gives organizations "*a competitive edge*"; while Anderson, Potocnik, and Zhou (2014, p. 3) referred to its ability to provide a "*competitive advantage*."[1]

Although they warned that innovation also involves substantial risks, in a meta-analysis, Rosenbusch, Brinckmann, and Bausch (2011, p. 445) identified both tangible benefits, such as new products, services, or production processes, and more process-oriented benefits, such as increased productivity, greater employee satisfaction, greater employee commitment, reduced staff turnover, and greater attractiveness to potential investors. Mumford, Hester, and Robledo (2012, p. 8) also pointed to a range of more indirect organizational benefits (i.e., benefits not referring directly to the bottom line but to factors that mediate success on the bottom line) that have been linked to innovation. These factors include *ability to respond to a crisis* and improved *teamwork, collaboration, and organizational citizenship*. Mumford, Bedell-Avers, and Hunter (2008) listed *improved planning processes*, and Amabile, Schatzel, Moneta, and Kramer (2004) mentioned *a more satisfied and intrinsically oriented workforce*. Thus, the benefits of innovation are not confined to the direct production, implementation, and marketing of new products, as desirable as these are, but also involve factors such as the general atmosphere in an organization, staff motivation, or job satisfaction.[2] These aspects will be referred to as press later in this book (e.g., Chapter 5).

[1] In all of these examples, the emphasis given to the italicized words has been added by the present authors.

[2] Benefits of this kind are not confined to organizations involved in commercial activity. A. J. Cropley (2012) reviewed the effects of "creative" teaching methods on the classroom workforce (pupils) and reported analogous benefits such as improved motivation, better concentration, reduced absenteeism, and decreased incidence of disruptive behavior.

TABLE 1.1. *Examples of Specific Benefits of Innovation for Organizations*

Outcome Benefits	Process Benefits
• Increased productivity	• Better response to crises
• Competitive advantage	• Improved planning
• Increased demand	• A more satisfied workforce
• Improved export performance	• A more intrinsically motivated workface
• Increased revenue	• Better teamwork and collaboration
• Greater profitability	• Improved organizational citizenship
• Improved ability to attract investors	• Reduced staff turnover
• Greater ability to attract high-quality staff	

The benefits that have been reported as accruing from greater creativity and innovation are summarized in Table 1.1. This table is not intended as an exhaustive list of all possible organizational benefits associated with innovation but as an indication of the kind of thing organizational writers have discussed. The outcome benefits are purely commercial and global in nature. The process benefits involve psychologically oriented concepts such as intrinsic motivation, to be sure, but they are also global in nature. Later in the book, some of these outcomes and processes will be examined in a more psychological way, and the dynamic relationship between the two domains will be spelled out in a more differentiated manner.[3]

CONCEPTUALIZING INNOVATION

Some writers (e.g., Read, 2000) have complained that innovation in organizations is discussed in such diverse terms that its meaning is difficult to grasp. It is true that in the organizational literature *innovation* refers both to (a) a novel *product* such as a new device, service, or procedure and (b) the *process* through which such products are devised, brought into existence, brought to market, or put into practice. The OECD guidelines (OECD, 2005, p. 46) define *organizational innovation* in a two-track way, as involving "a new or significantly improved *product* (good or service), *process*, new marketing method or a new organizational method in business practices, workplace organization or external relations" (emphasis

[3] An example of a more differentiated, noncommercial, psychological outcome benefit would be "an increased number of effective and novel ideas."

added). Bledow, Frese, Anderson, Erez, and Farr (2009a, p. 305) defined it in *process* terms as "the development and intentional introduction of new and useful ideas." Dillon, Lee, and Matheson (2005) and Kim and Mauborgne (2004) made the idea of usefulness clearer by referring to "value innovation," which focuses on customers, conceptualizing innovation as a process through which organizations find novel and effective products that serve their current customers and identify new markets. Thus, organizational innovation is typically regarded as having two elements: the process component and the product component. The products will frequently be referred to here as solutions because they often involve the meeting of previously unmet needs in societies (Nussbaum, 2013, p. 38) or the solving of social and organizational problems such as those outlined above.

Incremental Versus Disruptive Innovation

An important consideration in this context is the distinction made by Christensen (1997) between incremental innovation and disruptive innovation.[4] Leifer, McDermott, O'Connor, and Peters (2000) made a similar distinction by referring to radical innovation. As Miron-Spektor, Erez, and Naveh (2011, p. 740) put it: "Innovation can vary from an incremental extension of current organizational capabilities to a radical one." In addition to being referred to as radical or disruptive, the latter kind of innovation is also called breakthrough (e.g., Mascitelli, 2000) or discontinuous (e.g., Veryzer, 1998). Luecke and Katz (2003) defined two forms of innovation: incremental (exploiting "*existing* forms or technologies" [emphasis added]), and radical or disruptive, defined as "*a departure from* existing technology or methods" (emphasis added). These two forms of innovation correspond to a considerable degree to Pink's (2005) distinction between information (building on existing knowledge) and conceptualization (seeing things in a novel way).

The crucial point is that incremental innovation is merely sustaining (e.g., Light, 1998) or evolving (e.g., Veryzer, 1998). It involves further developing, polishing, or expanding *already existing* forms or technologies. Radical or disruptive innovation, by contrast, involves a decisive, probably sudden and nonlinear *departure* from what already exists. Horibe (2009) used the metaphor of getting rid of mice; the classical approach is

[4] We will argue in Chapter 4 that this distinction greatly aids understanding the differences between older members of organizations (e.g., managers) and younger colleagues.

encapsulated in the traditional saying: "Build a better mousetrap and the world will beat a path to your door." This involves incremental innovation because it is based on improving what already exists by making the known solution – a mouse trap – better. Disruptive or radical innovation, by contrast, would involve a completely new approach – a novel line of attack that might well make the old technology irrelevant; thus, improving it would then be of little use, as Smith Corona discovered. As an amusing, impracticable example of a radically new approach, Horibe suggested using supersonic waves to beam the mice back to where they originally came from.

An example can be taken from the automobile industry. Although hailed in some quarters as a major innovation, the hybrid car is still a rectangular box with a wheel at each corner. Thus, it represents only incremental changes in the known way of transporting goods and people. Firing people into the air to hang in space while the earth turned below them so that they landed at a distance from their starting position would involve a new paradigm and would thus represent radical innovation, even if currently impossible to implement. A. J. Cropley (2006) and D. H. Cropley and Cropley (2005) pointed out that highly effective sustaining innovation is possible by means of conventional thinking alone (see also the discussion of product in Chapter 2), so that of necessity the main focus of interest in this book is on disruptive, radical, breakthrough innovation, although the value of incremental or sustaining innovation is not denied.

Business-Oriented Models of Innovation

A. J. Cropley and Cropley (2009) reviewed traditional innovation research and showed that it frequently focuses on economic factors and concepts or on structural factors such as the trajectory that innovations follow, where in the innovation process idea generation and opportunity recognition occur, the degree of formality and linearity of the process, the organizational structures that support the process, and the resources and competencies required (e.g., Leifer et al., 2000); skills, strategy, structure, systems, style, staff, and shared values (e.g., Higgins, 1995); or resources, processes, and values (RPV) (e.g., Christensen, Anthony, & Roth, 2004).

Herzog (2008) reviewed a number of more recent models of innovation in business and organizations, and he and Bledow et al. (2009a) drew attention to aspects of the organizational environment such as a shared vision, innovative organizational culture, emphasis on exploration rather than exploitation, investment in R&D, team diversity, task-related conflict, and rewards. However, even these models have continued to see innovation as explained by *structural and process-related aspects of the organizational environment.* A. J. Cropley and Cropley (2009) summarized these models as: (a) attributing innovation to rational, economic push and pull factors; (b) regarding it as arising from continuous but unpredictable change and adaptation; (c) attributing it to the work of forward-looking management; or (d) seeing it as depending mainly on knowledge and skills.

Even where conventional, traditional models of organizational innovation refer to noncognitive psychological factors (for instance, motivation or tolerance for uncertainty), these are looked at more from the point of view of the organization (e.g., the flexibility of institutional goals, the openness of organizational climate, the pattern of rewards provided by the organization). A good example can be seen in the contribution of Bledow et al. (2009a; see, for instance, their Table 1). They examine psychological factors in terms of the individual, the team, and the organization and in relation to their function as antecedents, processes, and outcomes associated with innovation. Although it is true that these authors refer to the individual and to personal properties that are frequently discussed in psychological research (e.g., divergent vs. convergent thinking or openness to experience), Bledow et al. (2009a) discuss such variables mainly in terms of the organization's structure and function, and little emphasis is placed on psychological processes within the individual actor or on personal properties of the actor.

According to D. H. Cropley and Cropley (2014, p. 25), from a psychological point of view, business-oriented descriptive frameworks for studying organizational innovation are of limited value because they do not adequately address:

- The psychological resources of the individual person that contribute to the process of innovation.
- The organizational factors that have an impact on these psychological resources.
- The role of the individual in the detailed steps involved in the innovation process.
- The manner in which the importance of certain psychological factors changes during the innovation process.

The purpose of this book is to expand existing perspectives by applying psychological concepts to examining the:

- products that innovation yields
- thinking processes within individual people that generate the ideas that give rise to such products
- values, attitudes, motives, and the like, of human actors that affect the way they carry out the processes and develop the products

As Read (2000, p. 106) stated clearly: "The encouragement of innovation is a *management function*" (emphasis added), so that the final element in the expansion of perspectives involves the forms of management that encourage people to be innovative (or inhibit them from doing so). This area is intimately linked to what is often referred to as innovation management, and indeed the ultimate purpose of this analysis is to provide managers with a tool for understanding and promoting the introduction of beneficial change into their organizations.

A SHIFT IN EMPHASIS

Innovation does not occur in a vacuum but is embedded in a system. This system is frequently conceptualized as involving levels, but in this book we treat it as encompassing three interacting environments. It is true that the elements of the system differ quantitatively, as the term *levels* implies. For example, one element involves the entire external world; another, an individual person. In addition, the relationship among the elements of the system is hierarchical, with the individual person, for instance, being both an independent element of the system but also simultaneously a unit contained within the society at large. For the purposes of this book, however, the most important differences among the various elements of the system are *qualitative* not quantitative; what is important is the *kind* of thing that happens in a particular element of the system, not how large it is. For this reason, these elements are referred to here as environments. The external world outside the organization that, for commercial organizations often means customers, constitutes the social environment; the organization itself defines the organizational environment; and the individual person functioning within an organization constitutes the personal environment. The person is an environment in the sense that psychological processes such as thinking take place within the person. The interrelationship of these environments is shown in Figure 1.1.

Barreto (2012, p. 356) argued that organizations typically try to deal with modern pressures by focusing on the social and organizational environments and *improving what they already do*. This often means, for instance,

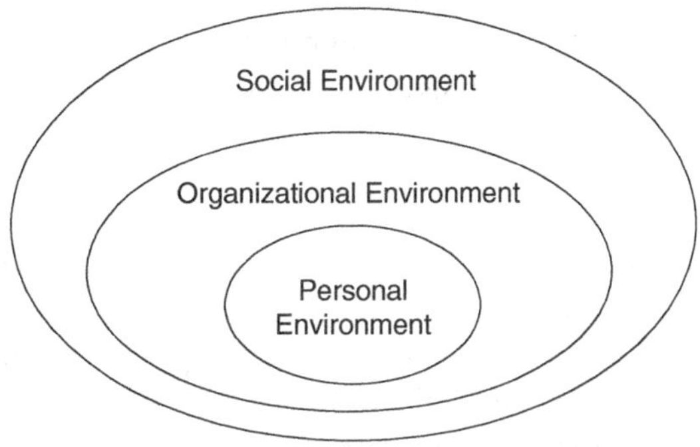

FIGURE 1.1. The Interrelationship of Environments

"squeezing another penny out of costs, getting a product to market a few weeks earlier, responding to customers' inquiries a little bit faster, ratcheting quality up one more notch" (Hamel, 1996, p. 69). More recently, Nussbaum (2013, p. 234) made a similar point when he complained that organizations are still trying to drive profit mainly "through efficiency, outsourcing and cost-cutting"; the result is that "*creativity and innovation are shunted to the periphery*" (emphasis added).

In a comprehensive review of the organizational literature, Barreto (2012) focused on individual actors (the personal environment), to be sure, but saw their role as mainly a matter of interpretation of information provided by the social and organizational environments in the form of the exogenous or endogenous shocks already mentioned. According to this model, the innovative impulse set in motion by a shock leads either to *identification* of opportunities – which are more or less lying around waiting to be recognized (discovery) - or to *generation* of opportunities through search and action (creation). Barreto thus saw the individual actor as mainly *reacting* when forced to do so by a shock. Looked at in this way, innovation involves little more than identifying and attempting to apply existing but previously neglected possibilities in order to relieve the pressure of the shock.

Nussbaum (2013, p. 38) referred to the reactive approach to innovation just outlined as the old model. By contrast, his new model *starts from* ideas originating in people's "creative intelligence" rather than being imposed from outside. Thus, he adopts a *proactive* approach, which requires that innovation management actively foster the generation of ideas and promote their transformation into valuable products rather than waiting for the external world to impose demands that cannot be ignored and then responding by making changes in the way the organization is run (such as decision-making processes, reward systems, or structure of the workforce) or waiting for internal defects to demand such changes and then reacting to these demands in a last-ditch fight for survival.

Innovative Thinking

Chang and Burkitt (2005) called for examination of the generation and implementation of *ideas* in innovation rather than, for example, acquisition of improved technology for doing familiar things or streamlining already existing processes and systems, thus in effect calling for increased emphasis on the personal environment. In their assessment of the "state of the science," Anderson, Potocnik, and Zhou (2014) also emphasized the importance in organizational innovation of ideas generated by employees. According to Liedtka (1998, p. 120), "traditional processes have *choked* initiative and favored incremental over substantive change. They have emphasized analytics and extrapolation rather than creativity and invention." He called for more attention to be paid to innovative thinking, which he contrasted with strategic thinking. Chapter 3 will examine such thinking more closely.

Smith (2009) gave an example of thinking that was fixated on a particular strategy – that of Polaroid. Their tried and trusted, highly successful strategy was to get cameras into people's hands and make money through rapid provision of hard-copy pictures taken with the cameras. Their tactic for realizing this strategy was to offer a technology for rapid printing (Polaroid film). The firm reacted to the emergence of digital imaging by maintaining its rapid printing strategy and merely seeking to improve the printing technology through which this strategy was implemented: They spent years and substantial amounts of money developing a miniaturized printer that could produce instant hard-copy prints of digital images, much as the Polaroid process had done for photochemical images. Thus, Polaroid innovated by improving what already existed. Unfortunately, digital photographers print very few of the countless pictures they take. Thus, there was no market for the printer, even though it was an effective cog in the – unfortunately outdated – existing strategy of instant hard-copy pictures. Polaroid eventually went into bankruptcy protection.

Personal Resources for Innovation

The idea of innovation as being essentially proactive is not new in the organizational literature. Parker, Williams, and Turner (2006) defined it as "proactive behavior" (p. 636) and then went on to examine the key issue for this section: what they called the antecedents of proactive behavior located within the individual person. They identified "proactive cognitive-*motivational* states" (emphasis added), including especially "role breadth self-efficacy," "control appraisals," "change orientation," and "flexible role orientation" (p. 637). Frese and Fay (2001) focused directly on the individual actor by referring to "personal initiative" (p. 133). Lynch, Walsh. and Harrington (2010) used the term *innovativeness* to refer to this property, and gave "open-mindedness," "willingness to change," and "willingness to engage in risky behavior" (p. 12) as examples of what it involves.

Other writers have also made a similar point but have used different terminology: Williams (2007, p. 34), for instance, identified a property of individual human beings that he called a propensity for entrepreneurship. Rosenbusch, Brinckmann, and Bausch (2011, p. 441) used the term *entrepreneurial orientation* in a similar way and, indeed, this term is widely used in the organizational literature. However, the use of the words *entrepreneurship* or *entrepreneurial* may cause some misunderstanding because, in the organizational literature, these and related terms are used mainly to refer to the foundation of new organizations. To take a single example, even though their discussions in the prestigious *Academy of Management Review* make use of psychological concepts, McMullan and Shepherd's (2006) use of the term entrepreneurship still has a clear orientation toward foundation of new organizations. This focus on new organizations has tended to be the case even in more strongly psychological discussions. For example, Amabile (1997, p. 20) restricted innovative creativity to the special case of creativity applied in order "to establish *a new venture*" (emphasis added), thus focusing on the organizational environment. In this book, by contrast, the emphasis is on the personal environment so that, within this environment, innovation is treated as involving a constellation of psychological resources within individual people that enhance their ability and willingness to generate *commercially* useful products, regardless of whether this involves founding new organizations.

The crucial point for this book is that, in the personal environment, generation and implementation of profitable novelty in organizations are intimately linked to (a) special thinking processes and (b) psychological resources of individual people. The psychological resources can be seen as antecedents of innovative behavior in the form of personal resources that help people involved in innovation to seek and generate proactively novel ways of adding value (Figure 1.2).

Nussbaum (2013) referred to these personal resources as involving creative intelligence, but this book will argue in later sections and in

FIGURE 1.2. Personal, Psychological Resources Drive Innovation

subsequent chapters that, although Nussbaum took a valuable step in the right direction, conceptualizing the personal factors in innovation as a matter of *intelligence* is too narrow. Behaviors such as taking risks, adopting a flexible role orientation, or displaying openness to change go well beyond what is usually understood as intelligence, which, as will be shown in Chapter 3, is more commonly associated with knowing the single best answer, sticking to it, and reapplying it in new situations (i.e., with information rather than reconceptualization).

Although a focus on new knowledge and fresh ideas leads to interest in *the people who have the ideas or acquire the knowledge* rather than physical resources, management methods, work organization, and the like, properties of an organization such as those just mentioned form a set of background conditions that cannot be ignored. They will be referred to in later sections as press (see especially Chapter 5). As O'Shea and Buckley (2007) put it:

> A central issue for organizations who value innovation is how to select, develop, and motivate individuals capable of formulating ideas in the first place, and also to *create the supportive environment* in which groups can productively and swiftly implement them. (emphasis added) (p. 102)

What is needed in order to achieve this is a model for thinking about, understanding, and discussing the nature and interplay of the various factors involved in innovative thinking, including:

(a) administrative, structural, work process-related factors involving the organization itself
(b) interpersonal and intrapersonal factors related to the innovative individual
(c) the ultimate result of the interaction between (a) and (b)

Later chapters will develop a more detailed model of this interaction, which is shown in Figure 1.3.

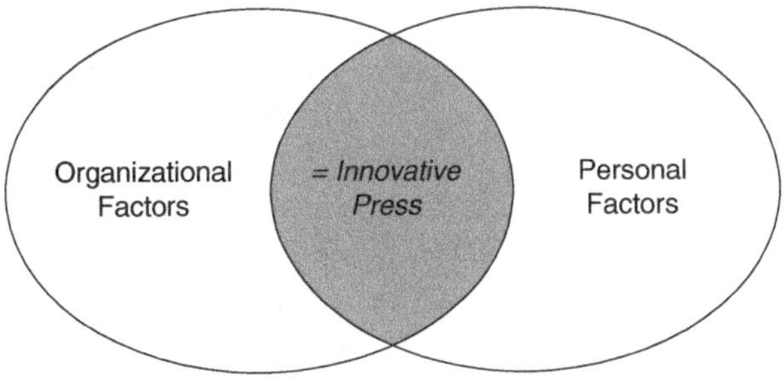

FIGURE 1.3. The Interaction of Factors Defines the Innovative Press

INCORPORATING IDEAS FROM THE PSYCHOLOGY OF CREATIVITY

Although research on organizational innovation has produced major insights about the social and organizational environments, this book is mainly concerned with promoting an understanding of the interaction between personal factors that foster innovation and the managerial actions likely to promote it, that is, between the personal environment and the organizational environment. This raises two key questions:

1. Where can we find the insights needed for developing an understanding of the generation and implementation of ideas?
2. How can such generation and implementation of ideas be fostered?

In a critical review of current research on innovation, Blackburn and Kovalainen (2009) answered the first question by advocating turning to core disciplines such as economics or sociology, and – of central interest for present purposes – psychology to provide a conceptual framework for working out an answer. This book provides such a framework by turning to psychological research. Andriopoulos (2001, p. 834) gave a rather broad hint about where to look in psychological thinking by concluding that:

> ... organizations increasingly aspire to become more *creative* and capitalize on the benefits of *creativity*, and perceive the development of conditions that encourage *creativity* within their working environment [as important] (emphasis added).

Nussbaum (2013) placed the emphasis squarely on creativity: After rejecting the old model, he argued (p. 234) that "we need to switch from efficiency to *creativity* models" (emphasis added).

Creativity and Innovation

The psychological literature on creativity provides major insights into how to promote innovation. This is scarcely surprising: the terms *creativity* and *innovation* are sometimes used almost interchangeably and the link may seem self-evident. After conducting an extensive and intensive review, Anderson, Potocnik, and Zhou (2014) concluded that, although creativity and innovation are not identical, they are definitely related. Ward (2004) went further by concluding that it is legitimate to study the two together and to use similar concepts when discussing either area, or to transfer concepts. Haner (2005, p. 290) specifically concluded that the application of concepts from creativity research to understanding innovation is justified: "Creativity processes and innovation processes are . . . different, but they display common characteristics and patterns that allow for joint reflection." Despite this, O'Shea and Buckley (2007, p. 102) conclude: "While much research has been conducted in both the areas of innovation and creativity, one of the primary problems is that *there has been little integration between the two areas*" (emphasis added). In a recent overview, Chan and Thomas (2013, p. 1) also complained that the "link between creativity and innovation has not received sufficient attention."

In general terms, it has often been argued (e.g., Florida, 2004) that creativity drives the broader innovation process of modern economies by functioning as a fundamental source of novelty. As Christensen (1997, p.95) put it, the task of creativity is "to find ideas for new products and services that will be unique and valued in their markets." Zhou and Shalley (2008) came to a similar conclusion based on their view that creativity is an indispensable foundation for innovation. In fact, it is tempting to treat creativity as simply the first step in a more extensive process referred to as innovation, as a precursor to the real business of innovation.

More qualitative approaches to differentiating between creativity and innovation see creativity as generating novelty out of thin air, so to speak (i.e., as more a matter of radical innovation). By contrast, *innovation* is used to refer to the generation of novelty by means of a process of expanding, adapting or reapplying the already known (i.e., as a matter of incremental innovation). One special manifestation of the latter kind of novelty production occurs when ideas that are well known in one organizational setting and are thus not inherently novel are transferred to another setting where they were previously unknown. Some authors have also conceptualized the distinction between creativity and innovation as resulting from the fact that, according to them, creativity derives from *cognitive*

TABLE 1.2. *Theoretical Distinctions between Creativity and Innovation*

Creativity	Innovation
• generates entirely new ideas	• expands or adapts existing ideas
• is dominated by intrapersonal factors such as thinking and motivation	• is dominated by social factors such as communicating and "selling"
• is not bound by conventional logic	• is strictly bound by conventional logic
• is not confined by the constraints of reality	• is strictly confined by the constraints of reality
• does not need a concrete product	• must yield a concrete product

processes such as getting ideas, whereas innovation is seen as mainly dependent on *social* processes such as persuading others to make changes (i.e., "selling" the novelty).[5]

These attempts to distinguish creativity and innovation are summarized in Table 1.2, where they are referred to as theoretical distinctions because the contrast listed in each row is based on theory rather than an empirically demonstrated difference. The rows in the table derive from separate discussions and can be read independently of each other. However, summing each column by reading down its rows produces an interesting stereotype of creativity (left-hand column), on the one hand, and innovation (right-hand column) on the other. Thus, creativity is often seen as generating new ideas without being bound by logic or the constraints of reality and without necessarily leading to a concrete product (although this is not forbidden). In contrast, innovation is regarded as expanding what already exists; mainly social (because it requires persuading other people); strictly logical; highly constrained by the demands of the real world (especially the commercial world); and absolutely requiring a concrete, indeed commercial, product.[6]

However, establishing the details of the relationship between creativity and innovation is not as straightforward as might have been expected at first glance. Mumford, Hester, and Robledo (2012, p. 8) identified three reasons for this: (a) creativity and innovation are complex phenomena; (b) creativity and innovation are multilevel phenomena and are influenced

[5] As will be shown in later chapters, the conceptualization of creativity in this book does not accept this view at all. Creativity is regarded here as encompassing not only cognitive processes but also personal properties, motivation, feelings and attitudes, and social interactions.

[6] This taxonomy is discussed in greater detail in Chapter 2, which is focused on products.

by variables operating in the personal, organizational, and social environments simultaneously; and (c) the two interact in different ways in the various environments just mentioned. For instance, the conditions that foster conversion of creativity into innovation in the personal environment (i.e., within the mind of the individual attempting to generate effective novelty) are frequently at odds with those that promote it in the social environment (i.e., in the society at large). To take a single example: Lack of concern about the precise details of how a proposed product would actually work would make it easy to come up with unexpected ideas in the mind of an inventor (personal environment) but would make it very hard to persuade customers to buy the product (social environment).

Nonetheless, Anderson, Potocnik, and Zhou (2014) showed that there has been a vigorous discussion of innovation and creativity for more than a decade now. Their discussion goes well beyond cognitive factors, referring not only to thinking but also to inter-individual social processes, intra-individual personal dispositions, and motivation. However, their treatment of such factors remained global and rather undifferentiated. D. H. Cropley (2015) likened the whole structure of the innovation process to an iceberg. The visible part may be striking, it is true, but what goes on under the surface is what is truly crucial. The argument here is that much of the invisible section of the innovation iceberg consists of psychological phenomena that have been overlooked in the past because of the focus on the visible tip but can readily be discussed in terms of concepts adapted from creativity theory. (The relationship of innovation to creativity will be discussed in greater detail in Chapter 8.)

OVERVIEW AND OUTLOOK

Innovation involves the generation and implementation of novel products or processes (solutions) in organizations. It is commonly regarded today as the key to human well-being as well as to the success of organizations. Technological advances have made a huge contribution to human welfare and the prosperity of many organizations, but in an age of reconceptualization they are not enough. Innovation may include new or improved technology, to be sure, but goes beyond it to incorporate the personal creativity that leads to new paradigms.

However, business imperatives mean that innovation is frequently examined purely from the point of view of *implementation* of novelty, with little account taken of its *generation*, whereas creativity research has tended to pay more attention to the generation of effective novelty, although not exclusively. Some writers even regard successful *implementation* of novel solutions as incompatible with creativity. Discussions of innovation within organizational theory have also largely been limited to examination of *organizational* factors such as organizational culture, company structures, work organization, or structure of the workforce (e.g., age and gender distribution, level of education, and training). Where psychological discussions exist, they have tended to focus on the way the organization functions (e.g., tolerance vs. intolerance of failure, openness of communication channels, provision of free time for acquiring information and thinking about it, provision of constructive feedback on ideas) rather than on properties and processes within individual actors in the organization (e.g., ways of thinking, forms of motivation, personal properties such as flexibility).

Nussbaum (2013, p. 15) argued that what is required is to "*deconstruct* the creative act" (emphasis added), and this book will indeed deconstruct creativity in order to tease out the key ideas that can be applied to enlarging understanding of innovation. Although this deconstruction is compatible with Nussbaum's full support of the importance of creativity research for understanding innovation, his analysis of creativity is relatively superficial. In fact, as will be shown in later chapters of this book, creativity theory offers a complex and encompassing framework for a highly differentiated analysis in terms of products, the processes that lead to the products, the psychological resources of the individuals who carry out the processes, and the external conditions acting on the individuals to foster or inhibit the processes.

The basic framework for deconstructing creativity and achieving understanding of the link between creativity and innovation is to be found in the work of Barron (1955) and Rhodes (1961). It involves the Four Ps of creativity: *product* (for our purposes, what the innovative process leads to; see Chapter 2), *process* (i.e., special forms of thinking that give rise to a useful novel product; see Chapter 3), *person* (i.e., the psychological resources of the individual that support the process of the generation of useful novelty; see Chapter 4), and *press* (i.e., the influence of the environment in which the innovative individual operates (including the person's psychological resources; see Chapter 5).

In this book, these Four Ps will be expanded into Six Ps by deconstructing person into personal characteristics, personal motivation, and personal feelings (see Chapter 4). Furthermore, product will be restricted to products that are not simply novel and in some way useful (the classical definition in creativity theory) but are also commercially useful (see Chapter 2). Every innovation is constructed from a combination of commercially useful product; processes that lead to the product; properties of persons who carry out the processes; and the effects of the environments in which the person operates, the processes occur, and the products are conceived, brought into existence, marketed and accepted (or not). Thus, the expanded catalog of Ps encompasses what are called the building blocks of innovation.

Both creativity research and innovation research show, however, that the connection between personal innovativeness and managerial behavior is not simple or straightforward; in fact, it is beset by paradoxes, as will be shown in Chapter 6. A taxonomy of innovation derived from creativity theory offers insights that help to make sense of the paradoxes of innovation and suggests how to cope with them (Chapter 8). Finally, the discussion in this book will turn to the question of how to analyze organizations in order to diagnose their strengths in overcoming the paradoxes and show where their weaknesses lie, and how to apply such a diagnosis in order to promote innovation.

PART 1

BASIC CONCEPTS

2

Products: What Does Innovation Lead To?

Chapter 1 argued that the Four Ps model of creativity needs refinement if it is to prove useful in understanding innovation. The purpose of the next four chapters of the book is to carry out the necessary reworking of the Ps approach in order to develop a model of innovation based on the building blocks of product, process, person, and press. The present chapter begins the necessary reworking by examining the most obvious building block: the public face of innovation – product.

THE USEFULNESS IMPERATIVE

The nineteenth-century French novelist Théophile Gautier stated in the preface to a product of his own aesthetic creativity – his novel *Mademoiselle de Maupin*, published in 1836 – that "nothing is truly beautiful unless it is *useless*" (emphasis added). This rejection of usefulness is typical of the notion of creativity seen in the art for art's sake movement, of which Gautier was a leading representative. In the early years of the modern creativity era, that is, in the 1950s and 1960s, there was still resistance to the systematic study of creativity on the grounds that it is ineffable and inscrutable, a mystical, divine phenomenon beyond the understanding of mere mortals and thus above trivial considerations such as usefulness. A modern version of the rejection of concrete products and endorsement of the idea that creativity is purely spiritual was articulated by Rothman (2014). He complained about what he called creativity creep, defining the term as a shift away from conceiving of creativity as a way of being – a position of which he approved – to seeing it as a way of doing – a position of which he disapproved. In rejecting the linking of creativity to tangible products he stated: "If you're really creative, really imaginative, you don't have to make things. You just have to *live, observe, think, and feel*" (emphasis added).

However, within the framework of a discussion of innovation in organizations, simply feeling creative without actually doing anything is of limited interest, and uselessness in a product is not a virtue at all. Levitt (2002) was particularly scathing in his comments about people within organizations who are eager to advance novel ideas but regard the question of whether they can be implemented as an unnecessary hindrance to their creativity. To put the matter plainly, in the organizational environment, novelty is generated with the deliberate intention of producing something useful in a concrete sense, especially in a commercial sense. Burghardt (1995, p. 4) turned thinking in an appropriate direction when he wrote of "creativity with a *purpose*" (emphasis added), and Horenstein (2002, p. 2) gave a good idea of what that purpose is: the production of "devices or systems that perform tasks or solve problems." In this book, generation of such useful novelty is regarded as depending on the creativity of human actors in the production process. However, the products of this creativity must be capable of being implemented in order to benefit an organization; otherwise, they are merely – possibly attractive or exciting – flights of fancy.

The idea of not merely novel but also useful products is probably most obvious when it is applied to tangible, functioning physical objects such as a structure; a machine; an appliance or a tool; or an effective, complex system of some kind (such as a jet aircraft or a business information system) or, on the other hand, a process in the sense of a service, technique, or method (a manufacturing process, a control process, a logistics service). Of course, as D. H. Cropley, Kaufman, and Cropley (2008) pointed out, the idea of benefit is not as clear-cut as might be thought at first glance: One person's benefit may be another's curse. The innovations involved in an effective new weapon of war or a novel software tool that is effective in using the Internet to steal money may well benefit one group but harm another.

Although the reference to weapons of war and theft may be rather extreme, it must be admitted that organizations that benefit from creativity not seldom do so at the price of disastrous effects for some other organization, such as a rival firm whose products are made obsolete or whose systems are rendered ineffective by the new product. The example of Smith Corona has already been mentioned (see Chapter 1); the word processor rendered their product obsolete, even though a Smith Corona typewriter was an excellent machine. The beneficial effect of the microprocessor for Microsoft and Apple spelled doom for Smith Corona.

Creativity Is Not Enough

The fact that innovation involves novel products makes the innovation–creativity link seem obvious. However, as Levitt (2002, p. 137) emphasized in a dictum that can be regarded as the guiding principle of this chapter: "Creativity is not enough." Silvia (2008, p. 139) was even more concrete: Unlike Gautier, he derided useless products and made the blunt point that "some ideas should never see the light of day," no matter how creative they are, for instance, because they are silly or useless. As an example of such an idea, Silvia mentioned artificial testicles for neutered dogs! Although Staw (1995, p. 163) too criticized excessive faith in creativity, he made it plain that his purpose was not to reject any discussion of creativity but "to let the air out of some of the rhetoric" and thus achieve a more down-to-earth discussion. This chapter offers such a discussion. The central point is that in the organizational environment, creativity must lead to two outcomes: a novel idea, on the one hand, to be sure, but also an object, process, or system that utilizes this novelty in a commercially effective and profitable way, on the other, or, at the very least, the recognizable potential for such implementation.

UNDERSTANDING INNOVATIVE PRODUCTS

Very early in the modern creativity era, Morgan (1953) examined a large number of definitions of creativity and concluded that the single universal element in all discussions is novelty. According to Runco and Jaeger (2012, p. 92) the standard definition of creativity in current psychological research goes a step further and focuses on generation of products that are not only novel but are useful too. In commercial organizations, this typically means products that can be implemented for profit.

Even when they are free of commercial intent, however, noncommercial products of creativity, such as paintings, musical compositions, poems, or novels, or systems of ideas as in, let us say, philosophy or mathematics, also perform tasks or solve problems, such as capturing the essence of beauty or communicating a feeling to another person, or revealing the order or structure underlying the world; such products can also be useful in their own way. Thus, the general idea of usefulness is not enough on its own to define innovation because noncommercial creative products can also display usefulness or, according to Runco and Jaeger, must do so. The fundamental difference lies in what is meant by the term *usefulness*. In the organizational sense, good ideas are all very well, but they must culminate in a product that is capable of being implemented for commercial gain, which is critical (Puccio, Murdock, & Mance, 2005). This requirement for creativity plus commercial usefulness is at the heart of Levitt's dictum that creativity on its own is not enough: The embodiment of innovation in the organizational environment is not just a novel product and not just a useful novel product but a value-adding novel product.

Thus, it is not so much that creativity theory ignores products but that there is a qualitative difference between the way the term *useful* is understood in creativity theory and in innovation research. Yue, Bender, and Cheung (2011, p. 26) captured the essence of this difference by distinguishing between products characterized by what they called aesthetic salience and those displaying meritorious salience. Aesthetic salience is typical of artistic, literary, philosophical, and similar products, whereas meritorious salience is generated by scientists, inventors, and – of vital interest for the present book – businesspeople. Yue, Bender, and Cheung's use of the term *meritorious* may disturb some readers because the generation of, for example, artistic, literary, or intellectual beauty is often also meritorious in its own way. The crucial point for the purposes of this book is to focus on products whose usefulness is practical, concrete, and commercial. In an extension of Yue, Bender, and Cheung's terminology, these products could be said to display not just meritorious salience but commercially meritorious salience.

Some of the most obvious differences between the two types of product are summarized in Table 2.1. The left-hand column typifies the way products are often conceptualized by creativity researchers; the right-hand column demonstrates the more or less universal point of view of innovation researchers.

RECOGNIZING COMMERCIALLY SALIENT NOVELTY WHEN YOU SEE IT

Christensen (2013) emphasized the importance in innovation of being able to evaluate the results of novelty generation. To evaluate results, it is vital to be able to:

(a) recognize products that are novel, of high quality, and task appropriate, even when they are surprising and deviate from the usual way of doing things and may thus seem ignorant, absurd, or even threatening;
(b) identify where the special strengths of particular products lie or where they need to be improved;
(c) state the results of (b) in a systematic way that is understandable to everybody involved; and

TABLE 2.1. *Examples of Characteristics of Contrasting Kinds of Novel Product*

Aesthetically Salient Products Involve . . .	Commercially Salient Products Involve . . .
• novel artworks, literary works, films, scientific theories, philosophical systems, and the like	• machines, appliances, devices, structures, processes, and systems that perform existing tasks better
• systems of ideas or representations of the world that cast new light on existing issues	• novel machines, appliances, devices, structures, processes, organizational systems, and the like
• systems of ideas or representations of the world that reveal new issues	• objects, structures, processes, and systems that reveal new tasks
• systems of ideas or representations of the world that help to deal with new issues	• machines, appliances, devices, structures, processes, and systems that perform new tasks effectively
• novel techniques for producing the above	• novel technologies for effectively producing the above

(d) communicate all of this to colleagues, including those who generated the novelty.

However, the potential of products to be implemented is not always recognized. To take a well-known example, Victor Kiam is said to have been offered the rights to Velcro but to have refused because he could not see any practical use for it. Art Fry had to work hard to gain recognition of the usefulness of the Post-it® note, even though it ultimately became a commercial success. It is also known that groups that have produced a number of good ideas (for instance, by means of brainstorming) not infrequently have difficulty distinguishing the good ones from the bad (Rietzschel, Nijstad, & Stroebe, 2010). Such examples raise the question of (a) how to recognize potential innovations when you see them and (b) how to identify in a differentiated way specific properties of products that make them commercially salient (or not). The importance of innovation for organizations in the fight for survival emphasizes the need for ways of recognizing, evaluating, and characterizing appropriate products (Horn & Salvendy, 2006). How is this to be done?[1]

[1] Of course, it is easy to recognize an effective novel product after it has been successfully introduced, captured a large share of the market, produced increased profits, and led to higher share prices. It is also easy to recognize *bad* products after a company has gone bankrupt. The present discussion is concerned with recognizing, defining, articulating, and refining the strengths and weaknesses of products before the fact.

Properties of Commercially Salient Creative Products

The overarching quality of all creative products, whether they are commercially salient or not, is novelty. As A. J. Cropley and Cropley (2009) pointed out, there is more or less universal agreement on this – creativity always leads to something new. To be judged as possessing commercially meritorious salience, however, products must go further than being merely novel and must also be appropriate and correct (Amabile & Tighe, 1993, p. 9); that is, they must also display relevance, for example, by being related to some issue or purpose. In addition, they must also be useful or valuable (Amabile & Tighe, 1993, p. 9), in other words, capable of doing what they were designed to do or effective.

Products that are novel but lack relevance and effectiveness in the sense just outlined involve only pseudo-creativity, which typically means that the novelty derives only from nonconformity, lack of discipline, blind rejection of what already exists, or simply letting oneself go. Pseudo-creativity can easily become self-indulgence or may involve a special kind of conformity to stereotypical creative patterns of behavior and be no more than pretentiousness. In a recent TV interview on creativity, a psychology professor wore a baseball cap sideways throughout the interview. The professor's behavior was certainly unusual because not many professors wear baseball caps sideways when appearing in scholarly discussions on TV, so his action possessed novelty. However, this novelty did not have any clear connection to what he was discussing and did not make his arguments more compelling. It may have been a flag to indicate the presence of the "watchful, inner kind of creativity" that Rothman (2014) called for – which might otherwise have gone unnoticed – or might have demonstrated the ability to think and feel creative (see p. 34).[2] Despite being unusual, however, the action of wearing the cap possessed neither relevance nor effectiveness and was thus a matter of pseudo-creativity.

A second form of ineffective novelty generation – quasi-creativity – can be added to this discussion. Quasi-creativity goes beyond pseudo-creativity because the novelty is related to some practical problem or task. However, it offers no prospect of a genuinely applicable solution. If a child drew a fantasy spaceship that could travel the cosmos driven by, let us say, the energy released by a super candle that provided sufficient power for faster-than-light speed, the child would be giving expression to an idea that is

[2] No doubt first-year undergraduates recognized his creativity immediately from his nonconformer's uniform!

novel and relevant because some form of faster-than-light travel in some form of transport device is an imaginative approach to interstellar travel, and the idea of utilizing the energy in a candle for this purpose is certainly unusual. However, in the present state of knowledge of physics, the idea lacks effectiveness (unless the child designed an engine of this kind that actually worked). The novelty generated in daydreams sometimes involves pseudo-creativity. Pseudo-creativity may yield solutions to a genuine problem only if the solutions were capable of being implemented (effective).

In the case of aesthetic products, something novel, such as a new painting technique using human feces as the medium, might be rejected by the general public because it is disgusting (i.e., it might be ineffective in the social environment), but it might still be regarded by art insiders as a bold and creative attempt to widen horizons, break the shackles of conventionality, or change the prevailing paradigm (i.e., as aesthetically meritorious). In organizational/management discussions, by contrast, commercially meritorious novelty must be accompanied by relevance and commercial effectiveness. It must work not only by pleasing specialists (such as within the art world in the example just given), but – unlike mere aesthetically meritorious novelty – it must also work in the broader social environment, for example, by increasing market share and increasing sales.

Few engineers would acclaim the Tacoma Narrows Bridge in Washington State or the Westgate Bridge in Melbourne as triumphs of engineering innovation, even though the former was beautiful to look at (thus satisfying one of the requirements in the left-hand column of Table 2.1) and the latter introduced novel building technology (thus satisfying one of the criteria in the right-hand column of the table), because unfortunately both bridges fell down. In the case of the Westgate Bridge, the structure's collapse caused substantial loss of life and was Australia's worst industrial accident. In organizational innovation, relevance and effectiveness take on additional contours that go beyond those in aesthetically salient creativity, contours that may extend to literal or metaphoric life-and-death issues.

Situation versus Domain Relevance and Effectiveness

Relevance and effectiveness may be of two broad kinds. A useful distinction is between situation-relevant and domain-relevant products (for a more detailed discussion, see A. J. Cropley & Cropley, 2009; D. H. Cropley, 2015). Situation-relevant products solve a specific concrete problem applying to a particular situation. Domain-relevant products, by contrast, expand the way a domain is conceptualized, emphasize new issues not previously noticed, suggest new ways of solving problems in the area, or carry out other similar functions. The specific situation may even be relatively unimportant. For instance, the French painter Henri de Toulouse-Lautrec introduced a highly effective new technology for printmaking in Paris late in the nineteenth century and the novel product (a new production method) gained him business supremacy over his greatest rival for customers. From the commercial point of view, the exact subject of the prints (the Moulin Rouge and especially its dancers) was irrelevant. What gained income and commercial success for Toulouse-Lautrec, compared to artistic acclaim (which is a separate issue), was his expansion of the domain of transfer screen lithography by introducing spatter painting using a stiff brush (apparently Toulouse-Lautrec used a toothbrush).

It is possible for the two kinds of creativity to exist separately – a novel product could be situation-relevant without being domain-relevant (i.e., it could get the job done in a new way without meeting any of the criteria in the left-hand column of Table 2.1). It could also be domain-relevant without being situation-relevant (i.e., it could satisfy one or more of the criteria in the left-hand column but none in the right-hand one). Products that display domain relevance unaccompanied by situation relevance are probably more acceptable in aesthetic and philosophical domains where the opening of new perspectives, development of new ways of attacking problems, introduction of new techniques, and the like, may have at least equal status with utilitarian issues such as getting traffic across a river. In commercial settings, however, situation relevance is an absolutely indispensable prerequisite before domain relevance can even be considered.

Of course, a product may possess both kinds of relevance, as was the case with Toulouse-Lautrec's prints; they revolutionized printmaking technology (domain relevance) while also doing the specific job of establishing him as a successful manufacturer of saleable lithographic prints (situation relevance). In his case, his creativity went further because it gained him long-term acclaim as a great artist as well as commercial success. In terms of the distinction introduced in Table 2.1, Toulouse-Lautrec's products displayed both aesthetically and commercially meritorious salience. However, the commercial salience of his novelty is scarcely remembered today, except perhaps by historians in university departments of design, despite the fact that his commercially salient innovation is still applied in printmaking.

Critics who focus on situation relevance (i.e., the product should do its concrete, practical job) are sometimes regarded by those who focus on domain relevance (the product expands horizons) as philistines or money grubbers, while those who give greatest priority to domain relevance may be regarded by those who emphasize situation relevance as head-in-the clouds dreamers. It is important for those managing innovation in organizations to be aware of the difference between the two kinds of relevance and usefulness and to be able to recognize and possibly implement both kinds in products.

CREATIVITY IN PRODUCTS

In discussing what they called functional creativity, D. H. Cropley and Cropley (2005, 2014) and D. H. Cropley (2015) focused on four properties of a product that take it beyond mere aesthetic salience into the realm of commercially meritorious salience. Their taxonomy can readily be adapted for the purposes of a discussion of the creativity of innovative products. Its first level involves relevance and effectiveness, properties that have already been discussed. These are indispensable for solving practical problems. Indeed, problems can be solved through relevance and effectiveness alone. Such solutions are reminiscent of incremental, sustaining, or evolving innovation. However, breakthrough products involve at least one other element in addition to relevance and effectiveness: novelty. From a functional point of view, this is a relevant and effective product that not only does the job but also does it in a new way. These qualities of a product (relevance, effectiveness, and novelty) are joint prerequisites for the lowest level of genuine creativity compared to pseudo- and quasi-creativity.

However, D. H. Cropley, and Cropley (2005, 2014) argued that a solution can go further by being elegant. *Elegance* is an aesthetic term. and this aspect of a novel product is easy to understand in an aesthetic context, but it requires some explanation in a commercial sense. Han, Hwan Yun, Kim and Kwahk's (2000) discussion of what they called usability (p. 477) is helpful here.[3] These authors decomposed usability into two components, objective performance (i.e., relevance and effectiveness; the novel product does what it is supposed to do) and – of greatest interest for the point being made here – subjective impression on customers. They referred to the defining characteristics of subjective impression as "human interface

[3] Although they focused on consumer electronic products, Han and colleagues expressed the view that their approach could be applied to products in other commercial fields, a view that has been supported by D. H. Cropley and Cropley (2008, p. 155), who argued for the existence of a *universal* aesthetic (emphasis added) of functionally creative products.

elements" (p. 477). In a commercial sense, it is the human interface elements associated with a product that are at the core of elegance; in an elegant product, as Oman, Tumer, Wood, and Seepersad (2013, p. 65) put it in a down-to-earth way, the human interface elements "*delight* customers" (emphasis added).

Especially in the case of commercial products, elegance is thus a quality that "bridges the gap between form and function" (Oman et al., 2013, p. 65). A product not only functions well (it is relevant and effective), but its form also delights customers (it is elegant). People find an elegant product attractive in appearance; it gives the impression of working, and it has an air of being up to date or fashionable, to give a few examples. No doubt these properties also help to convince customers that a product is effective (whether it is or not). They may also mean that the product defeats a rival, for instance, in the marketplace, not necessarily because it works better but because it delights customers, to use the words of Oman et al. (2013).

Finally, in the Cropley and Cropley taxonomy (e.g., D. H. Cropley & Cropley, 2005, 2014) comes genesis: The property of a relevant, effective, and novel (and possibly, but not necessarily, elegant) solution that makes it transferable to different (quite possibly unanticipated) situations, opens up new ways of looking at known problems, or draws attention to the existence of previously unnoticed problems. In organizational terms, a genetic product solves more than one problem or shows the pathway through which solutions to more than one problem may be reached. The special quality of genesis as a criterion of creativity is that a genetic product not only offers new possibilities for the situation for which the novelty was generated but also:

1. applies to other apparently unrelated situations (i.e., it is transferable to other situations whether or not the innovator intended this);
2. introduces a new way of conceptualizing a whole area or opens up new approaches to existing problems, possibly in many areas (i.e., it is germinal);
3. demonstrates the existence of previously unnoticed problems and suggests the need for new work (i.e., it is seminal); and
4. lays a foundation for later innovations for which the original novelty is a prerequisite, although the original innovator may have had no idea of the future innovation (i.e., it is foundational).

For the purposes of the present discussion, however, the idea of functional creativity does not go far enough. In the case study presented earlier, there is little doubt of the aesthetic salience of Toulouse-Lautrec's creativity: His paintings were novel, relevant, and aesthetically effective (they captured the verve and spirit of the life of the Moulin Rouge in products of great visual beauty and yielded lasting insights into the life of a particular social milieu and a particular time). In addition, his posters extended existing painting techniques. However, the interesting thing about the novelty generated by Toulouse-Lautrec for present purposes is that it went a step further. It was also commercially salient: It was relevant to his need to produce commercially successful posters, it was effective (in crude commercial terms, customers liked it), it was elegant (it was pleasing to look at), and it was genetic (it opened up new possibilities in printmaking). The key point here is that it could be implemented in a commercially successful way. It defeated Toulouse-Lautrec's business competition and gave him a steady source of income. Thus, it displayed a second kind of effectiveness, aesthetically salient effectiveness to be sure, but commercially salient effectiveness as well – it went beyond mere functional creativity and displayed not just creativity but innovative creativity.

The Hierarchy of Creative Products

D. H. Cropley and Cropley (2005) treated relevance and effectiveness as a single dimension of functional creativity. However, the distinction made earlier between pseudo-creativity (novelty alone) and quasi-creativity (novelty plus relevance but without effectiveness) shows that relevance and effectiveness are distinct qualities of a product, and they will be treated separately here. A further differentiation arises from the distinction between aesthetically salient effectiveness and commercially salient effectiveness. These divisions yield six dimensions of creativity: novelty, relevance, elegance, genesis, aesthetically salient effectiveness, and commercially salient effectiveness, which make it possible to construct a hierarchical model ranging from the pseudo-creative (merely novel) at the lowest level through the quasi-creative (novel and relevant), to the merely aesthetically salient (novelty, relevance, aesthetically salient effectiveness, and possibly – but not necessarily – elegance and genesis). To this point, products are merely creative. Products displaying novelty and relevance plus commercially salient effectiveness (with or without aesthetic salience) are innovative. The general category of innovative products can be further differentiated into merely innovative products, elegant products (innovative plus elegant), and genetic products (innovative plus genetic, with or without elegance). For present purposes, elegant and genetic products are more highly differentiated variants of ordinary innovative products so that all three kinds of product can be referred to as innovative.

This hierarchical taxonomy of functional products is shown in Table 2.2. In the table, a plus sign means that the property indicated with the plus sign is indispensable to the kind of product depicted in the column in question, a minus sign indicates that the property is not present in this kind of product (otherwise it would be a different kind of product), and a question mark indicates that the property may or may not be present in this particular kind of product. Products which are merely routine (relevant and commercially salient but lacking novelty) are not shown in Table 2.2 because, although they possess relevance and commercially salient effectiveness, novelty is missing. Rather than representing creativity, routine improvements to products involve simply evolutionary change that polishes what already exists. They are more closely allied to information than to conceptualization. This does not mean, however, that routine products are useless. In organizations, they may be very valuable, even though they are devoid of novelty, because they are effective. Indeed, they may be the preferred form of change and may be mistaken for innovation, as examples like Smith-Corona and Polaroid show. Although pseudo-creative and quasi-creative products are novel, they are not innovative either because, despite the fact that sheer novelty may lead to applause in some social settings, it does not lead to anything concrete and useful (it lacks relevance and commercially salient effectiveness), except in the case of occasional lucky breaks.

A Unified Model of Creativity and Innovation

Chapter 1 pointed out that creativity and innovation are somehow separate and yet so closely related that they can be discussed using the same concepts (see O'Shea and Buckley [2007] for a particularly clear review of the situation). The analysis of products just presented decomposed creativity of products hierarchically by distinguishing among products according to differing combinations of novelty, effectiveness, salience, elegance, and genesis. All these products possess the minimum property of novelty and thus satisfy the weak or lenient criterion of creativity stated by Morgan (1953). All products beyond quasi-creativity are effectively novel and thus satisfy Runco and Jaeger's (2012) stronger or stricter criterion of creativity. They are not all innovative, however, and only products displaying commercial salience, with or without some

TABLE 2.2. *Differing Kinds of Novel Product*[a]

Property of the Product	Kind of Product					
	Aesthetic			Innovative		
	Pseudo-Creative	Quasi-Creative	Merely Aesthetically Salient	Merely Commercially Salient	Elegant (Commercially Salient and Also Pleasing at the Human Interface)	Genetic (Commercially Salient and Also Seminal/Germinal)
Novelty	+	+	+	+	+	+
Relevance	–	+	+	+	+	+
Aesthetic effectiveness	–	–	+	?	?	?
Commercial effectiveness	–	–	–	+	+	+
Elegance	–	–	?	–	+	+/?[b]
Genesis	–	–	?	–	–	+

[a] This table is an expanded and more differentiated version of a table in D. H. Cropley and Cropley (2005).

[b] Genetic products may be elegant, but need not be; genesis both with and without elegance is imaginable.

combination of elegance and genesis, satisfy the strongest or strictest criterion of innovation spelled out here.

This analysis suggests that creativity and innovation really are closely allied as facets of a single broader phenomenon – generation of useful novelty – so that their similarities are scarcely surprising. In fact, their most striking differences may well arise from something that is not, in itself, an inherent element of the generation of novelty at all: the intention or purpose of the generator of the novelty, the reason for generating the novelty in the first place. This simultaneous difference and similarity can be represented visually by placing various forms of generation of novelty at different points along a continuum defined by the intention of the generator. The continuum ranges from a pole involving generation of novelty with no intention whatsoever of producing a product of any kind – mere spiritual creativity in the sense of Rothman (2014) – to an opposite pole involving complete and total intention of producing a specific product. The model can be further differentiated by introducing a second aspect of the generator's intention, the intended level of commercialization: Spiritual creativity has no intention of producing a product and no commercial intention either, whereas in the case of innovation, a product is fully intended and is also fully intended to be commercially effective. Innovation is thus a special case of creativity: In a whimsical way, it could be said that innovation involves committing creativity with intent or perhaps that innovation is creativity with attitude.

Between these two poles lies pseudo-creativity (see the section titled Properties of Commercially Salient Creative Products), which involves an intention of producing a discernible effect (a product in the loosest sense), but apart from its capacity to attract attention, the product is of no interest. Quasi-creativity has the intention of producing a concrete product, but the practical relevance and effectiveness of the product are given little consideration. Everyday creativity[4] involves the intention of producing an effective and relevant product, but there is no serious thought of commercialization (the novelty is generated for the pleasure of the creator, his or her immediate circle of relatives and acquaintances, and the like). Aesthetic creativity definitely aims at a relevant and effective product. It can have commercial motivation too, but the creator is often more interested in personal satisfaction, the feeling of having shown the world a new way, expanded society's horizons, challenged conventions, or expanded

[4] See Richards (2007) for a more detailed discussion of everyday creativity.

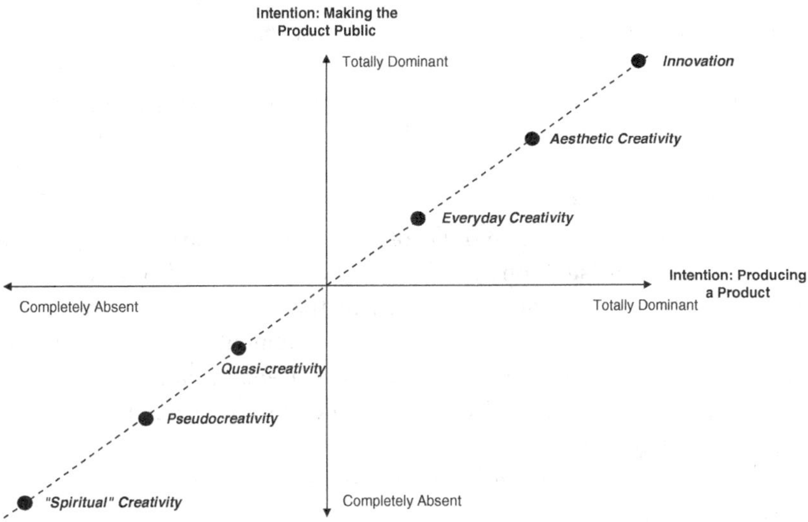

FIGURE 2.1. The Link between Intention and Kind of Creativity

methods or techniques than in making money. Indeed, in some circles, such as those Gauthier moved in, commercial motivation would be regarded as unworthy or as selling out.

Figure 2.1 shows how various kinds of creativity can be placed on a grid defined by these two dimensions of intention.

DIAGNOSING INNOVATION IN PRODUCTS

This hierarchical organization of novel products (which was outlined in Table 2.2) introduces an important principle into the discussion. There are levels and kinds of creativity. Different products can be creative to greater or lesser degrees, but they can display different kinds of creativity. The relationship among the criteria is also dynamic. To take the most obvious example, novelty increases a product's commercial usefulness. Elegance transforms mere novelty and effectiveness by making the products delightful, and genesis provides a further transformation by giving a product the power to change the way a family of products is conceptualized. Thus, although elegance and genesis are not absolutely indispensable for commercial salience, they add value to a product. This is important because a change in the social environment (the external world) can quickly destroy the relevance and effectiveness of a product, whereas its delightfulness and generic properties are likely to make it more persistent.

The fate of Polaroid's chemical instant print technology is an example. The system was novel and effective, and it was highly commercially successful in its day. Unfortunately for Polaroid, however, changes in the environment (the rise of digital imaging) meant that photochemical imaging was no longer modern and attractive (delightful) and no longer represented the new paradigm, and that alone, despite all other virtues, was fatal for the company.[5] A more recent example is Nokia, which refused to recognize that mobile phones are now part of the fashion industry, and insisted on building technologically advanced mobile phones rather than devices that satisfied the desire of their customers for ever smaller, more streamlined, fashion statements. That is, by ceasing to delight their customers and introduce transformational (genetic) products, Nokia overlooked the importance in commercial salience of elegance and genesis.

In fact, elegance and genesis are important in a commercial sense for several reasons:

1. Elegant and genetic novelty may add so much value to a product that it is immune to value subtractions resulting from a rival's novelty.
2. Elegant and genetic novelty may also give a product the capacity to subtract value from a rival product (i.e., to nullify the rival's effectiveness).
3. Genesis may make it possible for a product to cope successfully with changes in the external environment (such as in business practice and conditions, in societal tastes, or in availability of resources, or even paradigm changes in which what has long been regarded as the right approach is now discarded as no longer relevant).

Latent Commercially Salient Novelty

The nature of the rival may be unknown at the time a product is being developed, and thus added value resulting from even innovative novelty may not be immediately apparent; that is, the usefulness of the product may be latent. Despite earlier insistence in this chapter on the necessity of commercially salient effectiveness in innovation, there may be two

[5] There is still a small market for Polaroid film among specialists, and it is readily available on the Internet. Thus it has not become totally irrelevant.

kinds of commercially salient relevance and effectiveness that need to be considered: one kind that involves immediately obvious commercial salience and another kind where the commercial salience is not yet apparent but may eventually be recognized (i.e., the product has potential for commercial success, or latent commercial salience). Large numbers of valuable products cannot be dismissed as lacking usefulness simply because they do not provide a solution to a current problem in an already existing situation. Even highly effective novel products could initially fail to be recognized as relevant and effective, for instance, because current technology needs to catch up before the practical usefulness of a solution can become apparent. Thus, even seemingly irrelevant or ineffective novelty could possess hidden or latent relevance and effectiveness. A discussion on the Web site www.u-sit.net puts the point succinctly: "it behooves the creative thinker to go the extra mile and find a new vantage point *solely for the potential value of the new perspective*" (emphasis added). The following section turns to the question of how this can be done.

Indicators of Innovative Creativity in Products

In their discussion of the usability of products (see above), Han et al. (2000, p. 477) pointed out that understanding objective performance (i.e., what are called relevance and effectiveness in this book) and human interface elements (elegance) could be used to (a) "identify important design elements," (b) "diagnose usability problems," and (c) "predict the level of usability of consumer [goods]." The taxonomy presented in Table 2.2 expands their criteria and strengthens the possibility they discussed of adopting a diagnostic approach to innovation management. However, such an approach requires that managers can recognize the innovative creativity of products when they see it and can especially differentiate between kinds and levels of it.

Kim and Han (2008) provided an overview of procedures for carrying out commercial assessment of novel products and showed that the procedures mainly focus on aspects of usability in the sense of Han et al. (2000). Kim and Han identified two broad approaches to assessing the usability or, using the terminology of the present book, the commercial salience of novel products: measures of consumer satisfaction (usually questionnaires) and performance measures (frequently involving complex techniques requiring high levels of expertise and/or specialized labs and workshops). In other words, consumers either like the product or not, and the product either works or it does not. The adapted and expanded functional model of creativity presented earlier (see Table 2.2), which now encompasses innovative creativity, goes well beyond such an approach and identifies a number of properties of industrial/commercial products that can be used to describe the level and kind of commercial salience the products possess.

The Creative Solution Diagnosis Scale (CSDS)

What is needed in organizational innovation is a systematic and relatively simple way of recognizing the presence or absence of the dimensions of innovative creativity outlined earlier in this chapter. D. H. Cropley, Kaufman, and Cropley (2011) presented a scale that they called the Creative Solution Diagnosis Scale (CSDS), which can be applied in this way. The scale is discussed in greater detail in Chapter 7. In essence, it deconstructs the innovativeness of products by identifying five dimensions of innovative creativity: relevance and effectiveness, problematization, propulsion, elegance, and genesis.

These dimensions are themselves deconstructed into indicators that help to identify the properties involved in the dimensions. D. H. Cropley, Kaufman, and Cropley (2011) and D. H. Cropley and Kaufman (2013) demonstrated that the scale is satisfactorily reliable and that its dimensions reflect the theoretical model of functional creativity outlined earlier in this chapter.

The indicators include properties related to relevance and effectiveness (such as correctness or operability), problematization (e.g., diagnosis, prognosis), propulsion (e.g., redirection, redefinition), elegance (e.g., convincingness, pleasingness), and genesis (e.g., germinality, seminality). These indicators can be regarded as a checklist of properties indicating the presence, amount, and kind of novelty (as outlined in Table 2.2) that are possessed by a product. They can be used to concretize diagnosis of a product in the sense of Han et al. (2000, p. 477): to distinguish between alternative or competing products (e.g., one product might be, let us say, stronger than another on problematization but weaker on propulsion) or between differential strengths and weaknesses within an individual product. For instance, a product might be strong on problematization but weak on elegance and thus be a good source of challenges to existing ideas but unlikely to please customers.

It is not being suggested here that managers should carry a copy of the CSDS with them and use it to score every idea they encounter in their daily work or in discussions of product development or similar themes. However, the scale does offer a set of concepts for systematic understanding of the innovative potential of novel product ideas and for identifying their strengths and weaknesses, both internally as well as in comparison with rival innovations or with existing products. It also offers terminology for communicating such strengths and weaknesses and discussing where and what kind of further development is needed.

OVERVIEW AND OUTLOOK

Innovation research on products covers much of the same ground as creativity research. In the case of innovation, however, commercial usefulness in products is absolutely essential (e.g., generating saleable new products, solving production problems, defeating opposition products, or meeting the needs of customers more effectively in order to improve the bottom line, drive up share price, and the like); without usefulness, there is no innovation in the organizational sense, only creativity for its own sake, or spiritual creativity. Both creativity and innovation can be treated as special forms of the general process of novelty generation, although this general process is usually referred to as creativity. Creativity and innovation are both concerned with generation of useful novelty; the difference between them can be understood in terms of the intention of the person generating the novelty in question.

In managing innovation, it is important that managers can recognize when a product is innovatively creative and can specify where its innovative creativity lies, as well as to say what it lacks and where it lacks it. Otherwise, the danger exists of missing opportunities or of failing to exploit them to the fullest. The Creative Solution Diagnosis Scale (CSDS) is a tool for recognizing the properties defining innovative creativity and assessing their relative prominence in a product. Such assessment provides a basis for making systematic judgments of suggestions for change, and such judgments are indispensable for effective innovation management.

3

Process: How Are Innovative Ideas Formed?

The ideal output of the innovative process is a novel, relevant, commercially effective, elegant, and genetic product. The question that now arises is: What processes give rise to the ideas for such products? In answering this question, the present chapter will focus on the building block of thinking. Reduced to its barest essentials, thinking involves obtaining information, sorting/categorizing and storing it, recalling it, and (re)applying it. As a building block of innovation, thinking involves special or particular cognitive actions such as making associations between or among remote pieces of information, seeing unexpected implications of facts, transferring existing knowledge to new situations, or interpreting events broadly. An amusing if rather disgusting example of the application of such processes to generate the novelty for a commercially successful product was given by Gordon (1961). He described how the problem of the last drops dripping onto the table cloth after tomato ketchup has been poured out of the bottle was solved by seeing a link between this problem and the way a horse's anus controls the flow of feces, and designing a nondrip tomato ketchup bottle cap based on this insight!

COMPONENTS OF THE PROCESS OF INNOVATIVE THINKING

In an early discussion written from the point of view of organizational theory, Roberts (1988) made a distinction that is helpful for present purposes: He divided the process of innovation into two subprocesses that he labeled invention and exploitation. Invention is related, as the term itself indicates, to production of novelty, while exploitation is linked to identifying and utilizing the novelty in a commercially successful way. More recent writers have also described two components of innovative thinking. Bledow, Frese, Anderson, Erez, and Farr (2009a, p. 309), for example, divided the process into idea generation, on the one hand, and idea implementation, on the other. Ward and Kolomyts (2010, p. 94) identified generative and exploratory processes. Davila, Epstein, and Shelton (2012, p. xiv) distinguished between "value *creation*" and "value *capture*" (emphasis added). In fact, Anderson, Potocnik, and Zhou (2014) made it clear that the idea of a two-component process is now well established in the organizational literature. Turning to psychological thinking, in an influential discussion, Finke, Ward, and Smith (1992) distinguished between generating novelty and exploring it once it has been generated. Lonergan, Scott and Mumford (2004) concluded that this idea is now widely accepted in psychology too.

Luecke and Katz (2003) extended this approach by introducing the important idea that innovation does not simply have two subprocesses but several components arranged in a sequence of steps or phases that they referred to as "idea generation," "idea evaluation," "opportunity recognition," "development," and "commercialization" (p. xii). It is apparent that what they call idea generation and idea evaluation are more concerned with invention, while opportunity recognition, development, and commercialization are more closely connected with exploitation. Although they were discussing creative problem solving rather than innovation, Mumford, Antes, Caughron, Connelly, and Beeler (2010) listed eight subprocesses or phases: problem definition, information gathering, information organization, conceptual combination, idea generation, idea evaluation, implementation planning, and solution appraisal. Once again, it can be seen that the first five steps involve in essence invention, the latter three, exploitation. The question of the number of steps, stages, or phases in the generation and implementation of effective novelty briefly discussed here will be examined more closely later in the book (see Chapter 6, which presents a seven-stage model in Figure 6.1). However, a division of the process of innovative creativity into two phases provides a helpful starting point for the present discussion.

Working at the commercial level more than 100 years ago, Prindle (1906) studied inventions and concluded that they emerge in a series of steps, with each step building on earlier ones. Writing directly in an organizational innovation context, West (2002, p. 356) envisaged the relationship between generation and implementation of novelty (invention and exploitation, or value creation and value capture) as sequential: "Innovation then can be defined as encompassing ... the development of ideas . . . *followed by* their application" (emphasis added). Indeed, the idea of innovative thinking occurring in a series of value-adding steps that build on the one before in an orderly sequence is attractive.

However, case studies have shown that individuals engaged in creative activities do not usually have a sense of working in discrete phases, one step after the other (Glover, Ronning, & Reynolds, 1989). Thus, it seems that in practice different phases, however many there are, do not simply follow each other in a lock-step sequence but that there may be, at the very least, an iterative or cyclical process of idea generation and implementation (e.g., Paulus, 2002). The steps of generation of novelty and application of the new idea may, for instance, alternate, or the two may occur simultaneously (Benner & Tushman, 2003; Burgelman, 2002; Bledow et al., 2009a).

According to Gupta, Smith and Shalley (2006), synchronous production and exploitation of novelty involves organizational ambidexterity, whereas sequential processing involves punctuated equilibrium. Understood in the simplest way, when applied to organizational innovation (e.g., Gersick, 1991), punctuated equilibrium involves long periods of stability interrupted by occasional bursts of divergent thinking, after which stability is reestablished. The bursts of divergent thinking generate disruptive novelty; in the long periods of stability, this is checked out and perhaps adapted incrementally by means of convergent thinking. The alternation is seen as a recurring sequence. Organizational ambidexterity, on the other hand, involves constant switching back and forth between divergent and convergent thinking.

Other organizational writers have made a similar point and referred to "oscillation" (Martindale, 1989, p. 228), "alternating psycho-behavioral waves" (Koberg & Bagnall,1991, p. 38), and "dynamic shifting" (Bledow, Frese, Anderson, Erez, & Farr, 2009b, p. 365). Organizational researchers such as King (1992) and Van de Ven, Poole and Angle (2000) have shown that the innovation process is often, at the least, disorderly and repetitive, or as Anderson, Potocnik and Zhou (2014, p. 5) put it in a down-to-earth way: "the innovation process as it unfolds over time is messy, reiterative, and often involves two steps forwards for one step backwards plus several side-steps." Nonetheless, the basic idea of a sequence of different but somehow coordinated subprocesses is a helpful starting point for the discussion that follows. As has already been mentioned, the idea of phases in the generation of effective novelty will be discussed in more detail in Chapter 6 (see Table 6.1) and Chapter 8.

DIVERGENT AND CONVERGENT THINKING

The question that now arises is what actually happens in the phases or subprocesses, regardless of how they are organized with regard to each other. Writing from an organizational point of view, Raisch, Birkenshaw, Probst, and Tushman (2009) began to examine the psychological processes involved. They emphasized the cognitive processes of synthesizing knowledge and integrating knowledge across domains, which are obviously connected with invention, but examined these processes not in terms of the personal environment of the individual actor but mainly in terms of the structural and procedural aspects of the organizational environment that are thought likely to promote the processes – such as the flexibility of organizational boundaries and the coordination of knowledge bases. Plsek and Bevan (2003) identified a number of more or less psychological aspects of processes within the organizational environment that they regarded as vital for innovation, including taking risks, providing resources, sharing knowledge, setting innovation as a goal, supporting innovative processes, providing rewards for innovative thinking, fostering the formation of networks, and promoting intrinsic motivation. All of these obviously provide favorable external conditions for the process of generation of effective novelty but, once again, they do not look directly at the psychological nature of the cognitive processes within individual people.

However, as Raisch, Birkinshaw, Probst, and Tushman (2009) themselves pointed out, merely identifying organizational conditions that correlate with generation and implementation of novelty (such as, let us say, showing that there is more innovation when organizations make it easy to share knowledge, or that rewarding people for having novel ideas is associated with an increase in the number of such ideas produced) involves a static approach. What is needed is a dynamic approach that accounts for the following:

(a) Aspects of the organizational environment such as, let us say, sharing knowledge or providing rewards (as desirable as these may be) have different effects on different individual actors because of differences in the psychological resources that different people possess (see Chapter 4).

(b) The cognitive processes within the person (the personal environment) that are necessary for the generation and implementation of commercially salient novelty differ at different points in the sequence of events involved in the process, as is explained in following section (see also the discussion of phases in Chapter 6).

Various psychology writers have made a distinction between two kinds of thinking: the one leads to unexpected or unusual conclusions and is therefore more closely linked to invention, and the other is more closely linked to what already exists and is thus related to exploitation. Early examples include the distinction made by Bartlett (1932) between closed and open thinking. Wallach and Kogan (1965) referred to modes of thought, and A. J. Cropley and Field (1968) distinguished between two thinking styles. In a more picturesque way, Hudson (1967) drew attention to contrary imaginations. More recently, Rothenberg (1983) used a classical metaphor to describe Janusian thinking: The Roman God Janus (after whom the month January is named) had a face on both the back and the front of his head so that he could simultaneously look backward to the old year and forward to the new, thus combining information from what is already known and what is as yet unknown, in a process that Rothenberg called homospatial thinking.

Although his work is essentially popular in nature, de Bono (1993) made a catchy and widely quoted contribution to the discussion by distinguishing between rock logic and water logic. Application of the first kind of logic leads to thinking step by step in a straight line. Decisions on what the next step should be are based on correctness, and this is decided in terms of absolute norms such as truth, justice, or beauty, which change only slowly. Water logic, by contrast, allows ideas to flow together from many directions according to the natural pathways in the material in question, just as water flows along cracks and depressions in the ground wherever there is no resistance, and forms pools and eventually rivers (creative ideas).

De Bono is probably best known for his distinction between conventional thinking and what he called lateral thinking. The former is strictly sequential and follows logical steps, whereas lateral thinking involves detours or side steps. Marginal characteristics of a concept or object that are not central to its usual definition are emphasized and brought into juxtaposition with similar characteristics of other concepts and objects to yield unexpected associations. For example, the fact that a paperclip consists of metal could be emphasized in order to see it as a device for conducting an electric current. A matchbox can be regarded as a nonconductor with movable parts. Seeing these two objects in this way would make it possible to utilize them in an emergency situation for the construction of an electric switch.

However, the dominant psychological conceptualization of this issue was introduced by Guilford (1950). Although he drew attention to the importance in creativity of factors such as the person (see Chapter 4), in his seminal address to the American Psychological Association in 1949, Guilford emphasized the idea of two contrasting thinking styles, which he referred to as convergent and divergent thinking. Guilford's terminology quickly came to dominate psychological discussions, and indeed many writers treated *creativity* and *divergent thinking* as more or less synonymous terms, with convergent thinking being regarded as the antithesis of creativity. The dialectical pair, divergent thinking versus convergent thinking, has come to dominate psychological thinking about the special characteristics of creative cognition, and these two contrasting concepts will provide the basis for the following discussion.

A. J. Cropley (1999) summarized the differences between the two kinds of thinking in the following way:

1. *Convergent thinking* involves deriving the single best (or one and only correct) answer to a clearly defined question. It emphasizes speed, accuracy, logic, and the like, and focuses on accumulating information, recognizing the familiar aspects of new situations, reapplying already proven techniques, and similar processes. It is thus most effective in situations where the required answer can be worked out from what is already known by applying conventional and logical search, recognition, decision-making and evaluation strategies. One of the most important aspects of convergent thinking is that answers are either right or wrong. Convergent thinking is also intimately linked to knowledge because it involves manipulation of existing knowledge by means of standard procedures, which are themselves part of existing knowledge, and its typical result is improvement or extension of the already known along known lines. Thus, convergent thinking produces at best incremental innovation in the sense explained in Chapter 1.
2. *Divergent thinking*, by contrast, involves producing multiple or alternative answers from available information by, for instance, making unusual combinations, recognizing remote links among pieces of existing information, transforming existing information into unexpected forms, or seeing obscure implications. Divergent thinking may lead to a variety of conclusions based on the same starting point, and the ideas it yields may vary substantially from person to person. The results of divergent thinking may never have existed before: Sometimes this is true merely in the experience of the person producing the variability in question or for the particular

setting, but it may also be true in a broader sense, in which case the novelty is genetic (see Chapter 2).

Both divergent and convergent thinking can themselves be conceived of as consisting of families or clusters of subprocesses. Ward and Kolomyts (2010, p. 94), for example, decomposed divergent thinking into component processes such as information retrieval, imagery, analysis, abstraction, and analogy. They pointed out that these components could be further decomposed into even more specific components such as alignment, retrieval, mapping, and projection. At a more formal level, Boden (1996a) distinguished between ordinary thinking and thinking that makes a leap in the way a topic is conceptualized. Examples given by Boden of subprocesses that lead to such leaps include:

- retrieving a broader than usual range of facts from existing knowledge;
- building unusual chains of associations;
- synthesizing apparently unrelated elements of information;
- transforming information in unlikely ways;
- shifting perspective so as to see ideas in a new light; and
- constructing unexpected analogies.

A. J. Cropley (1999) suggested that the leap may not be a single cognitive action but could involve a chain of smaller steps that ultimately produce what is perceived as a leap.

An exact, highly specific description of divergent and convergent thinking would go far beyond the purposes of the present book. However, Table 3.1 contrasts subprocesses of divergent and convergent thinking at a descriptive level in more everyday language in order to give a sense of what is understood by the two terms here.

A. J. Cropley and Cropley (2009, p. 72) presented a case study of the French entomologist, René de Réaumur, as an example of synthesizing apparently unrelated elements of information to yield an important commercial innovation. In Réaumur's day, it had been known for more than 2,000 years that plant fibers that have been separated and suspended in water form a kind of interlocking mat upon drying out (i.e., paper). In France, before Réaumur, old rags were used as the source of fiber from which paper was made – an expensive manufacturing process because the raw materials had already been subjected to considerable value adding, with the result that paper was scarce and expensive. In the early 1700s, Réaumur noticed that certain wasps, today known as the paper wasp, chew up wood, digest it, regurgitate it, and use the resulting material to build

TABLE 3.1. *Typical Processes in Convergent and Divergent Thinking*[a]

Convergent Thinking	Divergent Thinking
• Thinking logically	• Thinking unconventionally
• Homing in on the best answer	• Branching out to generate multiple answers
• Recognizing the familiar	• Seeing the known in a new light
• Grasping the facts accurately	• Finding a new perspective on the facts
• Retrieving relevant information	• Retrieving a broad range of information
• Staying within the limits	• Going beyond the limits
• Combining what belongs together	• Combining the apparently disparate
• Making associations from adjacent fields	• Making remote associations
• Reapplying set techniques	• Devising new techniques
• Playing it safe	• Taking a risk
• Preserving the already known	• Challenging or transforming the already known
• Ensuring feasibility	• Ensuring novelty

[a] This table is based on A. J. Cropley and Cropley (2009, p. 48).

their nests. The material dries out to form a paperlike substance. Réaumur realized that chemical processes in the wasps' stomachs make paper directly from raw wood. He proposed transferring the wasps' chemical approach to human papermaking and thus invented modern techniques (although it must be admitted that he himself never succeeded in getting the process to work properly).

CONVERGENT THINKING AND INNOVATION

The crucial idea for analyzing the role of process as a building block of innovation is that it can be conceived of as essentially oriented to generating novelty (divergent thinking) or to maintaining the status quo (convergent thinking). Although this dichotomization involves a simplified way of looking at process, it is helpful for the present purposes. Intuitively, and especially after reviewing Table 3.1, there seems to be a close concordance between creativity and divergent thinking. After all, generating novelty is obviously essential for the production of new devices, systems, procedures, and the like.

Although Guilford himself acknowledged the importance for creativity of the acquisition of knowledge of facts and logical reasoning – subprocesses of convergent thinking – in psychological theory and research, creativity quickly came to be equated with divergent thinking. Divergent and convergent thinking were even sometimes presented as conflicting or competing processes (e.g., Getzels & Jackson, 1962), and convergent thinking was sometimes seen as bad or, at best, a necessary evil that is greatly exaggerated in education and business (e.g., A. J. Cropley, 1967). Both convergent and divergent thinking lead to production of ideas, although there is a major qualitative difference. As A. J. Cropley (2006, p. 391) put it, convergent thinking usually generates orthodoxy, whereas divergent thinking always generates variability; otherwise its results would not be divergent.

The Myth of Innovation through Pure Divergent Thinking

Indeed, the idea that effective novelty as outlined in Chapter 2 can be generated through simple unfettered divergent thinking alone, without any of the time-consuming and even mundane activities typical of convergent thinking (such as acquiring information, puzzling things out, checking feasibility, and so on; see Table 3.1), is attractive, probably especially to the pseudo- or quasi-creative (for a discussion of these terms, see the section titled Properties of Commercially Salient Creative Products in Chapter 2). Some writers (e.g., Hausman, 1984) have seemed to support this position by arguing that true creativity is always so novel that it is unprecedented and thus has no connection to anything that has gone before. However, writing about students in an apparel design course, Kawenski (1991) drew attention to a pervasive problem to which faith in pure divergent thinking gives rise and that possibly contributes to the antipathy to generation of novelty discussed in greater detail in Chapter 6. She reported that her students' "romantic notions led them to believe that creative thinking consisted of just letting their minds waft about dreamily, waiting for the muse to strike them" (p. 263).

It is certainly possible to imagine lucky hits or flukes, successful wild speculations, or dreams that turn out to be effective. A well-known historical example that looks at first glance like a lucky fluke is the discovery by Charles Goodyear in 1842 of the process for vulcanizing rubber, which is reputed to have taken place in the kitchen at his home as a result of an accidental spill of raw rubber onto the stove and caused him considerable trouble at first because he was not sure exactly how he had done it. However, Goodyear had been working hard along a consistent line of attack (treating raw rubber by combining it with various chemicals under exposure to heat) for years, and his discovery of the effective solution was simply the logical conclusion of a long line of inquiry, even if it came about in a haphazard way. In fact, there are many examples of apparently lucky combinations of events that led to acknowledged creative solutions (Rosenman, 1988). For instance Pasteur, Fleming, Roentgen, Becquerel, Edison, Galvani, and Nobel all described chance events that led them to breakthroughs.

In his now classical stage model of the generation of effective novelty, Wallas (1926) identified a stage of incubation during which ideas seem to churn and work in a person's head without the person being aware of them, until – apparently out of the blue – an answer pops up: a process of fermentation until an idea is suddenly there, even seeming to come from nowhere. However, as A. J. Cropley (1999) argued, far from representing generation of effective novelty without convergent thinking, intuition may well derive from convergent thinking at least as much as from divergent thinking. He concluded that even people who have not consciously acquired specialized knowledge and experience in an area often know a great deal through the convergent process of implicit learning (of which the learner is unaware), for instance through broad experience in a domain. Implicit learning leads to tacit knowledge that people do not know they possess. As a result, an apparent bolt from the blue may really involve logical extension of what the person in question already knows (without noticing that he or she knows it). In other words, the basis of intuition – which appears at first glance to be the epitome of creativity coming from nowhere – is knowledge, and knowledge is acquired via convergent thinking.

Despite the position of writers such as Hausman (1984), others such as Bailin (1988) have concluded that creative products are always conceived by both the creative person and external observers in terms of existing knowledge. Indeed, it is clear that many innovations are based on what already exists, even if existing knowledge is transferred to a field quite different from the one in which it is already known (see the Réaumur case study for an example of such transfer). In fact, the Canadian Intellectual Property Office (2015) reported that 90 percent of new patents are improvements of existing patents. In an aphorism that was printed in *Harper's Monthly* in 1932 (Josephson, 1959, p. 97), Thomas Alva Edison concluded that "[innovation] is 1% inspiration, 99% perspiration," thus clearly acknowledging the importance of more than simply letting ideas run free in a process of unfettered divergent thinking.

In fact, there has been increasing recognition of the fact that commercially salient novel products are not brought into existence solely by application of the family of divergent thinking subprocesses listed in the right-hand column of Table 3.1 but that they also require convergent thinking subprocesses such as those listed in the left-hand column (e.g., Rickards, 1993; Brophy, 1998; A. J. Cropley, 1999). This raises the counterintuitive question of how convergent thinking acts as a building block of innovation because it seems intuitively obvious that checking facts, assessing workability, calculating accurate cost estimates, assessing downstream effects, and similar processes would discourage branching out, taking a risk, trying something unexpected, and other divergent thinking subprocesses.

This book takes the view that production of commercially salient effective novelty does not occur by what Simon (1989, p. 377) called brute force: making blind associations among already known elements and occasionally recognizing, perhaps by sheer good fortune, that a new combination offers the required solution. As has already been pointed out, and echoing Levitt (2002, p. 137), "creativity is not enough." Within the organizational environment, simply lashing out mentally in an almost blind manner incurs the costs of innovation discussed in Chapter 6 with only vague hopes of compensating gains from implementation. As discussed in Chapter 6, the disorder involved in inserting novelty into an organizational environment must be introduced in an orderly fashion!

In more psychological terms, divergent thinking must be guided by convergent heuristics or what are often called metacognitive processes (e.g., Flavell, 1976, p. 232). Such processes involve, essentially, thinking about your own thinking. In the present context and as will be explained more fully in the section titled The Perils of Unfettered Divergent Thinking, such processes also include regulation and control of your own thinking through activities like checking feasibility. Silvia (2008) summarized this process clearly by referring to the importance of discernment (p. 139) or, in process terms, evaluating your own ideas. What then are the processes through which existing knowledge is converted into effective novelty?

Converting Existing Knowledge into New Ideas

Sternberg, Kaufman, and Pretz (2002) analyzed the role of creativity in "propelling a field" (p. 83), a concept that is close to what is understood here by innovation. They suggested a number of processes though which this can occur:

1. Conceptual replication (the known is transferred to a new setting)
2. Redefinition (the known is seen in a new way)

3. Forward incrementation (the known is extended in an existing direction)
4. Advance forward incrementation (the known is extended in an existing direction but goes beyond what is currently tolerable).
5. Redirection (the known is extended in a new direction)
6. Reconstruction and redirection (new life is breathed into an approach previously abandoned)
7. Reinitiation (thinking begins at a radically different point from the current one and takes off in a new direction)

Of these, only the last involves something quite new. All the others are based on modifying existing knowledge.

Savransky (2000) also discussed the processes through which existing knowledge is used to develop effective novelty: He argued that inventive solutions to problems always involve a change in what already exists. He discerned six ways in which this can occur. These include improvement, diagnostics, trimming, analogy, synthesis and genesis (his list is modified slightly for the purposes of this book).

The Russian researcher Altshuller (1988) also emphasized the role of the already known in his procedure for finding creative solutions to problems, known as TRIZ (a transliteration of the Russian acronym for "theory of inventive problem solving"). This procedure is based on an analysis of thousands of successful patent applications, that is, on effective novelty that is already known. It argues that all engineering systems display the same systematic patterns of change. Creativity is the result of development of what exists according to these patterns. TRIZ identifies these systematic processes of novelty generation so that people working with a new problem can apply them in order to derive their own novel solutions.

THE PERILS OF UNFETTERED DIVERGENT THINKING

Divergent thinking produces novelty, to be sure, but on its own it can easily lead not to creativity but to pseudo-creativity or quasi-creativity (unless there is a blind hit – see the section titled The Myth of Innovative Creativity through Pure Divergent Thinking). A. J. Cropley and Cropley (2009) gave the whimsical and fictitious example of a civil engineer who noticed that steel reinforcing rods and spaghetti are both long, have a circular profile, and under certain circumstances are flexible, and thus made an unexpected link between spaghetti and steel reinforcing rods. There really are similarities between the two, and settings may conceivably exist where this variation from the usual perception of steel and spaghetti could lead to effective novelty (even if it is difficult to imagine what these settings might be). However, most civil engineers would probably reject out of hand the actual use of spaghetti instead of reinforcing rods in building large concrete structures and would predict a catastrophe if spaghetti were used to replace steel (i.e., they would explore the novelty and would judge it to be incapable of implementation). Although forging an unexpected link and seeing spaghetti in a new way involve divergent thinking, rejection of the novelty generated in this way would be based on the engineers' knowledge of basic principles of civil engineering, such as strength of materials (i.e., on convergent thinking). Thus, checking out divergent thinking by means of convergent thinking would lead to avoidance of a structural disaster.

The situation just described would involve novelty generation followed by (or accompanied by) exploration of the novelty from the point of view of acceptability, practicability, affordability, marketability, or similar criteria in order to determine if it is effective. Only if both processes were carried out and led to satisfactory results would it be possible to speak of innovation. It is thus tempting to think of the phase of exploration as essentially a process of evaluation, as Luecke and Katz (2003) did. Runco (2003) supported this view. He argued that creativity requires a combination of divergent and convergent thinking, and argued further that the convergent thinking involves "critical processes" (p. 432), that is, what has just been called evaluation.

The importance of divergent thinking in production of effective novelty cannot be denied. However, although generation of novelty is necessary, Levitt's (2002) dictum holds true: "Creativity is not enough." Sheer generation of novelty is not sufficient on its own, except perhaps for occasional flukes when blind luck leads to effective novelty. Convergent thinking is necessary too because it makes it possible to explore, evaluate, or diagnose novelty and identify its effective aspects. In the enthusiasm for divergent thinking it is thus important not to forget the contribution of convergent thinking. Table 3.2 gives examples of vital convergent thinking processes in both the generating and exploring phases of generation of variability.

In aesthetic creativity, in many cases novelty that turns out to be ineffective can be implemented without disaster. Indeed, it may be hailed as a brave attempt to push back the frontier. In the case of organizational innovation, however, introduction of novelty that does not work can have disastrous consequences. It may be as lethal for an organization as failure to innovate, to continue the metaphor of organizational death introduced in

TABLE 3.2. *Contribution of Convergent Thinking to Innovation*[a]

Phase in Production of Effective Novelty	Convergent Process
Generating variability	• Accumulating factual knowledge • Observing closely • Remembering accurately • Drawing correct conclusions • Thinking logically • Processing information rapidly
Exploring variability	• Recognizing promising lines of attack • Rejecting unpromising lines of attack • Zeroing in on potential solutions • Seeing limits • Being aware of weaknesses • Weighing feasibility • Recognizing a workable solution when it occurs

[a] This table is adapted from A. J. Cropley (2006, p. 399).

Chapter 1. Thus, novelty generated in organizations via divergent processes must be fitted in with the demands of the external world. In a nutshell, organizations need to be free to generate novelty, but they cannot afford to do this in a vacuum: They face the necessity of engaging with actors and organizations in the wider social environment, including – crucially for most organizations – customers. Christensen (2013) gave examples of highly effective (and sometimes ultimately successful) innovations that nonetheless led to disasters for otherwise successful and well-run great firms because customers rejected the innovation. As Besemer (2006, p. 171) put it: "consumers don't like too many surprises." To be exploited, novelty must be made compatible with the existing framework, referred to in this book as the social environment, or to be shaped by the social press. This means that organizations must break away from what already exists while preserving the tried and trusted. As Gabora and Tseng (2014) pointed out, unfettered creativity can easily become too much of a good thing.

What are the risks for an organization if novelty is introduced without appropriate exploration (i.e., if divergent thinking is not accompanied by convergent thinking)? Figure 3.1 considers a number of possibilities. If no variability is generated (there is no divergent thinking), nothing changes and orthodoxy rules, avoiding dangers such as disastrous change, to be

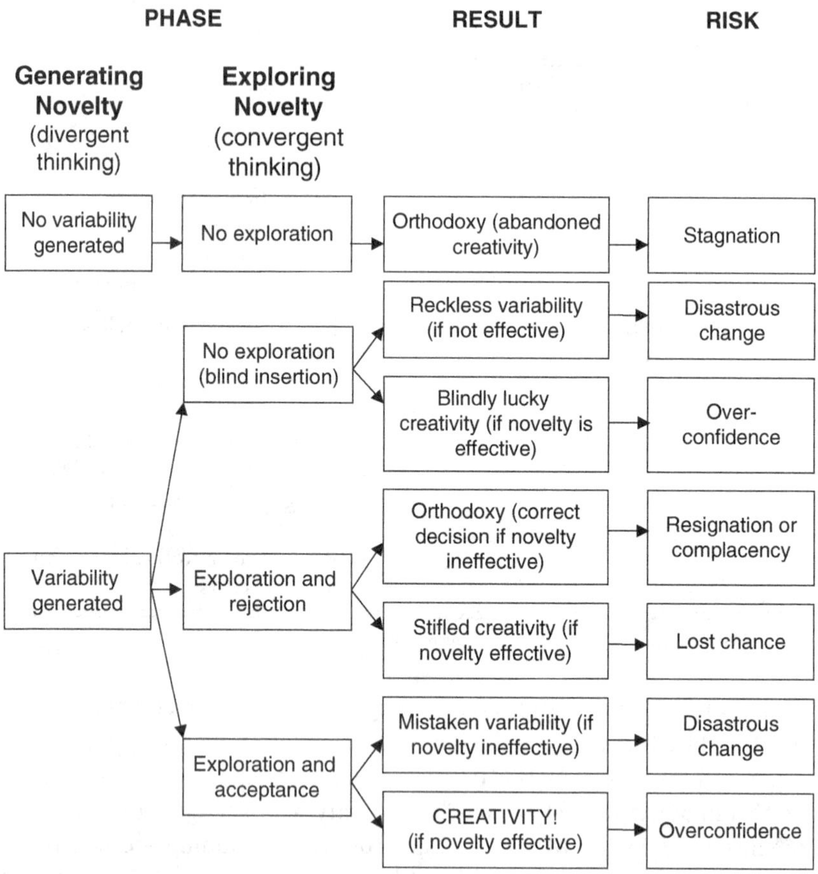

FIGURE 3.1. Consequences of Differing Combinations of Divergent and Convergent Thinking[a]

[a] This figure is taken from A. J. Cropley and Cropley (2009, p. 83).

sure, but bringing the risk of stagnation and similar problems. This is the situation depicted in the first row of the figure. It is, of course, the safest pathway in organizations, an environment in which errors are frequently punished but doing nothing is often tolerated without sanctions.

A new set of possibilities opens up when variability is actually generated. It is possible for this to be accepted without exploration (i.e., divergent thinking without convergent thinking). If such novelty proves to be ineffective, it is possible to speak of recklessness, which raises the danger of disastrous change. If the novelty proves to be effective despite the lack of exploration, this is more a matter of luck than judgment, and it is thus possible to speak of blind innovation, with the danger of overconfidence in the future. Not only does lack of knowledge reduce the possibility of generation of variability in the first place, but even where variability is generated, lack of exploration (convergent thinking) raises the possibility of reckless variability and exposes the organization to the risk of disastrous change or overconfidence.

Figure 3.1 also depicts the various possibilities if exploration does take place (i.e., divergent thinking accompanied by convergent thinking). Where convergent thinking leads to a correct decision to implement the novelty, there is a successful innovation, which is the ideal result. Where convergent thinking correctly leads to rejection of the variability generated through divergent thinking, the possibility of disastrous change is avoided but at the risk of resignation or complacency. Of course, the convergent thinking is not always correct: In the Computer Users' Committee at the University of Hamburg in the early 1980s, one of the present authors (A. J. Cropley) fought against the introduction of remote computer terminals on the grounds that desktop computing would never catch on! Fortunately, his objections were overruled and ignored. Errors of exploration (mistakes in convergent thinking) can lead to stifled innovation (false negatives) or mistaken innovation (false positives) and raise the danger of a lost chance or, on the other hand, a disastrous change.

An example of the latter is to be seen in the introduction of New Coke by the Coca-Cola Company in 1985. Faced with falling market share, mainly in favor of Pepsi, the company introduced New Coke in the United States in April 1985. Blind taste testing prior to the launch had indicated that consumers preferred the new flavor to the traditional one by a wide margin. Indeed, the initial reaction to New Coke in its first few weeks on the market was favorable. Market share increased substantially. However, a strong backlash quickly developed: No fewer than 400,000 protest calls and letters of complaint flooded the company's public relations department, and protest groups sprang up, especially in the South but in other parts of the United States too. Massive hoarding of the familiar variant of Coca-Cola also occurred. In July, regular Coke was reintroduced as Classic Coke and was marketed alongside New Coke.

The New Coke fiasco had a happy ending for Coca-Cola, and disastrous change was avoided. Although derided at the time as the greatest management bungle of all time, the introduction of New Coke actually achieved its strategic goal – rejuvenation of the Coke brand. After the retirement of the new form of the drink and the return to the old form, Coke regained its lost market share. There was even a conspiracy theory that the whole thing was a brilliant marketing ploy that worked exactly as planned. For the purposes of this chapter, the initially disastrous introduction of New Coke is seen as an example of the second-to-last sequence of events depicted in Figure 3.1 – implementation of novelty without adequate evaluation (although the ultimate outcome was not a disaster).

THE INTERACTION OF DIVERGENT AND CONVERGENT THINKING

The arguments advanced in earlier sections of this chapter imply that both divergent and convergent thinking are necessary for the production of effective novelty and that divergent *and* convergent thinking are vital parts of the process of innovation. As has just been shown, however, unfettered divergence unsupported by convergent processes opens up the danger of misguided innovation, which may be as dangerous for organizations as failure to innovate, or even more dangerous, as the near-disaster of New Coke shows. Thus, a combination of both kinds of thinking is needed. However, the way the two kinds of thinking work together is not straightforward, as will be shown in following paragraphs.

The Perils of Convergent Thinking

Although essential for successful innovation, convergent thinking has perils of its own. Quite apart from problems arising from, for instance, lack of knowledge, incorrect information, misunderstanding, and the like (i.e., not enough convergent thinking), too much convergent thinking can act as a set of blinkers and channel information processing into a narrow range of approaches – possibly without the awareness of the person concerned.

The results of convergent thinking such as possession of large amounts of information, perhaps through working successfully in an area over a long period of time, can provide a substantial knowledge base that can be manipulated to yield effective novelty, for example, through processes outlined by Sternberg and colleagues, and Savransky (see the section titled Converting Existing Knowledge into New Ideas). Thus, convergent thinking can benefit divergent thinking. However, preexisting knowledge can also act as a corset that blocks novel ideas so that thinking leads only to production of tried, trusted, and correct answers. What is needed is enough convergent thinking but not too much! Gabora and Tseng's (2014) too-much-of-a-good-thing principle applies here, too.

How do divergent and convergent thinking work together? The phenomena of punctuated equilibrium and organizational ambidexterity in organizations have already been referred to (see the section titled Components of the Process of Innovative Thinking). In creativity theory, Shaw (1989) discussed simultaneous or parallel, possibly conflicting, processes such as free generation of novelty in parallel with strict evaluation of the workability of the ideas generated and saw these as involving what he called loops. For instance, an idea might be generated (in present terms, divergent thinking might occur), and its workability could be assessed, flaws detected, and understanding of the flaws added to existing knowledge (all the latter via convergent thinking). The new state of affairs emerging from the generation-evaluation cycle just described could then act as the starting point for a new cycle. Shaw concluded that there may also be more complex loops involving three or more subcomponents of the process of production and implementation of novelty, such as recognition of the existence of a problem (essentially convergent in nature), redefinition of the problem (divergent), generation of novelty (divergent), and evaluation of the novelty (convergent). The complexity of the interactions among the subprocesses of innovative creativity is emphasized by the fact that, for instance, the information obtained when a product is tried in public could generate new problem awareness and set off a completely new cycle of invention, implementation, and evaluation in a variant of punctuated equilibrium, or it could lead to a restart at the level of implementation while preserving the existing invention: This would be something like institutional ambidexterity.

However, other possible forms of interaction can be imagined rather than the variants of a linear or loop model just outlined. For instance, knowledge (acquired by means of convergent thinking) may act as a pool of information or a wellspring, from which ideas are extracted and combined via divergent thinking. This approach is important because it implies that the first prerequisite for innovation would be a large supply of information, for instance, in the form of expertise,[1] with the amount of effective novelty generated depending on the degree of divergence of the processes carried out on the pool of knowledge once it has been acquired (such as linking apparently separate elements, seeing new kinds of relationships in data, or using unexpected combination strategies). It is conceivable, in fact, that convergent thinking could start the whole innovation process rather

[1] Expertise will be discussed in more detail in Chapter 4 as a personal resource for innovation.

than simply being applied in order to evaluate the products of divergent thinking after they have been generated.

Problem Finding

It also seems that divergent thinking may play a broader role than simply generation of novelty. For instance, the problem requiring an innovative response could be redefined in a divergent way so that the novel product could then be achieved by means of convergent thinking. A simple example is the solution achieved in an engineering situation where ultra-hard precast concrete slabs had to be bolted together. The concrete was so hard that it proved to be extremely difficult to drill the necessary holes for the bolts. The problem was initially conceived as the necessity of producing steel bits that were hard enough and sharp enough not to be blunted almost immediately when the concrete was drilled. Efforts to produce the required drill bits failed. At this point, the problem was redefined as that of avoiding the need for holes to be drilled at all, and the answer was fairly obvious: The concrete slabs were fabricated with precast holes, and the innovation proved highly successful, despite the fact that the solution was mundane.

The whole area of problem finding has been discussed for many years in creativity theory. Early writers such as Torrance (1963) argued that the special thing about creative problem solving is that it involves not solving problems as they have been constructed by somebody else but finding or defining your own problems in a process of problem recognition, problem finding, or problem definition. As Dillon (1982) pointed out, there are at least three possibilities in approaching problems: simply recognizing the obvious problem that is already evident in the existing organization of information, discovering problems that are hidden to other observers, or inventing problems where others see none. Merely recognized problems may sometimes prove to be insoluble. Discovered problems require going beyond the obvious, while invented problems seem to have the most to do with creativity (Jay & Perkins, 1997). Mumford, Baughman, Threlfall, Supinski, and Costanza (1996) identified problem construction as one of the main cognitive processes involved in creative problem solving.

While presumably better than nothing, simply finding problems is not enough for successful innovation. Tardiff and Sternberg (1988) went further and emphasized an additional element: finding *good* problems. More recently, Sawyer (2006, p. 47) concluded that the most important characteristic of creative individuals is "an almost aesthetic ability to recognize a good problem in their domain." A striking example is Einstein's recognition that existing theories in contemporary physics were inadequate for dealing with moving bodies. He (a) invented a problem where many others saw none and (b) identified the good aspect of this problem. This quickly led to the special theory of relativity, revealed the need for a general theory of relativity (the first solution was genetic), and ultimately resulted in lasting fame. Good problems are those that not only provoke a helpful answer to a specific situation but also yield or even require elegant and generalizable solutions. In the engineering situation where ultrahard precast concrete slabs needed bolt holes, for instance, the new design for prefabricated slabs was transferred to many other building sites.

The New Coke example shows how solving a bad problem or the wrong problem can be disastrous: The company's loss of market share was identified as involving a problem with the flavor of Coke, and this problem was very effectively solved by developing a new flavor, and it was judged by most people to be markedly superior to the old one. Unfortunately, however, the novel and effective, possibly elegant and genetic solution, did not solve the real problem, which presumably lay in the area of marketing, not taste at all.

OVERVIEW AND OUTLOOK

The process of innovation has been presented in this chapter in terms of phases, especially phases of invention and implementation. This approach obviously involves an oversimplification, as will be discussed later in the book (see especially Chapter 6). For instance, there may well be more than two phases, the phases may occur in a cyclical or recurring way and not in linear sequence, they may not be distinct from each other at all but may fuse or merge, or people actually engaging in innovative thinking may have no sense of working in phases at all. However, the phase approach provides a conceptual basis for a relatively straightforward discussion and has been adopted in this chapter for that purpose, especially in the form of a two-phase position based on the distinction in creativity research between convergent and divergent thinking.

Convergent thinking is understood here as encompassing a family of cognitive processes based on acquiring correct knowledge, processing and storing the knowledge logically, and retrieving it accurately. Divergent thinking involves using this information to generate novelty through subprocesses such as seeing unexpected links, understanding information in a new way, or redefining problems. As will be shown in the next chapter, these processes are supported (or not) by a cluster of personal resources such as willingness to take a risk, tolerance for uncertainty, or openness.

Innovation requires not only generation of novelty but also implementation of the novelty, and implementation requires both evaluation of the usefulness of novelty and also knowledge about how to implement it; both of these are convergent activities. In fact, naked or unfettered divergent thinking is dangerous for organizations and needs to be supported by convergent thinking – however, as will be discussed later in this book, the crucial action for management is to temper divergent thinking but not to curb it. Furthermore, novel ideas do not come from nowhere but are based on knowledge, except in the case of lucky flukes. In other words, divergent thinking not only needs to be moderated by convergent thinking but also arises from it. Thus, in the process of innovation, convergent thinking both precedes and follows divergent thinking; to put it slightly differently, in organizational innovation, the necessary divergent thinking is embedded in a field of convergent thinking. A more differentiated phase model of innovation (see Chapters 6 and 8) makes it possible to understand the interaction of convergent and divergent thinking more clearly and provides guidelines for the management of institutional creativity.

4

Person: The Personal Resources That Support Innovation

Innovation has been examined so far in terms of two building blocks: commercially salient products and the thinking processes leading to them. However, it can also be looked at in terms of the personal resources of individual people who engage in the process of generating commercially salient novelty. The need for an examination of such aspects of innovation was underlined by Dyer, Gregersen, and Christensen (2009, p. 60) in their review of the role of the person in innovation. They stated there that we "know very little about what makes one person more [innovative] than another." Although they actually used the word *creative* in the passage just cited, the focus of their discussions was unmistakably innovation. Bearing in mind Nussbaum's (2013) call for a proactive approach (Chapter 1), these personal properties can be thought of as psychological resources (Rauch, Wiklund, Lumpkin, & Frese, 2009) that function as "antecedents of proactive behavior" (Parker, Williams, & Turner, 2006, p. 636). Anticipating later sections, these resources include:

(a) personal styles, such as openness to experience or tolerance for uncertainty
(b) affective states, such as motivation or feelings
(c) cognitive properties, such as expertise and information-processing skills

CONCEPTUALIZING PERSON IN INNOVATION

In a discussion directly related to the person in innovation, Crant (2000, p. 440) referred to the proactive personality, and Parker, Williams, and Turner (2006) also described the proactive personality. More recently,

Lynch, Walsh, and Harrington (2010) defined innovativeness as an "innate human personality trait" (p. 7). Collis (2010) also discussed the role of personality in innovation. However, the use of the term *personality* may raise problems for readers. In psychological discussions, personality is usually understood as involving traits such as conscientiousness, agreeableness, adaptability, persistence, or imaginativeness, or broad dispositions such as extraversion/introversion, which are thought to be at least partly biologically determined (see, for example, Eysenck, 1952) or to be laid down in early years and to remain stable throughout life, except perhaps when they are modified through therapy. An example of the latter is the psychoanalytic model of personality. Thus, the idea of the creative personality seems to suggest that the personal resources of the innovative individual consist of specific personality traits that are laid down very early and are immutable or nearly so, and lead the person who possesses the necessary traits more or less inevitably to emit innovative behavior.

The title of Dyer, Gregersen, and Christensen's (2009) overview, "The Innovator's DNA," seems at first glance to support this conceptualization by implying that innovativeness as a personal property is in the DNA and is therefore something for the lucky few with the right genes. However, in an early psychological discussion, A. J. Cropley (1969, p, 4) argued that the personal disposition toward creativity can be thought of as encompassing a style, mode, or bias in ways of interacting with the external environment. Cropley particularly contrasted the divergent style with the convergent one (see Chapter 3). Gardner (1983) referred to creativity as a form of application of intelligence. In other words, the generation of effective novelty involves not what you have or how much of it you have but the way you use it! In a much more recent psychological discussion along related lines, Sternberg (2007, p. 3) described creativity as a habit that can be acquired in the same way as any habit and is therefore affected by the environment; he cited opportunities, encouragement, and rewards as crucial environmental conditions for fostering the habit.[1]

In this book, personal resources will be thought of in a qualitative way as involving a disposition to behave in a particular manner when confronted with a situation requiring generation of effective novelty. Dispositions are "consistent patterns in a person's behavior and thought" (Allport, 1961, p. 358) (e.g., approaching something new in a bold manner, feeling good about making suggestions for solutions to problems). Dispositions are learned as a result of experience in dealing with situations in life and differ

[1] Sternberg also made the point that, regrettably, creativity is sometimes seen as a *bad* habit!

sharply from person to person, even where personality traits may be similar. For instance, everybody possesses the trait of intelligence, although to a greater or lesser degree, but the way intelligence is applied is an acquired behavioral disposition that is shaped by experience. One person might acquire the habit of inventing new solutions (i.e., of innovating), and another person of equal intelligence might acquire the habit of improving what already exists (i.e., of adapting).

Turning directly to organizations, in a substantial overview and evaluation of the literature in which, among other things, they drew attention to the need for a solid body of widely accepted concepts, Rauch, Wiklund, Lumpkin, and Frese (2009), used the term *orientation* to refer to the personal disposition being discussed here.[2] Miron-Spektor, Erez, and Naveh (2011) echoed the style approach outlined above. They studied groups attempting to develop innovations and identified what they called cognitive styles. Where these styles come from was elucidated by Collis (2010, p. 3), who described them as resulting from learned rules and regulations in people's minds that can be unlearned and relearned through appropriate training – such training is in fact his main focus of interest. Despite their reference to DNA, Dyer, Gregersen, and Christensen (2009), in the article already mentioned, also went on to conclude that the antecedents of innovative behavior can be cultivated. Later chapters of this book (see especially Chapter 9) will discuss how managers can promote appropriate learning and unlearning.

PERSONAL RESOURCES FOR INNOVATION

Although some people would argue that it is an oxymoron, the term *organizational creativity* has become common in the literature and has been used by writers like Woodman, Sawyer, and Griffin (1993); Andriopoulos (2001); Mostafa (2005); Stenmark (2005); and, most recently, Mumford (2012) and West, Hoff, and Carlsson (2013), to give a few examples from the last few decades. However, as might be expected, discussions of organizational creativity are largely limited to organizational environment factors, even when they are based on psychological concepts. Examples are organizational culture (e.g., goals, values, degree of openness to the new, or kinds of decision-making process), management structures

[2] These authors focused on entrepreneurship. This term has been deliberately avoided in the present book because it is used almost exclusively to refer to the founding of new organizations, whereas the focus of interest here is innovation in existing organizations.

(e.g., distribution of power, reward systems, marketing strategies), or work organization (e.g., team structures, information flows, leadership styles). For example, Hunter, Bedell, and Mumford (2007) studied organizational climate, and Mumford, Scott, Gaddis, and Strange (2002) and Amabile, Schatzel, Moneta, and Kramer (2004) focused on leadership. In a review of around twenty studies, Damanpour (1991) emphasized the effects of organizational structure, and Taggar, Sulsky, and MacDonald (2008) examined the effects of organizational strategy. The extent to which qualities of an organization in such areas promote innovation define its level of organizational creativity. While it is clear that such organizational environment factors are by no means irrelevant, the position adopted here is that they do not take adequate account of the personal environment of the individual person.

Individual Creativity

Organizational researchers such as Bharadwaj and Menon (2000) and Andriopoulos (2001) moved toward a more person-centered approach in psychologically oriented organizational research by differentiating between organizational creativity as outlined in the previous section and individual creativity. In doing this, they moved away from a discussion based on organizational environment factors such as organizational culture, leadership style, reward systems, communication processes, and teamwork toward one emphasizing personal environment factors within individual actors such as knowledge, motives and feelings, and personal styles. Although the term *individual creativity* is helpful for the present discussion, because it focuses attention on attributes of the person not the institution, it does not distinguish among the following: someone who generates novelty with complete disdain for any kind of product at all (see the reference to Rothman [2014] in Chapter 2); someone like Gautier who wishes to generate novel products, to be sure, but shows disdain for usefulness (see Chapter 2); and the person who generates novelty for the express purpose of bringing into existence not merely a product but one that has at least the potential for practical implementation in a value-adding sense. All three patterns involve particular forms of individual creativity. The third situation – generation of novelty with the intention of generating a commercially salient product – is a special form of this individual creativity, and it differs from the general case through (a) its focus on a product and (b) its insistence on a commercially useful product.

Dimensions of the Personal Resources for Innovation

It is common in psychological discussions to look at generation of novelty in term of four components referred to as the Four Ps (product, person, process, and press); it can be seen that the Four Ps approach lumps all psychological dimensions of the individual person together to form a single P. However, A. J. Cropley and Cropley (2009) argued that this treatment of person is too undifferentiated because it confounds personal dispositions (such as confronting problems with confidence, opening one's mind to novel ideas, or going about things in an unorthodox way), motivational states (such as willingness to take risks, drive for closure, or tolerance of ambiguity), and feelings (such as pleasurable excitement versus anxiety in the face of incongruity, optimism versus pessimism, or the thrill of the chase versus trepidation); however, research suggests that these personal factors should not be conflated.

For instance, Baas, De Dreu, and Nijstad's (2008) meta-analytic findings showed that mood (feelings) modifies motivation. Among other things, mood can have an activating or deactivating effect; that is, it can enhance or detract from motivation. To take a second example, Baas, De Dreu, and Nijstad showed that feelings affect motivation differently according to the way a particular task is conceived of cognitively. In a thirty-year longitudinal study, Helson (1999) showed that personal dispositions such as openness and flexibility are only favorable for creativity when they are accompanied by motivational states such as tolerance for ambiguity and by feelings such as optimism. Otherwise they may even be detrimental to creativity. Thus, mood, motivation, and cognition cannot be treated as involving a single dimension of the person.

Accordingly, A. J. Cropley and Cropley (2009) deconstructed the P of person into personal properties, personal motivation, and personal feelings. These three elements are outlined in the next subsections.

Personal motivation

Many studies have confirmed that motivation played an important role in the creativity of famous creative people from the past (for an overview, see A. J. Cropley, 2001). According to Perkins (1981), creativity is driven by motivational factors such as (a) the drive to create order out of chaos, (b) willingness to take risks, (c) willingness to ask unexpected questions, and (d) the feeling of being challenged by an area. Newton, Copernicus, Galileo, Kepler, and Darwin were marked by tenacity and perseverance. Facaoaru (1985) showed that creative engineers were characterized not only by special intellectual characteristics but also by motivational factors such as determination. Mumford and Moertl (2003, p. 262) described a case study of innovative management practice and concluded that it was driven by intense dissatisfaction with the status quo, that is, by endogenous shocks (Barreto, 2012). Thomas Alva Edison constantly improved his own existing ideas and over the course of time, for instance, took out more than 100 patents for improvements to his original invention of the electric light bulb.

Personal feelings/mood

In an overview of research on mood and creativity, Kaufmann (2003) showed that generative feelings – such as the thrill of the chase when facing a challenge, the feeling of excited anticipation when generating novelty, or the feeling of satisfaction after achieving an effectively novel product – and also conserving feelings – such as anxiety in the face of uncertainty, frustration when progress is impeded, or disappointment when a product is not validated – play a role in generating effective novelty. Baas, De Dreu, and Nijstad's (2008) meta-analytic findings (already mentioned in this chapter) showed that mood (feelings) affects creativity in complex ways. Among other things, mood can be activating (e.g., anger, fear, happiness) or deactivating (relaxation, calm, depression); that is, it can enhance or detract from motivation. Hedonically negative moods such as anger or fear enhance creativity by increasing perseverance (they motivate people to put in greater effort), whereas hedonically positive moods affect people cognitively and encourage flexibility and daring thinking. Negative mood enhances performance on tasks that are presented as deadly serious and highly demanding because it encourages concentration, precision, and highly systematic divergent thinking; performance on tasks requiring speculation, taking a chance, and the like, is facilitated by positive mood.

Personal properties

Various authors have published reviews of the personal attributes that are important for generating effective novelty, and A. J. Cropley and Cropley (2009) reviewed several of these. The studies indicate that some personal styles for interacting with the world seem to be particularly helpful for creativity, including (a) resisting conformity (both in attitudes as well as in social behavior), (b) maintaining autonomy/inner-directedness, (c) following up intuitions, (d) tolerating ambiguity/preferring complexity, (e) being flexible, (f) following a wide range of interests, (g) taking risks, (h) accepting being different (i.e., self-acceptance), and (i) displaying a positive attitude toward work. Other researchers reviewed by Cropley and Cropley also included androgyny (displaying attitudes, values, preferences, and the like, that are typically regarded in the social environment as both male and female); this aspect of creativity will be discussed in more detail in Chapter 5.

Thus, for an analysis such as the one in this book, the P of person must be deconstructed into three components that, although they interact strongly with each other, have just been shown to be distinguishable. This deconstruction yields an expanded Four Ps model or, for present purposes, a model based on six building blocks of innovation. Table 4.1 provides an overview of the kinds of personal dispositions that are favorable for innovation within the building blocks of process, personal attributes and feelings, and press (from the point of view of the individual person) and contrasts these with characteristics of the organization (organizational environment). The contents of the table do not offer an exhaustive overview of the two environments but a summary of some of the main ideas about them in order to make the distinction between them clearer (later sections in this chapter will deal more fully with the personal environment).

The psychological domains are grouped according to various factors in the table (e.g., cognition, personal attributes, etc.). They are, of course, used in a metaphorical way when they refer to organizations (i.e., an organization does not itself think and does not have personal properties, but it does provide conditions that directly affect cognition or the way people's personal properties find expression). Much of the latter part of this chapter will be devoted to expanding understanding of personal environment factors by adding insights derived from psychological studies of creativity.

With properties such as rich information flows, coordinated knowledge bases, openness to novelty, encouragement of autonomy, lateral organization, and peer recognition, the organizational factors as summarized in Table 4.1 are no doubt highly facilitative of innovation, and there is no suggestion here that the organization environment is irrelevant. However, the organizational approach does not describe and define the personal properties of the human actors in the process of innovation. The main purpose of this chapter is to expand the left-hand column of Table 4.1 in order to develop a more encompassing description of the personal environment factors (properties of the individual actor) that need to be considered in developing an understanding of innovation.

The Crucial Importance of Openness

It is apparent that the list of relevant behavioral dispositions related to creativity is long. However, recent research has reduced the size of the field

TABLE 4.1. *Behavioral Dispositions Favorable for Innovation*

	Behavioral Dispositions	
Psychological Domain	In the Personal Environment	In the Organizational Environment[a]
Cognition (information acquisition, processing, and use)	• Spotting opportunities • Branching out from known facts • Making unexpected links • Employing thinking styles such as intuiting • Thinking both convergently and divergently • Building broad categories • Making remote associations	Nurturing knowledge by: • Providing resources and time • Facilitating rich information flows • Coordinating knowledge bases Maintaining an innovative culture by: • Taking novel ideas seriously • Maintaining flexible organizational boundaries • Setting flexible organizational goals • Providing constructive feedback
Personal[b] attributes (including attitudes, values, feelings)	• Displaying unorthodoxy • Enjoying autonomy • Being flexible • Maintaining a state of openness • Displaying self-confidence • Experiencing positive feelings about change and novelty • Preferring complexity	Human resources that support innovation by: • Displaying openness to suggestions • Tolerating "fooling around" • Tolerating errors • Responding positively to questioning and skepticism • Being willing to change

Personal motivation	• Being fascinated with a topic • Experiencing dissatisfaction with imperfection • Feeling an urge to produce something new • Having the courage to take risks • Being willing to go it alone	Management support for innovation by: • Providing rewards for generation of novelty • Encouraging autonomy • Encouraging questioning the customary way
Press (social factors)	• Possessing communication skills • Accepting feedback constructively • Being willing to work in a team • Possessing skill in collaboration But sometimes:[b] • Being impatient with those who have a different opinion • Feeling and displaying contempt for those who do not catch on • Being indifferent to peer relations • Showing defiance of authority	Encouraging participatory leadership by: • Maintaining open communication channels • Providing opportunities for participatory decision making Promoting networking by: • Providing opportunities for interactions with colleagues • Promoting lateral coordination of tasks • Encouraging peer recognition

[a] The subheadings in this column are based on Read's (2000, p. 104) overview of organizational environment factors.

[b] Negative aspects of innovative creativity will be discussed in greater detail in Chapter 6.

by examining more general ways of interacting with the external environment. Batey and Furnham (2006), for instance, reviewed research relating creativity to personality by studying the relationship between creativity and what psychologists now often call the Big Five components of personality: openness, conscientiousness, extraversion, agreeableness, and neuroticism. Hennessey and Amabile (2010) listed openness to experience, persistence, curiosity, energy, and intellectual honesty as having consistently been identified as vital for creativity. The relevant literature has also been summarized and reviewed recently by Martinsen (2011).

In a comprehensive review, Silvia, Kaufman, Reiter-Palmon, and Wigert (2011) showed that there is unanimity about the existence of a link to creativity on only one of the Big Five dimensions of personality: openness. The effects of personal properties such as inner-directedness, flexibility, or self-confidence (mentioned earlier in the section titled Personal Properties) are indirect because they are mediated by their contribution to openness. Silvia (2008) showed that openness is also strongly connected with people's ability to judge the value of their own creative solutions, what he called discernment. Ehrlinger and Dunning (2003) showed that one of the greatest weaknesses of incompetent people is how poorly they judge their own lack of ability. Thus, managers need to be able to explain precisely the weaknesses of the novelty such people generate, a process that would be greatly facilitated by application of the Creative Solution Diagnosis Scale (CSDS; see Chapter 2). Also interesting in the research just mentioned was that Silvia found that conscientiousness, no doubt highly prized in organizations, is *negatively* related to generation of novelty.

INNOVATION AND EXPERTISE

An obvious personal resource for innovation is knowledge of the field into which effective novelty is to be introduced. Scott (1999) listed a number of creativity researchers who all give a prominent place to knowledge (e.g., Albert, Amabile, Campbell, Chi, Gardner, Gruber, Mednick, Simonton, Wallas, and Weisberg). This aspect of innovative behavior was recognized very early: Rossman's (1931) study of inventors concluded that they "manipulate the symbols of ... past experience" (p. 82). He also showed that they combined "known movements" (p. 77). Feldhusen (1995) and Walberg and Stariha (1992), among others, made an important point by emphasizing the knowledge base (Feldhusen, 1995, p. 255) of creativity. As Ward (2004, p. 176) put it: "Creative ideas do not appear, ex nihilo, full-blown in the minds of their originators, but rather must be crafted from the person's *existing knowledge*" (emphasis added). Bailin (1988, p. 5) summarized the situation by concluding that novelty "always arises out of what already exists."

The idea of knowledge as the basis of generation of effective novelty has been put in more formal terms by Boden (1996a), using the language of artificial intelligence. What is required are detailed "cognitive maps [of a] conceptual space" (p. 8). The more structural features of a conceptual space such as, let us say, production methods are in a person's mind (the more the person knows about production methods), the more potential the person possesses for innovation in that area. In addition to providing a source of ideas about an issue, the knowledge involved in expertise provides information about which kinds of attack on a problem are likely to be fruitful (or are already known to be fruitless); defines the pathways, methods, and tools through which progress can be made; and specifies the nature of acceptable solutions.

However, the role of expertise in innovation is not purely cognitive. For instance, in their investigation of motivation for scientific creativity Park and Jang (2005) concluded that, scientists' special knowledge of their field provided them with motivation to seek new lines of attack and see things in a new way. Without this expertise they would not have been in a position to be motivated to develop the scientific innovations for which they strove. In particular, Park and Jang identified three ways in which expertise produces motivation: (a) by making it possible to recognize gaps in existing knowledge (incompleteness), (b) by setting off a drive to round out recently emerging novelty (development), and (c) by facilitating identification of contradictions in accepted knowledge (conflict/discrepancy). Thus, knowledge of the field is not only important in itself as a source of ideas; it also affects motivation, self-image, willingness to take risks, openness for the new, and similar noncognitive factors.

As with other aspects of innovation, however, there is a down side to expertise. In particular there is a danger that expertise will narrow and restrict thinking and guide it along fixed pathways that have worked well in the past (this will be discussed in greater detail in the section on age and innovation). The Post-it® note example has already been mentioned. One striking example of the way knowledge, although absolutely indispensable, can endanger innovation can be seen in Barker's (1993) account of how Sony initially decided not to proceed with the development of music CDs in the mid-1970s because they assumed that CDs would be the same size as the then currently available LPs and that such huge CDs would hold so much music that, for instance, they would be unaffordable. The designers' familiarity with provision of music on discs 12 inches in diameter channeled their thinking in a specific direction and made it difficult for them to envisage smaller discs, that is, compact discs, as they are now known.

INNOVATION AND AGE

Early in the development of modern cognitive psychology, Piaget and Inhelder (1969) identified contrasting patterns of behavior in dealing with novelty: (a) assimilating, which involves fitting new knowledge and ideas into existing mental structures, in effect updating what exists, and (b) accommodating, that is, forming new cognitive structures to make sense out of new information. Applying this distinction to innovation, assimilating behavior involves seeing new problems as variants of problems faced before, focusing on the similarities, and regarding expansion or adaptation of earlier solutions as the way to deal with the new situation. Innovation is achieved by making the new problem fit the old paradigm. Accommodating, by contrast, involves building new mental structures when confronted with a problem. Intuitively, the former is more closely connected to incremental innovation, the latter to disruptive innovation.

Kirton (1989) made a similar distinction between attacking problems by making use of the already known, which he called adapting, and attacking them by reorganizing and restructuring knowledge, which he referred to as innovating. He argued that both kinds of problem-solving behavior can lead to new products and processes but that innovating leads to higher productivity. Abra (1994, p. 10) made a similar distinction between perfecting and innovating. He also expressed this difference in a somewhat negative way, referring to plodders and visionaries. Some of the major differences between the two ways of generating effective novelty are summarized in Table 4.2. The differences described in the table are not absolute characteristics of two entirely discrete patterns of behavior but rather behavioral tendencies that are more pronounced or more frequently seen in one style of novelty generation than the other.

According to the Piagetian developmental psychology already summarized at the beginning of this section, many of the differences summarized in Table 4.2 are directly related to age: increasing cognitive maturity, which comes with increasing age (in most people, at least), is accompanied by a move away from accommodating toward assimilating. This move is highly adaptive because it means that, with increasing age, people are freed from the need to regard every event as a new puzzle that must be solved. They

TABLE 4.2. *Two Patterns of Novelty Generation*

Area	Kind of Behavior: Innovating	Kind of Behavior: Adapting
Cognition	• Forming new categories when confronted with new information • Working on several matters simultaneously • Changing focus easily • Jumping to conclusions • Seeking new solutions for old problems • Applying hunches and intuitions • Focusing on potential and promise • Judging situations optimistically	• Fitting new information into existing categories • Concentrating on the matter at hand • Focusing efforts narrowly • Drawing conclusions with caution • Making new problems fit old solutions • Focusing on weaknesses and risks • Dwelling on how easily things can go wrong
Motivation	• Taking risks • Pursuing short-term goals • Seeking to change the status quo • Risking failure • Trying to remedy inadequacies and shortcomings of the existing situation	• Avoiding risks • Pursuing long-term goals • Protecting the status quo • Avoiding failure • Accepting inadequacies and short-comings of the existing situation
Personality	• Accepting new ideas • Displaying brash confidence • Acting impulsively • Reacting excitedly to radical ideas	• Greeting new ideas with caution • Behaving in a disciplined way • Accepting change or ideas only after due consideration • Remaining level-headed
Social properties	• Rebelling • Risking losing face • Expecting to get away with it • Seeking to charge ahead • Expressing ideas openly	• Accepting authority • Seeking to save face • Accepting responsibility • Playing a gate-keeper role • Keeping ideas hidden

can draw on their accumulated experience and deal with new situations in terms of well-tested solution strategies. Applied to innovation, this means that increasing age is associated with an inherent tendency to expand and reapply the known, whereas youthful innovation involves developing something entirely new; indeed, this is necessary in youth because inexperience means that tried and trusted knowledge cannot be drawn upon because it has not yet been acquired. This implies a link between innovation and age, with younger people tending to accommodate (disruptive innovation) and older people tending to assimilate (incremental innovation).

Indeed, a finding in creativity research that has been reported again and again from early in the modern era (i.e., from about 1950) is that creativity diminishes with age. A. J. Cropley (1995) summarized the main thrust of early research. For instance, Lehman (1953) concluded that there is a rise in creativity until about forty, a peak between thirty and forty, and then a falloff thereafter, and that this holds true for all domains of creativity. Simonton (1999) later showed that, in fact, the peak age differs across disciplines but confirmed the existence of a general tendency for creativity to fade with increasing age. More recently, Kozbelt, and Meredith (2011) reported that musicians tend to produce their best work at about the age of forty. Franses (2013, 2014) calculated the ages at which two groups – famous artists on the one hand and winners of the Nobel Prize for Literature on the other – produced their best work, and reported an average age of 41.92 for the painters and 44.75 for the writers. Kanazawa (2003) showed that two-thirds of the men he studied who were acknowledged creators from a variety of fields, including natural science, visual art, literature, and jazz, made their most significant contribution by their mid-thirties, and 80 percent by around forty. The mean age was 35.4. Ruth and Birren (1985) confirmed the existence of age differences in creativity and showed that these exist for both men and women.

Despite calculating a mean age of peak creativity of 35.4, however, Kanazawa (2003, p. 264) showed that there are life-course persisters; that is, the age of peak creativity and/or a falloff in creativity are not matters of biological destiny. By means of a postmortem analysis of the work of 189 famous artists of the eighteenth to the twentieth century in which not calendar age but proportion of the person's total lifetime already passed was the independent variable (i.e., loosely interpreted for present purposes, how far the person had progressed along the career pathway), Franses (2013) showed that there may, in fact, be four different patterns of achievement linking peak creative output and age: precocious innovators (people who display their peak creativity around one-third of the way through their lives), mature innovators (who achieve their peak around halfway through their life), late innovators (who achieve it about three-quarters of the way through), and twilight innovators (who reach their peak of achievement in their last few years). Thus, under the right circumstances, it is perfectly possible for older people to be innovative.

Age Differences Favorable for Innovation

The most obvious difference between older and younger members of organizations is that older people have had more time to accumulate the preparatory experience mentioned earlier in the section titled Innovation and Age. Indeed, Walberg and Stariha (1992) identified use of existing knowledge (which is only possible after the knowledge has been acquired) as the single most striking cognitive feature of adult creativity. According to this view (see also Bailin, 1988, mentioned in the section titled Innovation and Expertise), effective novelty is most readily generated by processes like deepening, broadening, consolidating, and transferring existing knowledge (i.e., by accommodating). As Csikszentmihalyi (2006) pointed out, however, it is impossible to deepen, broaden, or otherwise manipulate knowledge you do not yet possess, and accumulating knowledge takes time, which implies not a negative but a *positive* link between creativity and age. Ericsson and Lehmann (1999) summarized this notion of the link between age and creativity by concluding that:

> the empirical evidence on creative achievement shows that individuals have not been able to make generally recognized creative contributions to a domain unless they had mastered the relevant knowledge and skills in the course of a long preparatory period. (p. 706)

A widely accepted idea is that there is a ten-year rule: A preparatory period of at least ten years is necessary for acquiring the fund of knowledge and skills (expertise) thought to be necessary for creativity.

On the other hand, the inspired shot in the dark, even if in a rough form, is possible without such intensive expertise and could even result from a lucky fluke. This suggests, in effect, two kinds of innovation: one based on expertise, the other on luck or inspiration. Galenson (2009) concluded that there are really two types of innovator, and linked the difference between them directly to age by labeling them *old* masters versus *young* geniuses (emphasis added): The former do their best work later in life, when they have had time to build up the necessary expertise, and the latter blossom early, when their minds are not yet trapped in the straightjacket of knowledge and the way for the inspired guess or the lucky hunch is still open. In a sense, it could be argued that, cognitively speaking, young innovators engage in disruptive innovation because they do not know how to do anything else!

However, it is important to note that the differences being discussed here are not simply the direct result of an inevitable linear correlation between innovation and age. As A. J. Cropley (1995) argued, differences in innovation-related behavior at different ages may be largely due to noncognitive differences in interests, motivation, self-image, and the like. For instance, with increasing age, adults often possess more clearly developed personal goals and better articulated ideas about which goals are worth pursuing. In addition, older managers are subjected to the pressure of social expectations: They have a responsibility to guard advances already made rather than engage in risk taking or trail blazing and have much more to lose, for instance, if they are made to look foolish. Older innovators may focus mainly on evolutionary innovation because they dare not do anything else!

Ruth and Birren (1985) summarized the situation by pointing out that, in addition to apparently biologically determined patterns of cognitive growth, three other kinds of influence lead to differences in the way people react to or generate novelty:

(a) Genuine age differences in the personal environment, such as reduced speed of information processing and a lower level of complexity in thinking among older people (i.e., genuine age differences in process) or lower willingness to take risks (genuine age differences related to personal motivation)
(b) The effects of education and social roles on people's behavior (i.e., differences that are artifacts of social norms and not biologically preordained at all)
(c) Interpersonal factors that are located in the organizational environment (of greatest interest for a discussion of innovation management), such as occupational status and roles within an organization (once again, social artifacts).

Implications for Managing Innovation

Intuitively, accommodation-based innovation would be facilitated by expressing impulses, rebelling against stifling authority, having no fear of losing face, or feeling excitement in the face of uncertainty. Assimilation-based innovation, on the other hand, would be promoted by knowledge and experience. Using the vocabulary of organizational innovation, older members of an organization such as senior managers may thus tend to favor incremental innovation, whereas younger members may be more prone to generate disruptive innovation. This would mean that, to senior staff members, younger people may sometimes seem to be reckless, unheeding or ignorant of traditional wisdom, careless about potential dangers, and quick to jump to conclusions (to accommodate), whereas older managers may seem to younger people to be excessively cautious and unable to change existing mind-sets because they interpret anything new in terms of what already exists (they assimilate). Such assimilating behavior of older managers is not absurd, of course. Their existing mental models of how to operate – their paradigms, as Collis (2010) put it (see Chapter 1) – have been successful in the past; otherwise, they would not be where they are now. Thus, in psychological terms, they have been conditioned to prefer assimilation.

Looking at the matter from a somewhat different angle, Root-Bernstein, Bernstein, and Garnier (1993) showed that innovative people often work on several problems simultaneously or change focus repeatedly; however, according to Walberg and Stariha (1992) mature-age creativity is more characterized by perseverance, discipline, and commitment, which seem to be incompatible with making frequent switches. The problem this age-related difference in process poses for older managers is exacerbated by social factors such as the expectation that, with increasing seniority, they will become gatekeepers guarding against the effects of recklessness, the possessors of level heads, and the like. It is almost required of older managers that they urge caution, damp down excessive enthusiasm, or draw attention to what could go wrong. Thus, both organizational and social norms frown on managers who display the kinds of behavior that facilitate disruptive innovation.[3]

Root-Bernstein, Bernstein, and Garnier (1993) studied the productivity of forty men who had all made enduring high-impact contributions in physics, chemistry, biochemistry, and biology, including several Nobel Prize winners and a number of men who had been nominated for the Nobel Prize without actually winning it, some of them on more than one

[3] In Chapter 6, it will be pointed out that these social expectations are not simply mindless stereotypes. They have survival value for organizations; that is, it is beneficial for an organization to have people who protect the good aspects of what the organization has achieved so far.

occasion. The contributions of these men were studied over a period of twenty years. Of particular interest for the present discussion is that those who ceased to be creative tended to be the ones who moved into management, whereas those who continued to be creative avoided administrative work! This may be exacerbated even more by the fact that research suggests that innovation is facilitated by working in a team, whereas older people may be more accustomed to working alone or at least to being the one who has to take responsibility when things go wrong. As Root-Bernstein (1989, p. 463) pointed out, the answer may be for senior staff members to learn to go back to behaving like novices; he spoke of achieving what he called the novice effect.

A major difference between older and younger managers involves what Sternberg (1998) and others (e.g., Baltes & Smith, 1990; Birren & Fisher 1990) call wisdom. This includes good judgment in difficult situations, understanding the way in which the events of life go together to form a consistent context, the ability to place events into perspective, a grasp of the fact that life is full of uncertainty and imponderability and that all planning must take this into account, and similar knowledge and skills. Wisdom also includes innovation-facilitating metacognitive skills for using this knowledge, such as skill in recognizing looming blind allies and tactics for avoiding them, or for teasing out emerging but not yet clearly formulated solutions and clearing the way for them.

In the internal (organizational) environment, older managers as a group (of course, there are individual exceptions) are more oriented toward mentoring and leading. Harsh experience may have taught them to be more skeptical when they encounter excessive self-confidence or arrogance. These may mean that older managers are often better at coordinating what already exists, know how to obtain financing, understand markets, can assess the potential value of as yet nonexistent products, know how to develop distribution channels, and have had experience in dealing with rejection and failure. Thus, managing innovative people involves balancing between the sober dictates of wisdom and the heady delights of doing things differently.

OVERVIEW AND OUTLOOK

The P constituted by the individual actor (person) is one of the building blocks of innovation. Person involves motivation, feelings/attitudes, and personal properties. Together, these lead to habits or styles for dealing with the challenges or shocks faced by organizations, which can facilitate or hinder innovation, according to their nature. These habits or styles are referred to in this book as behavioral dispositions. Examples of behavioral dispositions that are favorable for innovation are summarized in the left-hand column of Table 4.1 (e.g., making unexpected links, enjoying autonomy, experiencing an urge to do things better, being willing to defy authority). Although the topic is of little interest here, an unfavorable behavioral disposition would involve properties like sticking to conventional ideas of what goes with what, preferring to carry out clear instructions from other people, being satisfied with the status quo, and never rocking the boat.

Two clusters of personal resources form behavioral dispositions that are of central relevance to innovative behavior: the young genius or precocious innovator and the old master or mature/twilight innovator. These can be summarized as involving dependence on expertise built up through expanded knowledge in a process of assimilation in the case of the old master versus dependence on insights and sudden breakthroughs resulting from accommodation on the part of the young genius. These differing sets of antecedents to innovative behavior tend to produce different kinds of innovation (disruptive versus incremental). This, in turn, may be a source of friction between managers who are typically more experienced and more set in the ways that have produced success in the past (i.e., who tend toward being old masters) and younger members of an organization. The different patterns are not inevitably associated with age and are not a matter of biological destiny, however, and both are capable of generating valuable innovation.

5

Press: Where the Innovation Happens?

An important and unifying theme of the concepts presented in this book is the interrelatedness of innovation and the Four Ps, or (in the expanded model presented here) the six *building blocks* of innovation. As was pointed out in Chapter 1, the people who undertake innovation, the processes they engage in, and the products they generate all function as parts of a complex system. A system (Blanchard & Fabrycky, 2006) is defined as a set of interacting parts organized to achieve one or more stated purposes. The parts interact not only with each other – for example, exchanging energy or information – but also with their environment (Figure 5.1). An innovation system, therefore, is no different from any other kind of system.

Whether the system is a complex, tangible artifact – for example, a commercial aircraft – or the system that gives rise to the innovation, the role of the environment is critical. There are, in fact, two different but related contexts for this environment, or press. One is the social environment, which can be thought of as the broader, more general form of the environment in which innovation takes place. It characterizes the influence of various aspects of society on innovation. The other context is the organizational environment, which can be understood as the narrower, more specific and contextualized form of environment – the day-to-day workplace environment that has an immediate impact on innovation (Figure 5.2).

The external (social) and internal (organizational) environments together define the final element in the Four Ps model or, using the terminology of the present book, the final building block of innovation. This building block is referred to as press. To understand fully the role that press plays in helping or hindering innovation, it is necessary to unravel the suite of factors that define these two environments.

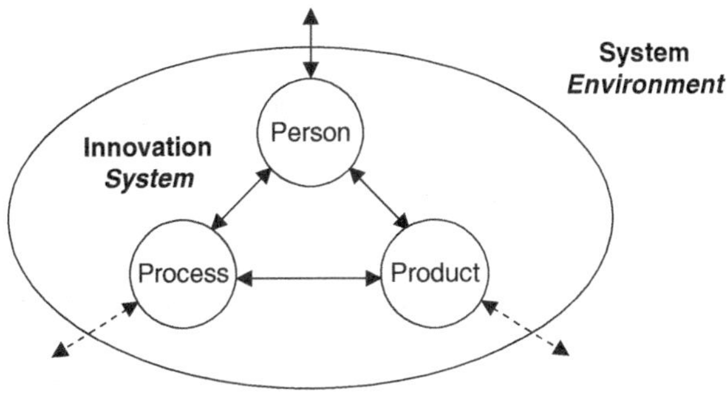

FIGURE 5.1. The Innovation System and Its Environment (Press)

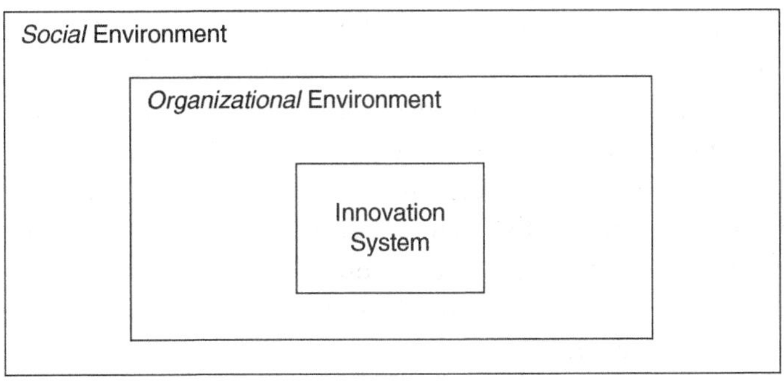

FIGURE 5.2. The Social and Organizational Environments

In their discussion of a systems model of creativity and of the organizational context, Puccio and Cabra (2010) described a similar interaction among the Four Ps, noting that "innovation comes about as the result of the interaction among people, the processes they engage in, and the environment in which they work" (p. 149). They make a familiar distinction in their discussion of press, noting two primary categories – the environment outside organizations and the environment inside organizations. In this chapter, the discussion will start by examining the social, or external, environment and then follow with an analysis of the organizational (internal) environment.

THE EXTERNAL (SOCIAL) ENVIRONMENT

Both creativity and innovation are defined by the society in which they occur. In this sense, creativity and innovation are, in fact, socially defined.

They are also, at least to a degree, socially motivated. Consequently, they can also be facilitated (or blocked) by the same social environment. This facilitation or blocking occurs because social settings differ in the degree to which they allow deviation from the usual and because innovation, at its core, represents the exploitation of ideas that disturb the status quo. Some societies accept more variability (i.e., novelty, surprise, unusualness) than others or are more willing to accept change.

The openness of a society for variability also depends on the nature of the person, and the organization, generating that variability: Is the person or organization respected or admired, or does he or she (or it, in the case of the organization) have permission to be different? The willingness of society to accept variability is also contingent on the effects of the variability on other people and organizations in that society; what is the impact on the society's prevailing way of life? A further complication is that the environment is not simply passive, either supporting or blocking whatever innovators choose to offer, but itself influences the amount and kind of novelty that is generated and exploited in the first place. There is a dynamic relationship between the press and the other parts of the innovation system. In fact, many of the factors that block or facilitate innovation in a society are reminiscent of factors encountered in the study of the creative person (see Chapter 4). This is hardly surprising given that societies are a reflection of the people who comprise them, and vice versa.

Any analysis of the external, social environment and innovation must thus start by revisiting the person as an antecedent of creativity and therefore of innovation. Creativity has frequently been treated as a form of self-expression or a way of understanding or coping with life that is intimately connected with personal dignity, expression of one's inner being, self-actualization, and the like (Maslow, 1973; May, 1976; Rogers, 1961). Moustakis (1977) summarized the individualistic approach to creativity by seeing it as a pathway to living one's own life in a desired way. Barron (1969) went further, concluding that creativity requires resistance to socialization, while Burkhardt (1985) took this theme of the individual against society further by arguing that the creative individual must fight against society's pathological desire for sameness. Sternberg and Lubart (1995) called this fight defying the crowd; they labeled the tendency of certain creative individuals to resist society's pressure to conform contrarianism. From the point of view of innovation in organizations, however, the social press is not the reactive need, or desire, to fight against society's attempts to squash innovation but a proactive desire to maximize creativity and innovation in situations where the factors in the social environment can sometimes act to hinder it. People, in other words, do not innovate in order to strike back at society but because of a desire to create value for their customers.

This proactive and forward-looking view of innovation and the social environment has a long tradition. As far back as the time of the Chinese emperor Han Wudi, who reigned until 87 BCE, there has been interest in innovation as a socially useful phenomenon. The emperor was deeply interested in finding innovative thinkers and giving them high rank in the civil service, and he reformed the method of selection of mandarins to achieve this. Both Francis Bacon (1909) and René Descartes (1991 [1644]), two of the founders of modern science, saw scientific creativity as harnessing of the forces of nature for the betterment of the human condition. In modern terms, this is the human capital approach, and this view of innovative people has become well known (Walberg & Stariha, 1992). Indeed, the driving force behind the modern interest in creativity that followed the *Sputnik* shock (see, for example, A. J. Cropley & Cropley, 2009; D. H. Cropley, 2015) centered on the consequences for society of lack of creativity and innovation.

Despite this, psychologists and educators in the post-Guilford phase of the modern era (see Chapter 3) tended to emphasize themes deriving from the psychology of the individual, such as cognitive aspects of creativity (i.e. Chapter 3) and creativity and personality (Chapter 4). This may have encouraged an individualistic approach to creativity and, to a lesser extent, innovation. Nonetheless, in recent thinking, creativity and innovation are seen increasingly as a force for developing society in desirable ways, not least as "the lever of riches" (Mokyr, 1990). Such an approach gives greater weight to the social aspects of innovation. Innovation, in other words, is the servant of society.

With these considerations in mind, analysis of the external, social aspects of innovation may be considered as having three dimensions:

- Understanding innovation as a social force with social responsibility
- Defining what is innovative in social rather than individual terms
- Attributing the driving force for innovation (i.e., the motivation) to social rather than intra-individual factors

These three dimensions are addressed in the sections that follow. Afterward, the discussion in this chapter turns to the role of the internal, organizational press.

ETHICAL ASPECTS OF INNOVATION

A good starting point for a discussion of the impact of the social environment on innovation – one that has a strong link to the context of organizations and business – is the question of ethics and social responsibility. Sternberg (2003) argued that creativity (along with intelligence) must be balanced or tempered by wisdom and assumed that creative people's wisdom ensures that their creativity serves the common good. Several authors have proposed a moral creativity (Gruber, 1993; Runco, 1993; Runco & Nemiro, 2003; Schwebel, 1993), while Moran, Cropley, and Kaufman (2014) explored a range of viewpoints of ethics and creativity/innovation. Well-intentioned innovation does not always produce unmitigated benefits for society; unintended negative effects of the introduction and exploitation of novelty are not uncommon. Even the highly acclaimed discoveries of Edward Jenner and Louis Pasteur about the transmission of disease, to take one example, laid the foundations for germ warfare! A more concrete example for engineers involves the numerous negative, unintended consequences that have resulted from the development of automobiles. Hundreds of thousands of people around the world are killed each year in traffic accidents. Thus, creativity and innovation have a dark side (McLaren, 1993) that needs to be explored and understood.

This dark side includes not only accidental harm but also creative activities that are carried out to satisfy personal vanity or pride, or that benefit narrow, short-term interests. Even more disturbing, it is also possible for effective novelty to be introduced in the full knowledge that it will damage others. This can occur without the damage being the primary object of the exercise, for instance, in business, when a new product is introduced in order to make a profit, in the full knowledge that it will inevitably harm a rival product. It is also often seen in criminal behavior. Fortunately, as Eisenman (1999) showed, prisoners rated by guards and other inmates as creative typically generated little or no effective novelty but rather showed lack of inhibitions and low levels of social conformity, that is, pseudo-creativity. This suggests that unsuccessful criminals (i.e., those who have been imprisoned) are not particularly novel or innovative. As a result, anticrime measures are reasonably successful, even without high levels of novelty, elegance, and generalizability. These issues have been explored in depth in D. H. Cropley and Cropley (2013) for both crime and terrorism. In the broader context of ethics, this has been explored further by a range of contributions in Moran, Cropley and Kaufman (2014), while D. H. Cropley (2014a) explored issues of ethics, creativity, and engineering innovation in more detail.

Unfortunately, it is also possible for the negative consequences of creativity not only to be fully intended by the person or group introducing the effective novelty but also to be the central purpose – harm to others as the main goal of creativity. Obvious examples of such creativity are seen in war. D. H. Cropley, Kaufman and Cropley (2008) have argued that terrorists, such as the perpetrators of the 9/11 attacks, are capable of generating highly effective novelty and successfully inserting it into a functioning system. As unsavory as it seems, they are creative and indeed innovative, despite their evil intentions. D. H. Cropley (2005) used the term *malevolent* as one way to describe such creativity and extended this more recently to the wider context of malevolent innovation (D. H. Cropley, 2010).

These examples raise particularly difficult issues, many with consequences directly relevant to organizational and entrepreneurial contexts. Suppose, for example, that an employee found effective, novel ways of bullying a colleague, through harassment or mockery, simply out of malice. Imagine a hacker applying skill in software development to devise a novel and effective way to distribute a virus that caused economic loss to millions of Internet users, simply for the thrill of damaging others. Along with particularly deadly weapons of war – the atomic bomb, for example – and effective, novel acts of terrorism, both of the situations just mentioned might well involve generation of novelty that was highly effective in achieving the goals of a particular individual; however, are they really examples of innovation?

A strictly individualistic approach might indeed conclude that they are. In the same way, effective and novel techniques of a mass murderer might be regarded as, in principle, having the same virtues as the innovative work of a creative businessperson because both reflect the workings of processes such as those discussed in Chapter 3 to generate and exploit effective novelty. However, such a conclusion is also unsatisfactory for the overwhelming majority of managers: Few of them will be interested in fostering the creativity of, let us say, an ax murderer!

What the preceding examples highlight is that the generation and exploitation of novelty really does require deviating from norms, so that in a sense it requires social deviation! The answer to the question raised above – were the 9/11 terrorists innovative? – can only be answered by going beyond a purely individualistic approach to innovation. An understanding of the social aspects of innovation helps to clarify where innovation comes from, what factors facilitate its appearance, how it can be fostered or applied in groups (for example, a service provider such as a bank, or a manufacturing firm), and so on. Emphasis on the social aspects of innovation does not deny the importance of the cognitive and personal aspects discussed in Chapters 3 and 4 but adds an additional dimension to these.

DEFINING INNOVATION IN SOCIAL TERMS

The essence of any kind of innovation is production and exploitation of effective novelty. In earlier chapters, novelty and effectiveness have been considered from a psychological point of view. The decisive property of novelty is that it causes surprise in beholders (Bruner, 1962); that is, people's surprise defines novelty rather than the product itself. Surprise occurs when something is unexpectedly different from the usual; that is, it deviates from the status quo. It is the contrast with what already exists that yields the surprise. In other words, the production of novelty does not occur in isolation but in a social context. The product or the process itself does not determine novelty; the particular setting does (the contrast of the novelty with the existing state of the art or the constraints of the external world). Without existing external norms, there would be no such thing as novelty, only variability (i.e., differences).

As was emphasized in Chapter 2 about the product, the term *creativity* is not simply applied to anything that surprises people. What is crucial for converting novelty into creativity, and therefore innovation, is effectiveness. This too is determined by the surrounding environment. Csikszentmihalyi (1999) described creativity as requiring "acceptance by a particular field of judges" (p. 316), arguing that creativity is essentially a positive category of judgment in the minds of observers, a term they use to praise products that they find exceptionally good. When a number of observers agree that a product is creative, then it is. Csikszentmihalyi called this social definition of effectiveness sociocultural validation.

Although social recognition or acclaim defines effectiveness and is thus necessary for creativity and innovation, the judges need not be experts. For example, it is not necessary to be a civil engineer to be capable of recognizing the effectiveness of a bridge. In other words, the everyday users of many products may well be in the best position to determine their effectiveness. As Wernher von Braun is reported to have said, "The eye is a fine architect; believe it!" (Rechtin & Maier, 2000). In effect, good products are recognizable as good products. It appears, therefore, that sociocultural validation can be carried out by a wide range of judges – novices, quasi-experts, and experts (for further discussion, see Kaufman, Baer, Cropley, Reiter-Palmon, and Sinnett, [2013]).

The Problem of Changing Standards

A practical problem with sociocultural validation as the means for establishing effectiveness – the criterion of effectiveness, in other words – is that what is regarded as creative in one era or in one society can be uncreative in another. There are many examples across many domains of creative activity. In music, for example, the composer Johannes Brahms was unable to obtain the post of director of the philharmonic orchestra in his native Hamburg because his music was initially judged too conservative. He had to go to Vienna to find acclaim. In Georgian England, Shakespeare's plays were regarded as indecent and had to be edited to make them respectable; in 1818, Dr. Thomas Bowdler published the *Family Shakespeare* in which he removed expressions that could not, with propriety, be read aloud in a family setting (he bowdlerized Shakespeare's work). Innovators are also no strangers to this phenomenon – many innovations have failed because products were judged ahead of their time or because the consumer was not ready for a particular product (the Besemer dictum). These can be seen as examples of society making a subjective judgment about the worth of a product and rejecting it, regardless of any technical effectiveness.

The Social Definition of *Who* Is Innovative

In addition to deciding what is creative and innovative, the social environment identifies certain people who generate and exploit novelty as innovators or entrepreneurs but anoints others as strange, mentally ill, or even criminal. One mechanism through which society determines who is innovative can be demonstrated by Schuldberg's (2001) discussion of psychopathology and creativity, especially his concept of diathesis. Some cause in an individual's development leads to psychological states that encourage behavior that differs from the average or normal, such as linking ideas usually kept separate, coming up with unexpected suggestions, freely expressing excitement and elation, and so on – concepts familiar from the discussion of person in Chapter 4. Quite apart from the individual definition is society's reaction to this sort of behavior. If society applauds the resulting behavior, the person is regarded as creative or innovative. If society frowns on the behavior, the person may be regarded as crazy or even criminal. This occurs despite the fact that the underlying behavior may be no different! An excellent example is Andres Serrano's infamous *Piss Christ* photograph in 1987 (D. H. Cropley & Cropley, 2013) that aroused considerable controversy – so much so that some people made death threats against the artist, while some organizations presented him with prizes. In the end, it would appear that it is not so much the actual deviation from norms that determines innovation but how the social environment reacts to the deviation.

The social group in which the innovator displays his or her deviation may be decisive. For example, someone who is active in a setting where uncontrolled expression of impulses or ignoring conventions may be regarded as odd or incompetent (e.g., business or engineering) would be treated differently from someone in a setting where such behavior was admired (e.g., avant-garde theater or modern dance). In the latter case, the person might be fortunate enough to have the behavior accepted as not only surprising but also effective and thus creative. D. H. Cropley and Cropley (2013) gave the example of an artist in Britain who stole human body parts from the corpses of people who had recently died so that he could use them in artworks. Many observers would probably find this abhorrent or disgusting, or would regard it as showing disgraceful disrespect for the dead or those mourning the person's death, but the artist himself was indignant at the interference with his work, and some commentators enthusiastically approved of his behavior, judging the results of the theft to be artistically powerful and technically daring. On the other hand, the artist was criticized for using plaster of Paris as his medium because it is regarded as artistically inferior.

Of course, this does not mean that it is necessary to abandon attempts to be creative in domains such as business or engineering for fear that the social environment might reject them. Instead, it further reinforces the importance of understanding, and being able to articulate to others the defining elements of innovation. This is also why it is important to understand innovation in the context of different domains – the domain extends to the social domain as well as the domain of activity. The Creative Solution Diagnosis Scale (CSDS; which was already mentioned in Chapter 2 and will be discussed in greater detail in Chapter 7) incorporates elements from the social environment into its conceptualization of a creative product (e.g., conceptualizing the elegance of a product as including the quality of delighting customers or users).

Social Determination of Amount and Kind of Innovation

Another filter through which to study the relationship between the social environment and innovation is the contrast between qualitative and quantitative points of view. For example, the very large departures from norms that might be labeled mental illness or criminality (compared to more moderate departures looked upon as innovation) can be understood in terms of the amount of deviation involved. This seems to be the case with the diathesis example described earlier. It is also possible, however, that it is not the amount of departure from norms but the kind of departure that is decisive in determining whether deviation is condemned or acclaimed as innovative. This seems to be more obvious in the case of the engineers versus dancers example.

It seems that society can tolerate only a certain amount of variability – there is a threshold, in other words – meaning that the quantitative point of view is a better model of the relationship. This may also be true of narrower social settings such as the family, social interactions with peers, recreational settings, work settings, and so on. Indeed, there is a level of analysis at which the social environment blends into the organizational environment. Within any setting, however, there may be considerable differences in the kind of variability (in addition to the amount) that is tolerated or applauded. One family may tolerate wild or undisciplined behavior, whereas another will not. Some circles of friends demand greater conformity from their members than others. Some vocational groups regulate the behavior of their members closely, others far less. As result, the social setting determines what kinds of new ideas emerge by setting limits on both the amount and also the kind of divergence that is permitted, or by guiding innovative thinking into particular channels. One way it can do this is via motivation. There is little incentive to innovate if there is, so to speak, no market for that innovation. Despite this social determination of the amount and kind of creativity, some exceptional individuals who defy the crowd are still seen to emerge. This tells us more about both the person and the press.

The Effect of the Amount of Innovation

It seems, therefore, that the amount of deviation from norms is decisive for public acceptance of innovation. Very large departures from what the group in question is used to may be socially unacceptable and even labeled in a variety of pejorative ways, as previously described. This suggests that an important ability for the innovator (whether an individual or an organization) is to learn how to link novelty to an existing framework, in other words, to understand how to introduce just enough novelty so that the amount of deviation is tolerated by the social group (or market). Not doing so risks the rejection of the innovation, not because it is inherently flawed or ineffective but simply because it is too different! A real example of this question of judging just how much deviation can be tolerated is found in the example of the Hungarian doctor Ignaz Semmelweiss (1818–1865). He discovered that the incidence of puerperal fever – a serious, often fatal infection to which women are prone immediately after childbirth – could be cut drastically simply by having doctors wash their hands before delivering babies. Unfortunately, this idea conflicted with the prevailing views of the day, and Semmelweiss was also unable to explain why it worked. Worst of all, this proposed deviation from a norm was seen as insulting to doctors, implying that they were dirty. As a result, Semmelweiss's highly effective and life-saving innovation was rejected. Here was a case of a level of deviation intolerable to a social grouping suppressing an innovation.

The Effect of the Kind of Innovation

The Semmelweiss example was a case of too much deviation. The kind of deviation may also be important. The socially derived distinction between kinds of innovation can be regarded as involving, on the one hand, socially radical and, on the other, socially orthodox effective novelty. From a social point of view, radical novelty arises out of willingness to venture into the area of socially frowned-on ideas or actions. Orthodox novelty involves generating effective novelty while remaining within socially prescribed limits. This distinction is similar to the one Millward and Freeman (2002) made between change that stays within the existing social system (what is called here orthodox innovation) compared to change that challenges the system (i.e., radical innovation). Sternberg (2006) linked his own cognitive approach to creativity with social factors when he divided the processes of his propulsion model (see Chapters 2 and 7 and the discussion of products) into those that accept current paradigms (i.e., orthodox creativity) and those that reject current paradigms (i.e., radical creativity). Sternberg also suggested the existence of a third variant, creativity (and ultimately innovation), that synthesizes current paradigms.

The social distinctions between amount and kind of innovation, and the labels that have been attached (orthodox and radical) suggest a 2 × 2 matrix as a mechanism for classifying examples of innovation in particular social settings (Table 5.1). The quadrant small/orthodox involves small amounts of change along the usual lines, small/radical involves small amounts of change but presented in highly novel ways. Large/orthodox involves large changes to the existing way of doing things, and large/radical involves large amounts of change to novel paradigms.

TABLE 5.1. *Domains and the Kind and Amount of Innovation*[a]

		Kind of Innovation	
		Orthodox	Radical
Amount of Innovation	Small	Pharmaceuticals, airlines, food finance, medicine	Retailing, manufacturing, advertising
	Large	Automobiles, energy	Information technology, entertainment

[a] *The placement of the domains in the various cells of the table is purely intuitive and has been carried out for illustrative purposes only*

Differences among different broad domains of the social environment (e.g., educational, justice, and financial systems); among groups within the social environment (e.g., teachers, students, and managers); or in the organizational environment, either within a single industry or across industries (e.g., pharmaceutical, energy, information technology, manufacturing, etc.) can all be classified using this grid. Some domains, for example, are open to high levels of radical innovation (e.g., information technology, entertainment), whereas others are mainly restricted to low levels of orthodox innovation (e.g., pharmaceuticals, finance). Thus, placement of the domain finance in the orthodox/small quadrant means that innovation in this domain typically involves lower levels of orthodox innovation – doing pretty much the usual thing in a slightly different way. The placement of IT in the radical/large quadrant means that innovation in this domain typically involves doing new things in a very different way.

Large amounts of radical innovation involve challenging existing norms and also pursuing the new goals in a dramatically different way. The entertainment industry, for example, is in the process of changing the basic model of large groups of people gathered at the same time in a single venue to one involving individuals selecting what they want to watch or listen to and choosing when they do this (a radically new way of doing things), and doing this by introducing very large changes in what constitutes looking and listening, such as streaming via iPhone (a large amount of novelty).

It is important to note that the placement of domains does not mean that other amounts and kinds of innovation are not possible within them. Instead, this is an attempt to compare the different domains with each other in terms of general trends and relative to social norms. Naturally, there can be radical/large innovation in a domain like finance, just as there can be orthodox/small innovation in information technology. What the table does suggest is that radical/large innovation is harder to achieve in some domains (finance or medicine, for example) – relative to the social setting – than it is in, let us say, communications or entertainment. In simple terms, the social environment is willing to accept more radical kinds of change and larger amounts of change in domains such as communications or entertainment than it is in finance or medicine, and the risk of the rejection of radical/large innovation is thus greater there.

This classification system can be expanded to account for another distinction. Research such as that of Simonton (1997) suggests that some societies are product-oriented (they focus on producing novel works such as art; literature; machines; and gadgets, preferably high-tech gadgets, etc.), whereas others are process-oriented (they focus on techniques, production, and management procedures, etc.). Different communities of experts or specialists may also reflect this difference. Engineers, for example, may place greatest value on product-oriented novelty, while philosophers may place it on process-oriented novelty. Glück, Ernst, and Unger (2002) showed that differences along these lines exist among other social groupings as well, and not just in commercial organizations – for example, between art and physics teachers. As a group, the former tolerate or encourage originality, risk taking, impulsivity, and nonconformity (i.e., radical innovation), whereas physics teachers as a group lean toward convergent problem solving, responsibility, and reliability (orthodox innovation or no innovation at all). These considerations suggest an extension of Table 5.1 by adding a third dimension: orientation (i.e., process versus product).

The classification relative to process/product orientation can also be applied to organizations. From the point of view of fostering innovation, the ideal situation seems to be an alignment among all players in the social setting – in other words, they all occupy the same quadrant. This would occur when manager, individual, and area of operations were all located in the same quadrant, especially in the case of innovative individuals. Harrington (1999) argued that there is no single best set of environmental circumstances that is favorable for everybody's creativity and innovation but that the decisive factor is the goodness of fit between the characteristics of the environment and those of the individual. Table 5.1, extended to cover orientation, can therefore be regarded as providing a starting point for developing a schema for diagnosing goodness of fit in terms of demands of the domain or area of operations, managers' orientation to innovation, and employees' production of innovation. This concept of goodness of fit for innovation will be explored further in Chapters 8 and 9.

Social Influence on the Content of Innovative Behavior

The social environment is not simply a passive recipient of the novelty that people generate, with its function confined to being surprised or not, and applying or withholding the seal of approval. As well as influencing – at least to some extent – the kind and amount of innovation that is produced, society affects the fields in which people become active, the novelty-generating tactics they employ, and the contents of their innovation. These effects are not only personal – affecting the creativity of a particular individual – but also general. In other words, environmental factors influence not just the novelty produced by individuals but also that produced in the society more generally. For example, there are documented cases of different people in a domain all adopting a similar novel approach or coming up with the same novel idea at about the same time. An example of this is the simultaneous but independent invention of calculus by Isaac Newton and Gottfried Leibniz, or the controversy surrounding the invention and patenting of the telephone by Bell and others. However, the phenomenon is more general than this. Research (Simonton, 1994) has shown convincingly that in times of economic prosperity or depression; before, after, and during political and social upheavals; or following a successful or an unsuccessful war, differing patterns of creativity occur. This involves not only the number of creators who emerge but also the domains in which creativity occurs and the kind of novelty that is generated. To take one concrete example, Simonton (1998) (p. 105) showed that melodic originality is higher among composers in wartime.

Such phenomena are commonly referred to as reflecting the zeitgeist ("the spirit of the times"). The internal explanation of the zeitgeist is that a domain possesses its own pattern or pathway of growth that is inherent in the domain in question; one thing leads almost inevitably to another. Closely related is the idea that each domain has its own system of internal logic and that growth in the field must follow this logic. For products, this would mean that novel products can only occur in a relatively fixed order and at the right time, after earlier events have opened up the field in a new way. Electronic devices, for example, obviously could only be invented after the discovery and harnessing of electricity. Of course, the discovery and harnessing of electricity did not guarantee that television would be invented, but it was a necessary precondition for its invention. This is a generalization of the argument in Chapter 1 that individual novel products are very frequently incremental extensions of what already exists rather than unprecedented breakthroughs.

Another wartime example serves to illustrate this point. In the Second World War, Great Britain first deployed the radar countermeasure now called chaff. This consists of small pieces of aluminum or other reflective materials that cause spurious contacts on a radar screen. Britain developed this in order to help protect Allied bombers from German radar-controlled anti-aircraft gunfire and fighter aircraft during mass bombing raids over Germany. Curiously, however, Britain did not use chaff immediately, despite having developed it, because they feared that if they did so, this would reveal the technology to Germany, who might then use it in bombing raids on Britain! When the British did introduce it, in July 1943, it was initially highly effective, although the Germans quickly learned how to disregard the spurious radar contacts, demonstrating a decay of novelty leading to decay in effectiveness (see D. H. Cropley, Kaufman, & Cropley, 2008). In the end, it turned out that the Germans had already developed the same technology themselves, at about the same time as the British!

A contrasting, external model of the appearance of effective novelty in various domains sees the influences on innovation as lying outside the domain itself, in the broader social environment. In this case, fluctuations in people's production of novelty are linked to broad social conditions, such as tolerance of variability by those who wield power in that society. A good example of this broad, social environmental influence, as distinct from a narrower, more domain-specific influence, is the influence in past centuries of the Catholic Church with regard to scientific opinions on the solar system. The prevailing view for many centuries – one that dominated thinking in entire nations – was that the sun orbits the earth. Deviating from this view could prove costly, as scientists such as Galileo discovered. In more recent times, we have seen similar whole-of-society effects on deviations from the norm in countries like the former Soviet Union. Societies seem to need certain kinds of innovation (or lack of innovation) at certain times in their social, economic, and political development and to transmit this need to innovative people in a global manner.

An interesting question for educators is how this occurs. An early answer was the proposal that all societies, as a kind of natural law, oscillate in long waves between a sensate and an ideational orientation (Martindale, 1990). The sensate orientation is empirical and deterministic; the ideational is intuitive and based on feelings. This is somewhat akin to a societal-level type indicator rather like the Myers-Briggs Type Indicator (MBTI), which will be discussed in Chapter 7. Differences between empirical and intuitive novelty production would hardly be surprising, but this pattern in the character of societies seems to be something that changes relatively slowly and is of limited value to an examination of the more day-to-day issues surrounding managing and fostering creativity and innovation. For the purpose of understanding how innovation is helped or hindered, it is sufficient to understand that societies directly influence people's innovation through various social mechanisms that in turn influence behavior. These have effects in both the long- and the short-term.

MOTIVATION: THE SOCIAL NATURE OF THE INNOVATIVE IMPULSE

Why do people seek to generate and exploit effective novelty? Why do they innovate? Motivating factors include those that are focused on the psychology of the individual. They also include factors that are individual and biological in nature. Berlyne (1962), for instance, argued that novelty and uncertainty act on the central nervous system to help people maintain an optimal level of neural activity. A certain amount of exposure to novelty production is biologically necessary. Studies of sensory deprivation (Zuckerman, 1969) and of the effects of monotony on children raised in orphanages (Dennis, 1973) have shown the effects of denial of novelty in a dramatic way. The effects include anxiety, hallucinations, bizarre thoughts, depression, and antisocial behavior. In the case of young children denied novelty, effects include apathy, dullness, and stunted emotional and intellectual development. Heron (1957) called this the pathology of boredom.

Of particular interest is that the nature of the novelty is important: Unexpectedness, incongruity, and the like (surprise), are more effective in promoting normal development than simple fluctuations in the usual (i.e., mere variability). In other words, the novelty must be relevant and effective! There is also a social component to the biological driver just mentioned – there is an interaction between the biological makeup of the individual and some aspect of the environment in which the person operates.

Social Motivation and Innovation

The impulse to be innovative is also determined by some or all of the following:

- Economic (entrepreneurial) factors (i.e., a desire to make money)
- Professional factors (because it is part of a person's job)
- Personal factors (e.g., because someone is curious)
- Social factors (e.g., because it brings status and acclaim)

Therefore, in addition to affecting the kind and amount of novelty produced, and determining which novelty is judged to be effective, the social environment also plays an important role in determining whether people are inclined to produce novelty at all, that is, in motivating (or not motivating) innovation. Many innovative products are developed "to satisfy the needs of ... social groups" (Sosa & Gero, 2003). The needs may be concrete and down to earth, such as cheaper power, or a cure for a particular disease. They may also be more general, such as better educational methods. They may also be more abstract, such as improved ways of expressing feelings through music. Generally, the social groups consist of people who are knowledgeable in a domain – specialists or experts – and users of the domain. In much the same way that someone with no knowledge in a given domain is unlikely to produce innovation in it, someone who does not know that a particular domain even exists cannot experience a need for innovation in it. The people who are motivated to solve the problems of a domain are most commonly people active in the domain.

The idea that innovation is linked with meeting the needs of social groups means that the problems innovative people seek to solve are at least partly socially determined. Where there is no social awareness that a problem exists, there may be no drive to produce solutions and thus no innovation. A simple example is the area of the design of everyday objects – tools, for example. A tool may be awkward to use and inefficient, or possibly even dangerous – a hammer is a good example. However, it may be so familiar to so many people that they have become accustomed to its disadvantages and may be able to use it very effectively, despite the disadvantages and inconvenience. They may even be incapable of imagining that a hammer could be different. In this case, there is no social pressure to introduce effective novelty and, in a sense, no problem, no matter how bad the design may be, because society has decided there is no problem.

Another good example is the automobile. The internal combustion (petrol) engine is very inefficient (only between 25 and 30 percent of the energy in the fuel is converted to mechanical work), cars are very dangerous, and they pollute the environment. However, innovation in automobile design is limited to tinkering with details – incremental improvements – with little genuinely radical originality seen since the introduction of the horseless carriage over 100 years ago. In fact, the car is only a coach or wagon with a motor replacing the horses! The basic design of a rectangular box, with a wheel at each corner, into which people climb, was well known thousands of years ago. Even the hybrid car is nothing more than a standard automobile with a different fuel system. This is, at least in part, because car manufacturers prefer the certainty of selling, for example, 100,000 standard (i.e., traditional) cars per year rather than the uncertainty of trying to sell jet-powered hover cars! This is not necessarily because jet-powered hover cars cannot be built but because society prefers the familiarity of the traditional design and does not see cars as inherently problematic. As a result, there is no social pressure motivating change.

Problem awareness in the individual versus in the social group is another factor that may be important for motivation. There may even be tension between the society's problem awareness and that of individuals. The problem may be apparent only to experts in an area or perhaps only to one such person and may not provoke a publicly perceived need for novelty. If only the insiders or even a single insider are dissatisfied and experience the urge to produce relevant, effective novelty, then the social motivation may trump the individual motivation. In this case, the society's lack of problem awareness may inhibit motivation to introduce novelty and thus block creativity. This suggests that a culture of problem awareness would foster creativity.

Society, the Individual, and Innovation as a System

Fredrick Winslow Taylor, the father of modern studies of work and work training, started his own work career as a machinist on the shop floor of the Midvale Steel Works and advanced through supervisory positions to become a member of senior management. He learned about scientific methods of observation and systematic drawing of conclusions when he studied engineering while an employee. He later transferred these to analysis of work practices in the steel works. Taylor's suggestions for scientific management came at a time when the new technology of fast steel cutting made new management practices possible. Because of its highly organized and systematic nature, the steel-cutting technology permitted the new style of management. At the same time, fast steel cutting could not be organized within existing management practices. Because of their highly organized and systematic nature, the new management practices made fast steel cutting possible. The conclusion is that there is a reciprocal relationship between the introduction of an innovation and the environment into which the innovation is introduced. It is important to note that the dynamics of the relationships do not all go in one direction: As has been shown, the environment permits or calls forth and directs or guides innovation, but innovation changes the environment.

Another variant of this interaction is to be seen in the way innovation not only is determined by social criteria but itself shapes the criteria. Among other things, especially among domain insiders, innovation may:

- Steer thinking about how to solve certain problems along a particular pathway. This may later become a constraint, possibly acting as a source of tension for those active in the area and paradoxically blocking the emergence of further innovation. Earlier innovation blocks later innovation.
- Alter the way other solutions in the area are judged, sometimes causing them to be judged as not innovative only because they are being judge relative to a successful innovation.
- Provide new criteria for judging later solutions, with the danger of the constraining effect mentioned above.
- Expand the way the domain is conceptualized in the society, thus opening up new possibilities for creativity (this is the idea of seminality; see Chapters 2 and 7).
- Suggest new issues not previously noticed (i.e., germinality; see Chapter 2 and 7).
- Suggest new ways of solving problems in the area.

Innovative products thus not only reflect social forces but may themselves alter those forces or even influence the way societies see the world. Sosa and Gero (2003) argued, for example, that the Sydney Opera House not only provided a solution to the problem of an opera house for Sydney and changed architecture and building techniques. It has also become a part of the Australian consciousness and an emblematic icon of Australian identity. The social aspects of innovation therefore exert their influence in both directions: The environment influences innovation and judges its effectiveness; innovation influences society's willingness to tolerate novelty and how it judges effectiveness.

This interaction between innovation and the criteria used to judge innovation is also seen at the level of the individual. Here are some examples:

- Remote associates arise out of deep domain-specific knowledge; broad, open perception; and networking in the processing and storing of information.

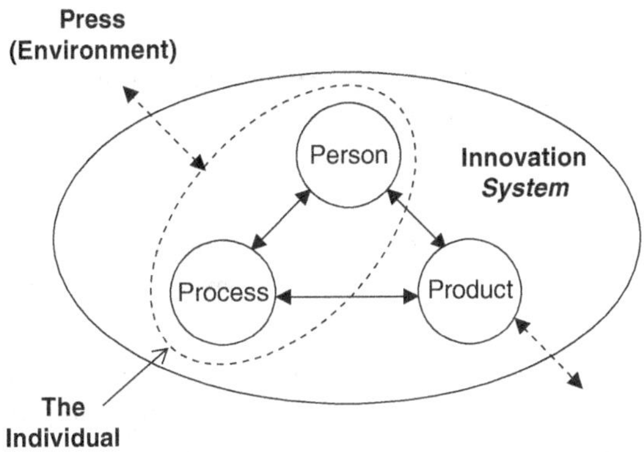

FIGURE 5.3. The Interaction between the Individual and the Press

- Resistance to group pressure is necessary for nonconformist behavior and autonomy of thinking – at least at certain times and in certain settings (such as the workplace).
- Readiness to take risks permits remote associations.
- Playfulness and willingness to experiment go with fluency and flexibility.
- Tolerance of ambiguity is supported by passion.

In fact, the influence pathways run in both directions. As Shaw (1989) put it, there are loops (see the discussion in Chapter 3).

The systems-like character of interacting factors discussed at the start of this chapter – especially that between the individual and her or his environment – and involved in the innovation process is shown in Figure 5.3.

Society's Ability to Tolerate Novelty

Society defines what is innovative in part as a result of its ability to accept the innovation. Returning to the example of the automobile, consider a design that arranges the seats so that all passengers except the driver face the rear. This design would also be effective in dramatically reducing deaths and injuries among occupants of motor vehicles involved in serious collisions. However, it has never even been tried by manufacturers because it is clear that car buyers would not accept it. Even more peculiar is the fact that infant capsules are made to face the rear, specifically because it is known that this is significantly safer – possibly by as much as a factor of five. Despite the value placed on creativity and innovation in many contemporary discussions, not all deviations from the commonplace are equally acceptable to a society.

This phenomenon goes beyond acceptance or not of specific pieces of novelty and extends to generation of novelty itself. Pseudo- and quasi-creativity (see Chapter 2) are often treated as harmless dreaming, letting off steam, and so on, even if they are regarded as having no social value. However, some behavior that deviates from the social norms awakens anger, resentment, and/or rejection; the example of Andres Serrano's controversial art makes this point. In fact, only certain departures from norms will be tolerated by a particular environment. Some people or organizations even have a vested interest in maintaining the status quo. For instance, scientists who have invested a lifetime's work in a particular paradigm are understandably likely to resist novelty, even if it is effective.

Of course, many of the behaviors that lie outside a society's norms and are labeled criminal really are unacceptable in anyone's terms. However, other proscribed behaviors are guilty only of deviating too much from what society will tolerate at the present time. A society's reaction to levels of novelty that exceed the limits – that introduce intolerable levels of surprise – is closely connected with the age, occupation, and/or social role of the person involved. For example, in typical Western society, an artist is allowed to be more outrageous than an engineer or a brain surgeon, while society is more tolerant of deviation in children than in adults. Indeed, as is discussed later in this chapter, there seems to be an inverse relationship between age and tolerance of deviation: The older people are, the less they are expected to innovate!

Social Mechanisms That Encourage or Discourage Innovation

In the course of psychological development, people learn specific behaviors for specific situations: how to obtain food or move about in safety; rules for living harmoniously with other people; cultural skills such as language; a concept of the good person; and techniques for dealing with stress, anxiety, and so on. These are acquired through interactions with the various elements of society: family, schooling, peers, role models, various forms of media. They are strengthened by having an affective (i.e., emotional) or evaluational component. Thus, children learn not only to do something in a particular way but that those who do it differently are ignorant, naughty, or evil. For example, a child in one social group may be taught to eat with the fork held in the left hand and the knife in the right, and to place food in the mouth with the fork but always with the tines curving downward. This child may also be taught that people who eat differently are ignorant and/or of a lower social class (a good example of this is holding a knife like a pencil rather than with the index finger running along the back of the knife).

In effect, generating variability – innovating – involves breaking the social rules. All people are capable of a wide range of responses to life situations, but in the process of growing up, they learn that most ways of behaving are actually forbidden, and they usually restrict their responses to a narrow range of socially tolerated behaviors; the preceding example about the knife and fork makes this point. Regardless of how the child viewed other people's eating habits, however, it is likely that he or she would quickly learn to change the behavior in question to fit in if the situation demanded this. A. J. Cropley (1967) studied the reactions of schoolchildren in social situations where a number of alternative courses of action were possible, of which one was highly socially desirable (e.g., "You have promised to visit your grandmother but are tempted to go to the movies instead"). He concluded that the children were guided by "stop-rules" (p. 46) that forbade most of the wide range of possible reactions in a particular situation in favor of the socially approved, correct one.

As Fromm (1980) put it, societies have filters that inhibit divergent behavior or even discourage thinking about different possibilities. According to Burston (1991, p. 145), the main purpose of these filters is maintaining the status quo. This is not confined only to obvious rules governing behavior – for example, in Australia cars are required to drive on the left side of the road. Visitors from North America could try driving on the right, but they would probably be arrested quickly, it is to be hoped before they caused an accident. However, there are rules not only about behavior but also about which opinions are correct, indeed about the right way of thinking and the contents of correct thought.

A simple example of the way society controls even what is thought can be seen in the phenomenon that is now referred to as political correctness. Ideas that can be interpreted as criticizing certain groups, showing lack of respect for them, or denying a particular status of that group are not discussed (or discussed at great risk). Political correctness is a form of social filter, but in some countries, it may actually be illegal to discuss certain ideas. This social filter is also seen in relation to issues such as the debate over climate change. A society's openness for novelty is frequently very limited. A result is that introducing effective novelty – innovation – requires a special form of courage, a willingness to challenge prevailing views even if this means being made a pariah.

A historical example (which has a reduced risk of offending against contemporary political correctness) involves Galileo's introduction of the novel idea that the earth orbits the sun (which is correct) and the reaction of the society in which he lived. Because this view conflicted with prevailing opinion, he was forced to withdraw publication of his findings and was even forbidden to think about his heretical views. He later denied that he had entertained thoughts about heliocentricity, and this was so patently absurd that he was threatened with torture for lying. In 1633, he was sentenced to prison, although this was commuted to house arrest. He remained under house arrest for the rest of his life.

There may be good reasons why societies have developed in this way. The idea has already been introduced that not every act of undisciplined, disruptive, or ignorant behavior, or every case of defiance, aggression, or nonconformity should be acclaimed in the name of creativity or innovation. Knowledge, accuracy, speed, good memory, and the like, are obviously important, most obviously for relevance and effectiveness. A society makes a substantial effort to train its members in its ways because then they can function effectively in a social environment. They can "enter into consensually validated ways of interpreting natural, social and interpersonal reality" (Burston, 1991, p. 145). Indeed, acquisition of the social rules has an important survival value. To take a simple example, if city children do not know how to cross the road safely in high-traffic areas, many of them would be killed or injured. Society has a strong interest in preserving most of the achievements of the past, as well as in limiting the extent to which people's behavior deviates from the well established. Some writers equate introduction of effective novelty exclusively with evolutionary change and imply that it cannot be introduced where the forces of preservation are strong. It is certainly true that most people would probably prefer the engineers at Boeing or Airbus to stick to the tried and trusted rather than introducing untested innovation into their designs! Nonetheless, even such areas are not completely static. Caution is not the same as a total absence of change.

A high level of conformity to social norms has the advantage that life becomes predictable because it is more or less known in advance what can be expected in everyday situations. However, the disadvantage is that unusual, unexpected behavior may become rare. In some societies, dislike of deviation may penetrate the public consciousness and become part of everyday, normal attitudes and values to such an extent that generation of novelty is subjected to extremely strong and widespread everyday sanctions. Gribov (1989) reported that the former Soviet Union was marked by

TABLE 5.2. *Opposing Forces in a Social Environment*

Force	Effect	Change Mode	Benefits
Conserving	Change: • is relatively slow • builds on what already exists • may appear to be blocked	*Evolutionary*	Despite change: • the world remains orderly and understandable • existing knowledge and skills remain useful • people's feeling of security is not threatened • experts' self-image of competence is preserved • power structures (and the like) remain intact
Renewing	Change: • is rapid (paradigm shift) • sweeps away what already exists	*Revolutionary*	As a result of change: • novelty is obvious • progress is often rapid • problems are often solved quickly • people are encouraged to introduce novelty • existing structures are threatened

a widespread public resentment of and hostility toward individuals who deviated from narrowly prescribed social norms and generated novelty. Burkhardt's (1985) concept of *Gleichheitswahn* ("sameness psychosis") also applies to a societal mass psychosis involving a drive to resist change.

There seem, in fact, to be two opposite forces at play in any social environment: forces of conservation and forces of renewal. The nature of these forces is summarized in Table 5.2.

Because these forces are logical opposites, they are often treated as being in opposition to each other. In fact, both are capable of producing change, and they can also work in a complementary fashion. From a practical point of view, the biggest difference between them is that the conserving pressures in a society allow only slow, gradual evolutionary change, whereas the renewing pressures encourage more dramatic changes that are larger and occur more quickly; that is, they lead to revolutionary change. This is the kind of change people usually have in mind when they talk of innovation.

Degree of Openness of the Society

What emerges is that openness to the new (or lack of openness) is a characteristic not only of individual people (see Chapters 1 and 4), but also of societies. People who produce and exploit novelty in societies – innovators and entrepreneurs – that are not open to it are likely to suffer various kinds of sanctions. The situation of such people is exacerbated by the fact that some behavioral dispositions associated with creativity and innovation may lead to disorganized, even chaotic behavior or to behavior that is regarded as antisocial or arrogant (e.g., impulsiveness, lack of concern about social norms, lack of interest in making a good impression, tendency to lose themselves in their work – again, see Chapters 1 and 6). Cognitive characteristics such as making remote associations that are too remote for most observers worsen the situation. The result may be that observers concentrate on the deviant or unpleasant, even antisocial behavior of the people concerned, and the link between their behavior and the innovation may become difficult for others to endure or even recognize.

Paradoxically then, there are rules about breaking the rules! People publicly acclaimed as creative or innovative break the rules but succeed in staying within acceptable limits. If they do not, they are likely to be regarded as eccentric, immoral, mentally disturbed, or criminal rather than creative, with the possibility of being criticized, shunned, or even locked away.

Socially Assigned Roles and Innovation

Another way that the external (social) environment exerts control over innovation is demonstrated by the apparent connection between innovation and gender. Discussions of gender-related differences in work in organizations are not uncommon, for example, in Lipman-Blumen's (1996) distinction between male and female achieving styles. Table 5.3 summarizes some aspects of gender stereotypes.

When the personal prerequisites for creativity discussed in Chapter 4 are juxtaposed with the stereotypes of male and female in Table 5.3, it quickly becomes apparent that the male stereotype fits the requirements for innovation much better than the female stereotype, which implies that women do not possess the psychological resources to be innovative. In fact, a recent white paper published by the Anita Borg Institute (2014) concluded that the empirical evidence is that firms where there are more women in key roles develop more products and services that meet the

TABLE 5.3. *Innovation-Related Stereotypes of Males and Females*[a]

	Stereotype	
Area	Female	Male
Cognition	• Concrete	• Abstract
	• Narrowly focused	• Broadly focused
	• Convergent	• Divergent
	• Intuitive	• Logical
Motivation	• Quick to give up under pressure	• Persistent
	• Seeks security (avoids risks)	• Willing to take risks
	• Seeks to avoid failure	• Seeks success
	• Reactive	• Proactive
	• Pursues long-term goals	• Pursues short-term goals
Personality	• Cautious	• Daring
	• Empathic	• Egocentric
	• Timid	• Aggressive
	• Sensitive	• Insensitive
	• Oriented toward feelings	• Oriented toward ideas
	• Lacking self-confidence	• Self-confident
	• Responsible	• Reckless
Social Properties	• People-oriented	• Task-oriented
	• Wants to be liked	• Wants to be looked up to
	• Communicative	• Taciturn
	• Self-effacing	• Seeks the limelight
	• Allows herself to be dominated	• Tries to dominate others
	• Gives in to authority	• Challenges authority
	• Fears criticism	• Fights back when criticized

[a] *This table is adapted from A. J. Cropley (2002, p. 83).*

needs of the market (i.e., that are relevant and effective). At a more concrete level, they reported that organizations with more women in leadership roles are able to reduce costs, enhance performance, and reduce staff turnover. In more psychological terms, the white paper concluded that, among other things, the participation of women added new knowledge and perspectives to idea finding in groups and thus promoted innovation.

Despite these findings, and even though the gender profiles in Table 5.3 may be no more than stereotypes, as Millward and Freeman (2002) showed, there is evidence that the stereotypes have consequences for the way female managers are regarded by their seniors (and thus for things like promotion) as well as for females' actual management behavior. In fact,

Schein (1994) concluded that the stereotypes dog female managers from the very beginning of their careers. Thus, one aspect of the effects of press at the social environment level may be a reluctance of organizations to utilize a substantial human resource for innovation.

An important mechanism through which stereotypes affect the behavior of females and males is role expectations in both external (social) and internal (organizational) environments. Scott and Bruce (1994) showed that these expectations have direct effects on some women's innovative behavior. For instance, not only do male managers expect their female colleagues to avoid risks, but the women too are familiar with the stereotype and the associated role expectations, and may behave accordingly. Thus, the unfavorable press factors may not be confined to pressures located in the external social environment but may also exist both in the organizational environment and within many women themselves (personal environment). Lipman-Blumen (1996) carried out an extensive analysis of male-female stereotypes and the way males and females are shaped into different achieving styles during the process of psychological development. She identified a number of psychological mechanisms that could be at work:

- Imitation
- Identification with the same-gender parent
- Differential reinforcement by parents, teachers, and the like, of what are perceived as gender-appropriate behaviors
- The belief that acquisition of clear gender roles is vital for healthy psychological development

Thus, even if they are no more than stereotypes, a society's ideas on gender can affect not only what others regard as normal in men and women, what duties women are assigned, and so on, but also – through internalization of the stereotypes by women themselves – the way women see themselves (personal properties), the ambitions they develop (motivation), their feelings and moods in certain situations such as exposure to a challenge (feelings), and their reaction to feedback from other members of a team (social), to give some examples, in other words, to their personal disposition to behave innovatively.

THE INTERNAL (ORGANIZATIONAL) ENVIRONMENT

At the start of this chapter and in Figure 5.2, it was explained that there are two contexts to the discussion of press. The broader, external social environment has been discussed, and attention is now shifted to the more specific internal organizational environment. Many of the same principles apply in this situation; however, some factors are more active in this narrower context. The organizational press is also of particular interest because innovation typically takes place within a well-defined institutional context. The environment in which people work or learn – the locus of innovation – plays a major role in encouraging or discouraging generation and exploitation of effective novelty. This environment goes beyond physical structures[1] and equipment, and includes the people in it, their attitudes, values, goals, and the like, and the way these are perceived (in other words, the organizational climate, or culture). Working with other people in groups and teams is another aspect of this press, and has both favorable and unfavorable effects on production and exploitation of effective novelty, largely through the roles people play, power, group processes, and the system of rewards. Thought leaders (managers, for example) can affect an organization's climate through the role models they offer, the way they acknowledge performance, and their effects on communication.

The Problem Facing Organizations

Turning to business, Higgins described ten challenges that he anticipated organizations would have to master with the help of innovation (and creativity) early in the twenty-first century. These challenges describe difficulties and potential constraints, but they also offer opportunities. The challenges include an accelerating rate of change, increasing competition, globalization, and the transformation of First World economies from industrial to knowledge-based economies. These factors mean that business is operating in an environment that is not only highly competitive but also unpredictable. Indeed, economic theory suggests that return on investment in wealthy nations should have been lower during the second half of the twentieth century than during the first half because the stock of capital was rising faster than the workforce (in other words, the workforce cannot keep pace with the available funding, putting a brake on returns). However, return on investment was considerably higher. How was this possible? The decisive factor that defeated the law of diminishing returns was the addition to the system of new knowledge and technology, i.e.,

[1] For further details about the impact of the physical environment on creativity and innovation, see Dul, Ceylan, and Jaspers (2011).

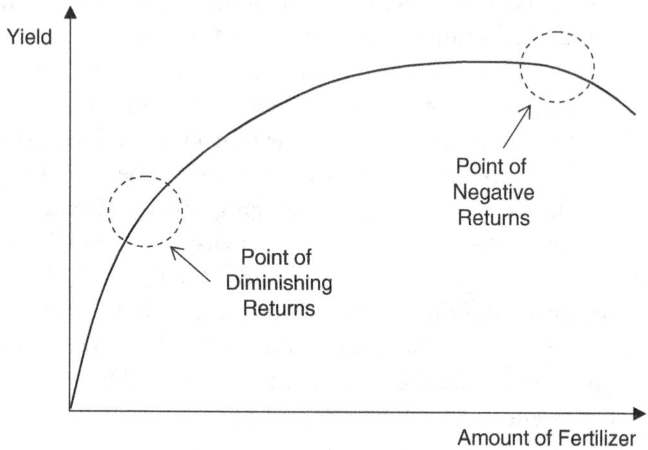

FIGURE 5.4. Innovation and the Law of Diminishing Returns

creativity and innovation. In fact, innovation currently accounts for more than half of economic growth (Thanksgiving for Innovation, 2002, p. 13).

The classic example of diminishing returns is fertilizer and crop yields (Figure 5.4). Without fertilizer, a given plot of land yields a certain output. Adding fertilizer increases the crop yield. More fertilizer results in a greater yield but only up to the point of diminishing returns.

At the point of diminishing returns, relative increases in yield become smaller and may even go into reverse (the point of negative returns). The same phenomenon might be observed in a manufacturing context – add more workers to a process and productivity increases. Keep adding workers and the relative productivity gains will drop off because there is a limit to how many people can work simultaneously. Add too many workers, and they may begin to get in each other's way and cause productivity to decline.

The key question in relation to creativity and innovation is how organizations avoid diminishing or negative returns. The addition of new knowledge and technology – innovation – has the effect of redrawing the curve. Steeper growth is maintained because as soon as the point of diminishing returns is reached, innovation restarts the relationship between input and output (Figure 5.5). In the crop example, this might be achieved, for example, by the introduction of innovative irrigation methods. This is reminiscent of the concept of S-curves in a product's life cycle. To keep the trajectory steep and positive, constant innovation is needed.

Pilzer (1990) describes the same phenomenon through the concept of economic alchemy. He argues that a society's wealth is a function of the

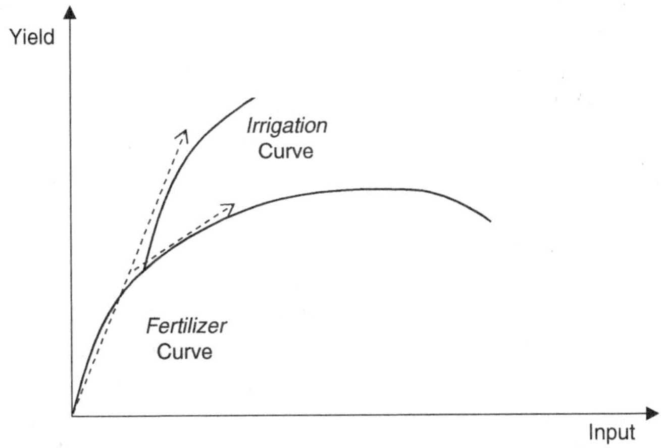

FIGURE 5.5. Innovation Defeats the Law of Diminishing Returns

physical resources available to it, with the availability of those physical resources determined by technology – "technology controls both the definition and the supply of physical resources" (p. 2). It follows, therefore, that "[i]n fact, for the past few decades, it has been the backlog of unimplemented technological advances, rather than unused physical resources, that has been the determinant of real growth" (p. 2). This can be taken a step further by suggesting that it is a lack of innovation (i.e. unexploited creativity), or poor implementation, that has prevented growth from reaching its real potential. Looking to business in the future, writers such as Oldham and Cummings (1996) concluded that innovation is a key factor in the prosperity of organizations exposed to the conditions that exist today.

Returning the role of the organizational press, the problem is that psychological analyses of organizations show that they resist the introduction of novelty (Katz & Kahn, 1978) or even minor change. Florida (2011, p. 19) refers to the work of Olson (1982), who discussed the way organizations resist change. Olson described the phenomenon that once an organization has prospered as a result of functioning in a certain way, it is difficult or even impossible for it to adopt novelty and innovate, no matter how effective it might be. Olson called this institutional sclerosis – a kind of organizational hardening of the arteries. Cultural and attitudinal norms become so powerfully ingrained that the organization rejects new ways of doing things. This frequently acts to stamp on innovative people and stamp out the introduction and exploitation of effective novelty. How can this be prevented, and how can an organization's natural resistance to change be broken down?

The processes involved in change can be mapped onto three key steps of innovation: (a) the generation of novelty, (b) the exploration of the novelty (including evaluation of effectiveness), and (c) the exploitation of the novelty. Organizational sclerosis first discourages the generation of novelty – we've always done things this way here, and it's worked for us! It then uses the process of exploration to discredit and belittle the novelty – those ideas are no good, our focus groups rejected them! Finally, sclerosis blocks exploitation – sorry, but we are prioritizing project X instead of yours! It must also be stressed, however, that change is not advocated simply for its own sake. Not all change is good, so that even in an organization open to creativity and innovation, the exploration phase is of great importance. Consider, for instance, how well the Coca-Cola Company explored its own decision to introduce New Coke in 1985. Ultimately, the company had to back down in the face of consumer resistance and reintroduce Classic Coke[2]. Was this a case of unexplored change that should have been rejected? Unexplored (or blind) change or incorrectly explored change can cause problems, as with the Coke example, while even successful change involves risks, such as overconfidence.

Organizations as the Site of Innovation

Focusing on organizational innovation, there are two broad strategies for approaching the task of the fostering of innovation. Sosa and Gero (2003) called these bottom-up (focused on dispositional characteristics of the individual such as intelligence, personality, interests or motives – necessary building blocks for innovation, so to speak) or top-down (focused on leadership, roles, group pressure, distribution of power, system of rewards, and so on, in the environment in which novelty is to be generated, explored, and exploited). As Sosa and Gero (2003) pointed out, behaviors that seem to be remarkable and to require a complex explanation in terms of personal dispositional factors (i.e., bottom-up factors) may seem unremarkable when looked at from a top-down perspective. The approach in this book has been a blend of bottom-up, in the sense that the Four Ps have each been examined in turn, and also top-down, in the sense that there is

[2] Of course, this may have been simply an innovative approach to marketing. If that is the case, then the example still serves as an important case study of innovation in a particular domain.

an acknowledged system-level interaction of the Four Ps that results in innovation. Isolating just the person and press for a moment, the point of the present discussion is to shift thinking about the interactions and to give temporary precedence to the top-down press factors.

One reason for taking this shift in focus is that the extent of the influence of the environment is often underestimated, especially in psychological discussions of creativity and innovation. This may be due in part to the so-called fundamental attribution error identified by social psychologists Ross and Nisbett (1991): When explaining behavior, observers tend to overestimate the importance of characteristics of the individual and to underestimate the effects of the environment. This tendency is known to be particularly marked when attempting to explain unusual behavior. Because innovation, by definition, involves the generation of surprise, its study would be particularly susceptible to the fundamental attribution error.

As already emphasized, however, the appearance of creativity and innovation in a given organizational environment depends on an interaction between personal properties and that environment. A key concern therefore is the way in which institutional settings in particular enable (or disable) people in their attempts to innovate. One way of conceptualizing this enabling/disabling function without disregarding personal properties has been suggested by Harrington (1999): It is a matter of goodness of fit, or alignment, between the conditions of the organizational climate and the properties of the individuals.

A Broad Understanding of the Term *Organization*

To understand how this alignment between organizational environment and person might be achieved, it is helpful to define more precisely what is meant by the term *organization*. For present purposes, an organization incorporates:

- Physical institutional structures and facilities such as workstations, laboratories, information-processing facilities, libraries, classrooms, workshops, and so on. These are found in every business, factory, workplace, and place of learning.
- People, not only managers or instructors, but also fellow workers or students.
- Intangible institutional factors influencing the interactions between physical structures and people, such as traditions, standards, norms and customs.

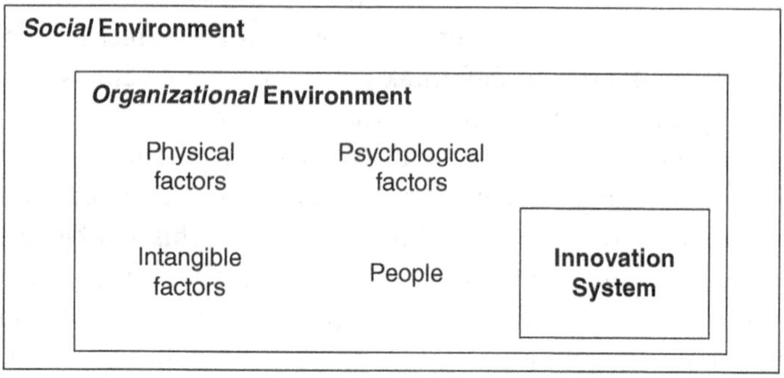

FIGURE 5.6. Factors in the Organizational Environment

- Psychological institutional factors influencing these interactions, such as roles, relationships, social hierarchies, interaction rules, communication pathways, and the like.

Figure 5.6 shows this organizational press in more detail.

The Congenial Environment

Reference has already been made earlier in this chapter to an environment that encourages the production and exploitation of effective novelty. The previous emphasis, however, was on the role of the external social environment in providing the conditions that can be manipulated to generate novelty, in deciding what is innovative, and in determining effectiveness. In this section, a congenial environment is now thought of as the specific, internal climatic conditions that permit, release, encourage, or foster the creativity and innovation of individual people or of groups, including:

- The amount of divergence or risk taking that is tolerated/encouraged
- The kind of variability that is tolerated/encouraged (for instance, routine extensions of the already known versus radical deviations)
- The resources that are made available (not only material, but also human) to support production of novelty
- The rewards (or punishments) that are offered to people who diverge from the usual

These are not substantially different from the factors that were discussed in the context of the social environment; however, the way in which they play a role is somewhat different in the context of the organization. The quality, quantity, and timing of these factors affect production, exploration, insertion, and exploitation of novelty by people functioning within the organization. For instance, the combination in an organizational environment of (a) encouragement of risk taking, (b) tolerance of radical novelty, (c) provision of ample time and other resources (funding, lab equipment, access to information), and (d) high levels of reward for those who depart from the usual (e.g. promotion, bonuses) would be highly congenial and, not surprisingly, would be expected to encourage innovation.

In fact, the beneficial effects of such circumstances are not restricted to encouraging divergent thinking (i.e., the cognitive aspects of innovation) but also promote other favorable characteristics, for example:

- A positive attitude to generation of variability in general
- Positive social status of creative individuals in teams and work and social groups
- A positive self-image among divergent thinkers
- Appropriate motivation (e.g., the urge to innovate, willingness to take risks, tolerance of ambiguity)
- Willingness to express personal characteristics such as openness, nonconformity, independence and flexibility

One of the better-known examples of the deliberate creation of a specific environment that we would call congenial in the context of innovation was the Lockheed Martin Skunk Works® concept. Responsible for the company's Advanced Development Programs, the Skunk Works traces its origins to the development of advanced fighter aircraft in World War II. The term has become synonymous with any small and loosely structured team of people engaged in the development of a project where a primary consideration is innovation. Typically, a Skunk Works operates with a high degree of independence from normal managerial and reporting constraints, and is protected from interference by a champion. By operating outside the normal rules of product development, physically separate from the main site of its parent company, and with minimal communication overheads and strong autonomy, a Skunk Works seeks to achieve rapid development of novel product concepts that subsequently may be reinserted into a normal product development cycle. Some of the rules of Skunk Works that are relevant to the present discussion are the following:

- Teams must have a high degree of autonomy.
- Project teams must be kept small (typically only 10 to 25 percent of normal teams).

- Reporting requirements must be kept to a minimum.
- A high degree of cooperation and communication between developer and customer must be maintained.
- Reward systems must be based on outcomes achieved.

Environments that are simultaneously challenging and supportive have been shown to sustain high levels of creativity and innovation in individuals and teams (West & Rickards, 1999). According to Mathisen and Einarsen (2004) (p. 119), creativity-fostering organizations are characterized by:

- Ambitious goals, which promote dissatisfaction with the status quo
- Freedom and autonomy in (a) choosing tasks and (b) deciding how they are carried out
- Encouragement of ideas
- Time (for creating ideas)
- Feedback, recognition, and rewards
- Lack of threat of sanctions when brave attempts go wrong
- Interest in excellence
- Expectation and support of creativity
- Permission to take risks
- Tolerance of errors
- Loosely specified objectives (or clearly specified objectives plus opportunities to challenge them)

The Bell Labs is another excellent example of how a highly innovative organizational climate can be created and nurtured (Gertner, 2012). There is also increasing evidence of the role that simple physical factors play in fostering creativity. Dul, Ceylan and Jaspers (2011), for example, have studied the impact of the physical environment (and the interaction of that with the social work environment) on creativity. Some of the physical factors that have a positive impact on creativity, and therefore innovation, include the presence of plants, the décor, visual access (to the outside environment), and appropriate lighting.

Assisters and Resisters

It is not just the way that the organization is structured – its physical setup, culture, hierarchies, and so on – that is important in encouraging innovation. Individual people also play an important role, not only as the active innovators but as facilitators of the innovation of others. Sergei Diaghilev, for example, is now remembered as the father of Russian ballet, while Igor Stravinsky is one of the most famous composers born and bred in that country. Both, however, were law students at the university in Saint Petersburg in around 1900! While still law students, both came under the influence of the revered musician Nikolai Rimsky-Korsakov, who advised each of them to give up law and focus on music, although he strongly advised Diaghilev against trying to become a composer as he intended. Diaghilev then focused on ballet. The result of Rimsky-Korsakov's influence on Stravinsky and Diaghilev was perhaps a loss to the field of law but a vast enrichment for the world of music. The point is that Rimsky-Korsakov's role was not as an active innovator in relation to the artistic output of either Diaghilev or Stravinsky but was critical to that output as an enabler or assister.

Another curious example is seen in the development of novel submarine technology in Germany both prior to and during the Second World War. In 1934, an engineer at Germaniawerft in Kiel, Hellmuth Walter, developed a novel, closed-cycle propulsion system for submarines based on hydrogen peroxide as a fuel. The advantage of such a system is that it does not require a source of atmospheric oxygen for combustion, meaning that submarines using this system could remain underwater for longer periods and operate at much higher speeds. Unfortunately for Walter (and fortunately for the Western Allies) the idea was rejected by the German naval high command – they found his claims for an engine that could power a submarine at a submerged thirty knots rather than the conventional seven knots, fanciful. Walter persisted and found a champion in Captain Karl Doenitz[3] in 1937. With Doenitz's help, Walter won a contract in 1939 to develop a prototype submarine using the new technology. Once the prototype demonstrated its performance, the naval high command was impressed and awarded Walter a contract to build six. The twist in the story is that Doenitz, now head of the German U-Boot service, did not want industrial resources taken away from the program building Germany's standard submarine and killed the project!

The facilitating role of people such as Rimsky-Korsakoff or Doenitz is well-known: Treffinger (1995) referred to the presence in organizational environments of resisters (people or circumstances that inhibit innovation) and assisters (people or circumstances that facilitate it). Although

[3] Doenitz, of course, subsequently became head of the German Navy's submarine service before assuming overall command of the German Navy in 1943. He was also, briefly, Hitler's successor as head of state in 1945.

assisters can be resources and other abstractions, the focus here is on human assisters: people who foster innovation merely by tolerating appropriate behavior, actively encouraging it, or even functioning as models of it.

A comprehensive study of twentieth-century British novelists (Crozier, 1999) concluded that differences in their productivity were largely attributable to the influence of social support factors. Csikszentmihalyi (1988) postulated that social support networks, including parents, teachers, mentors, colleagues, and managers, are vital determinants of creativity in the lives of individual creators. In a discussion of introduction of novelty into an organization, Mumford and Moertl (2003) emphasized the importance of, among other things, a "persuasive and effective advocate" (p. 264), in other words, what we would call a champion. These people are not always single individuals; they may also consist of groups or networks.

Assisters seem to be important for, among other things, development and maintenance of the intense motivation that is needed to sustain innovation. Petersen's (1989) study of hobby authors showed that support from other people – assisters – was vital in her participants' ability to avoid writer's block and maintain their motivation to write, thus demonstrating the importance of the social support system not only in acclaimed but also in everyday creativity (for a discussion of different levels of creative activity see, for example, Beghetto and Kaufman [2007]). As Bloom and Sosniak (1985) showed, assisters of creativity and innovation need not be powerful figures like Rimsky-Korsakoff or Doenitz, but in certain settings can be humble and unsung people such as a grade school teacher or perhaps a manager or colleague. Thus, some assisters energize, activate, or release creativity and innovation in others without necessarily producing effective novelty themselves. Facilitating the creativity and innovation of their colleagues is a major responsibility for managers in organizational settings.

An important function of assisters is to offer innovators a safe space where they can break the rules without punishment, protecting them from social and organizational sanctions (such as having project funding cut, being fired, or being shunned by coworkers). Another is to offer them a positive perspective on themselves, for instance, the view that their ideas are not crazy but innovative. This recognition can help to foster the courage to deviate from what everyone else is doing by, among other things, offering an opportunity to test the limits of the acceptable without risk or feelings of guilt. Assisters can also help innovative people to communicate their ideas to others by acting as an advocate.

Organizational Climate

In addition to relatively concrete and specific assisters and resisters, however, it is possible to speak of a more general element of an innovation-friendly environment: its climate. This was defined earlier in the chapter as the particular conditions in the environment. Siegel and Kaemmerer (1978), citing Litwin and Stringer (1968), focused on concrete aspects of climate by defining it as "a set of measurable properties of the work environment that are perceived by those working in the environment and influence their motivation and behavior" (p. 554). These include:

- Recognition of the value of generation of variability through, for example, promotions or pay increases
- Decision-making processes that do not stifle change by bogging it down in a quagmire of discussions and procedures
- Contact with models of innovative behavior
- Provision of appropriate opportunities to generate and exploit novelty
- The presence of people who encourage generation of variability

As Ekvall (1996, p. 105) explained, an organizational climate is also a perception in the minds of the people working in it: "a conglomerate of attitudes, feelings, and behaviors that characterize life in an organization." These include a feeling that generation of novelty is welcome and that people who generate it are respected. It also involves factors like feelings of tolerance and safety. These also define a congenial environment.

GROUPS AND INNOVATION

Another important aspect of the press that resonates with organizations is the question of groups (or teams) and innovation. As Harrington (1999) (p. 333) put it, groups can provide a "responsive" or "nourishing" audience. Paulus (1999) listed a number of beneficial effects on creativity and innovation that result from working in a group; the group can:

- Provide broader and more varied information than that possessed by a single person
- Motivate innovative activity
- Provide models
- Give feedback

One of the most frequently cited benefits of working in groups is the positive effect they are thought to have for the production of ideas, a key early step in the process of innovation. VanGundy (1984) pointed out that groups usually:

- Possess more knowledge than individuals working alone
- Arouse intense interest in group members
- Develop a broader perspective on the problem
- Generate more and higher quality ideas
- Come up with more candidate solutions
- Make riskier decisions
- Explore candidate solutions, to use our term, more effectively
- Enhance acceptance of novel solutions (in our terms, are more open)
- Lead to greater satisfaction with solutions

At the other end of the innovation process, groups also tend to enhance the implementation of solutions. This is not surprising given that a solution offered by a group has the support of a greater number of persuasive advocates (the members of the group) than a solution worked out by a single person. Altogether, VanGundy concluded that groups are most effective for solving problems that can be solved through division of labor, either because the problem can be broken into separate areas on which subteams can work simultaneously or because it can be broken into sequential stages that can be worked on and solved sequentially.

However, groups can also inhibit innovation. Larey and Paulus (1999) listed a number of creativity-inhibiting tendencies in groups that act to inhibit innovation:

- Free-riding (individuals reduce their effort and leave it up to the group)
- Evaluation apprehension (fear of negative reactions from the others)
- Production blocking (one person dominates and blocks others)
- Social comparison (people make sure that their ideas conform to the group tendency)
- Matching down (out of a sense of solidarity, the standard drops to that of the weakest member of the group)
- Focus on shared information (special knowledge of individuals is ignored or kept hidden because of the factors already listed)
- Premature closure (to keep the peace or because of the urge to be democratic or respectful, group members agree too quickly)
- Fixed roles or a fixed power structure (in the group there are leaders and followers; the former possess authority and the others do what they are told)

As an illustration of some of these inhibitors, in numerous studies, group brainstorming has been shown to produces fewer ideas that the same number of individuals brainstorming alone (Paulus, 1999). Apparently, some of the group members hold back their ideas, possibly because of the factors just listed. This is particularly the case where the individuals who come together to form the group all possess much the same knowledge base: The group does not broaden knowledge or add new perspectives but just has more people working on the same knowledge.

As Puccio (1999) pointed out, research also shows that the effectiveness of brainstorming groups in generating effective novelty (compared to producing a large number of ideas) depends strongly on the number of highly innovative people participating in the brainstorming: Groups without innovators do not generate much effective novelty, even if they do brainstorm and produce ideas. Thus, brainstorming makes use of what is available in the group rather than adding some new element that transcends the individuals in the group. The group is simply the sum of the links in the chain, not a new entity (or the whole is *not* greater than the sum of the parts). There is a growing body of work on groups/teams and innovation. For example, Baer, Oldham, Jacobsohn, and Hollingshead (2008) examined aspects of team composition and personality, while Paulus and Nijstad (2003) looked at a range of issues surrounding groups and creativity. Most recently, Mumford (2012) covered a wide range of topics relevant to organizations, including group/team factors in creativity and innovation.

Teamwork

If the group/team is the physical structure – the collection of people – then teamwork is a feature of what they do together. Thus, a group can fail to work together, or a group can work so that they achieve far more than they can as individuals. In other words, teamwork describes the outcome of a group, when the whole is greater than the sum of the parts. This is what many of VanGundy's (1984) advantages describe. Abra (1994) showed that achieving spectacular breakthroughs often requires cooperation with others. Sir Harold Kroto (winner of the 1996 Nobel Prize in chemistry for the discovery of Fullerenes) and William Phillips (winner of the 1997 Nobel Prize in physics for development of methods to cool and trap atoms with laser light) are two examples of contemporary Nobel Prize winners who emphasized teamwork when discussing their own processes of innovation. Kroto (Frängsmyr, 1997) argued that competition must be avoided at all costs. In the 1997 Nobel Lecture, Phillips emphasized that he always worked in a team. He gave as examples of the team's function testing out ideas, getting other people's feedback, getting their suggestions, asking questions, and answering questions.

Despite the benefits listed for working in teams, actions like taking a strong stand in favor of an innovation are risky, and the willingness of people to be innovative in full view of others is therefore affected by, among other things, fear of being publicly wrong, exposing themselves to criticism, or looking foolish. Production of novelty also depends on the dissatisfaction people feel for the status quo, which may require standing against the team or not accepting existing situations that the team sees as perfectly satisfactory. As a result, considerable courage and willingness is required to stand alone in a team. This is a situation in which the human assister can again be of great value. What seems to be clear is that there are great advantages for innovation when groups/teams are used, but that these must be managed with care and understanding (of what can inhibit innovation). A great deal of the work of modern organizations is done in teams, and it is therefore incumbent on managers to understand the interaction of groups and innovation.

OVERVIEW AND OUTLOOK

Press describes two environments within which innovation takes place. The external, social environment – society in general – defines a range of factors that determine who is innovative, what is innovative, and the amount and kind of innovation that is generally acceptable. This environment establishes a basic set of rules within which innovating organizations must operate. The internal organizational environment, shaped by the social environment, sets the immediate climate within which individuals interact to engage in the process of innovation. The press provides the link between the individual – characterized by person and drawing on process – and the organization as products are generated and exploited. Both the social and the organizational environment also act to encourage or discourage innovation through mechanisms such as the emergence of assisters (e.g., champions) and resisters, and the nature and composition of teams.

By adapting the Four Ps approach, which has become traditional in psychological discussions of creativity, to a Six Ps approach, the psychological analysis of innovation in organizations presented in this book has established six building blocks of innovation. These building blocks are the key to managing innovation, and the remaining chapters of the book now turn to using understanding of the building blocks for that purpose. However, this approach raises one fundamental puzzle that must be resolved if managers are to take control of innovation in their organizations. Within a given building block, mutually contradictory factors apparently facilitate innovation – for example, convergent and divergent thinking are both vital in the building block of process (Chapter 3). How is this possible? Such paradoxes exist in all of the building blocks, and this puzzle is addressed in the next chapter.

PART 2

MANAGING INNOVATION

6

Paradox: The Contradictions of Innovation

Application of the analysis that has been spelled out in the first half of this book is dogged by the problem that the building blocks of innovation involve numerous, apparently contradictory states of affairs that are nonetheless simultaneously true. Organization theorists have been aware of this issue and have been using the term *paradox* to describe it for decades. In a recent review Smith and Lewis (2011) analyzed research reports in twelve core organizational journals in the twenty years from 1989 to 2008 and identified no fewer than 360 articles that focused on the paradox approach. They also showed that in the selection of journals they reviewed, the number of paradox articles increased at a steady rate of about 10 percent per year over the twenty years they examined. Thus, there is no shortage of discussions about the innovation paradox in the organizational literature. In fact, paradoxes exist throughout the creativity/innovation system; some examples are listed in Table 6.1. The paradoxes listed in the table remain at a broad general level and will be outlined in a general sense in this chapter. They will be discussed in greater detail and in a more practical sense in subsequent chapters.

Of considerable importance for the present book is Smith and Lewis's (2011, p. 382) conclusion that there is a "lack of conceptual and theoretical coherence" to the discussions. *There is no clear theoretical framework for conceptualizing the paradoxes of innovation.* Fortunately, with its striking links to innovation theory, creativity theory – as it is understood in psychological research – is a promising source of ideas for establishing the necessary framework. The deconstruction of innovation that has already begun in earlier chapters and will be continued in later chapters shows that the paradoxes are neither arbitrary nor haphazard but are systematic and orderly, as paradoxical as that may sound. As a result, they can be managed; indeed, the position adopted in this book is that appropriate management of the paradoxes is crucial for organizational innovation.

TABLE 6.1. *Examples of the Paradoxes of Innovation*[a]

	Paradox	
Level	Conclusion	Counterconclusion
Meta-level (the inherent nature of innovation)	Innovation overthrows orthodoxy.	Innovation imposes orthodoxy.
	Innovation is a constructive force.	Innovation is a destructive force.
Social environment (innovation and society)	There is a pro-innovation bias in society.	There is widespread rejection of innovation in society.
	Innovation solves social problems.	Innovation causes social problems.
Organizational environment (innovation and the organization)	Organizations welcome innovation.	Organizations reject innovation.
	Organizations support innovative staff members.	Organizations suppress innovative staff members.
Personal environment [Cognition in the individual person]	Innovation requires divergent thinking	Innovation requires convergent thinking
	Innovative processes are inhibited by knowledge	Innovative processes depend upon knowledge
Personal environment (personal factors in the individual)	The innovative person tolerates ambiguity.	The innovative person seeks to eliminate ambiguity.
	The innovative person is open and flexible in setting and pursuing goals.	The innovative person pursues specific goals single-mindedly.
Personal environment (motivation in the individual)	Extrinsic motivation inhibits innovation.	Extrinsic motivation promotes innovation.
	Innovation requires tolerance for ambiguity.	Innovation requires drive for closure.
Personal environment (interpersonal factors)	The innovative person is a loner.	The innovative person works best in a team.
	Innovation requires defying the crowd.	Innovation requires acceptance by the crowd.

[a] The table does not contain a comprehensive list but is intended to give an idea of what is meant by the term *paradox* in this chapter.

THE PARADOXES OF INNOVATION ITSELF

D. H. Cropley, Cropley, Kaufman, and Runco (2010) drew attention to what could be called the meta-paradox of innovation, or in view of the German connection of one of the authors, the *über*-paradox. There is no doubt that innovation really has led to unprecedented levels of human well-being in many countries, in areas such as healthcare, food production, communications, transport, or leisure, to take a few examples. However, it has also brought nuclear, chemical, and biological weapons; environmental degradation; and new disorders, physical disorders such as repetitive-stress injury, psychological disorders such as obsession with computer games or online gambling, and social disorders such as online bullying or reduced ability to interact face to face with people. D. H. Cropley and Cropley (2013) also discussed new forms of crime and more effective terrorism resulting from or at least facilitated by innovations in, for instance, communications. Thus, despite its well-known benefits, innovation also has a dark side.

Innovation Comes at a Cost

Probably the most striking paradox at the meta-level is that innovation brings not only benefits but also costs, some of which are inherent to its core nature. Among other things,[1]

1. *Innovation consumes resources without any guaranteed benefit:* Generation and implementation of effective novelty is difficult and time consuming, and does not always bring a positive result.
2. *Innovation creates problems:* An innovative solution to one problem may generate new problems.
3. *People can become intoxicated with or blinded by innovation:* A hastily conceived innovation may possibly be implemented out of sheer infatuation with introduction of novelty.[2]
4. *Innovation produces conflict:* Innovation may lead to unrest or conflict between individuals, within groups, or in whole societies.
5. *Innovation destroys existing solutions that are functioning well:* Innovation may block the diffusion of perfectly good, already-

[1] This list is partly based on Gabora and Tseng (2104), although their discussion focused on creativity.

[2] This issue also appeared in Chapter 3, where the dangers of untested divergent thinking were discussed.

known solutions and thus confer no genuine benefit while incurring the costs just listed.

6. *Innovation blocks other innovations:* Innovation may hinder the emergence of alternative innovations, for example, by leading thinking along a particular path and thus establishing a new paradigm that closes the door to solutions based on a different paradigm.
7. *Incremental innovation may block radical innovation, even where the latter is needed:* Successful tinkering with what already exists may block radical rethinking of the whole situation. The success of the automobile and the constant incremental innovation such as improved safety measures or hybrid drive trains block any truly innovative approach to transportation of individuals.

Thus, at the meta-level, a degree of skepticism about innovation is not without basis. As Gabora and Tseng (2014, p. 4) put it, even though innovation is widely acclaimed, it is possible to have too much of a good thing. In addition to innovating, societies need to preserve the positive aspects of the way they already do things; a narrow focus of effort on attempts to develop and implement disruptive innovation at the expense of perfecting and disseminating what already exists (incremental innovation) may sometimes be inherently bad – innovation brings the risk of throwing out the baby with the bathwater. In evolutionary terms, a combination of novelty and continuity is essential for positive growth. Rather than ceaseless and unfettered innovation, there may be some optimum ratio of innovation to maintenance of the status quo. This would mean that, paradoxically, there is value for societies or even the species in both desiring and simultaneously rejecting innovation. In organizational terms, this tension is not infrequently referred to as the paradox of freedom versus necessity.

Innovation Blocks Innovation

Goncalo, Vincent, and Audia (2010) discussed a second meta-paradox: the problem that the generation of novelty, regarded as highly desirable and essential for social progress, can act as a "constraint on future achievement" (p. 114); that is, innovation can block innovation. Goncalo, Vincent, and Audia gave the example of Art Fry, the inventor of the Post-it® note. After fighting for years to gain acceptance of his idea for using a glue that did *not* stick – which seems to fly in the face of the very idea of adhesives – and eventually being hailed as the inventor of something highly innovative (the Post-it note), he became typecast as the Post-it man. Indeed after acquiring this reputation, he apparently saw all new problems as requiring a new kind of nondrying adhesive, thus never making any further paradigm change. Because it led to stereotyping of him as the Post-it man, his acceptance of himself in this role, an endless focus on the breakthrough that made him famous, and similar factors, the initial innovation introduced by Fry apparently blocked any further innovations on his part.

As was pointed out in Chapter 5, a product is publicly acclaimed as creative only when it is accepted by those who are knowledgeable in a field and it becomes integrated into the field. Thus, an innovation not infrequently changes the current paradigm in a field and thereafter redefines the norm. In so doing, on the one hand, it ceases to be novel itself (the process of acclamation as innovative makes a product familiar and therefore no longer novel) and, on the other hand, it sets new norms that not only render redundant earlier products that may have been, in their own time, innovations but also destroys possibly as yet unknown innovations in their cradle, as it were, by anticipating them and making the paradigm they represent obsolete in advance. The latter was true of digital imaging for Kodak's Advantix system, which was doomed before it came onto the market, despite being novel, effective, elegant and genetic (unfortunately it lacked only relevance).[3]

Hull, Tesner, and Diamond (1978) made an interesting examination of this inherent problem of innovation (innovation is its own worst enemy) at the practical level. Although their empirical findings were not clear-cut, they reviewed a number of discussions of the difficulty that existing paradigms pose for novel ideas and the resistance to such ideas they arouse. Put plainly, once an innovation becomes the paradigm in a field, it takes on the status of orthodoxy in that field and sometimes provokes resistance to subsequent innovation. According to Max Planck (1948), the older generation of true believers in the old orthodoxy (which was at one time itself an innovation) must die out before new novelty can prevail. Thomas Huxley went so far as to suggest – presumably with ironic intent – that all scientists[4] should be strangled on their sixtieth birthday before they become "clogs upon progress" (see Huxley, 1901, p. 117). He argued that the problem is worse in proportion to the level of creativity of the earlier contribution; that is, in terms of the

[3] One consolation is that a new product can reopen assessment of an earlier unsuccessful product, for instance by making observers look at it in a new way. This is the phenomenon that Sternberg, Kaufman and Pretz (2002, p. 83) referred to as reinitiation.

[4] In the present book, *scientist* should be replaced with *manager*.

present book, the more successful an innovation, the worse its clogging effect on future innovation.[5]

THE SOCIAL PARADOX

As Mueller, Melwani, and Goncalo (2012, p. 13) argued, creativity is widely "associated with intelligence, wisdom, and moral goodness." Kampylis and Valtanen (2010) reviewed 42 modern definitions of creativity and no fewer than 120 terms typically associated with creativity (collocations), and they concluded that the vast majority of discussions do not take any account whatsoever of negative aspects of creativity such as those mentioned in the previous section. Turning specifically to innovation, Mueller, Melwani, and Goncalo (2012, p. 13) showed that it is commonly identified as "the engine of scientific discovery" or the "fundamental driving force of positive change." Anderson, Potocnik, and Zhou (2014) reviewed the relevant literature and identified a pro-innovation bias, according to which innovation is always good.

Despite what has just been said, in the words of Mueller, Melwani, and Goncalo (2012, p. 13), "people desire but *reject* creativity" (emphasis added). A. J. Cropley (2009, p. 86) referred to "antipathy to creativity," Kim (2011, p. 285) warned of a "creativity crisis," Staw (1995, p. 161) discussed "why no-one [sic] really wants creativity," and Westby and Dawson (1995, p. 1) asked whether creativity is an asset or a burden. Thus, policy makers, social commentators, business leaders, educators, and members of the public proclaim the vital necessity of innovation, but in practice they consistently reject all but the most obvious incremental innovation.

The New Coke case study in Chapter 3 provides a commercial example of the rejection of change in the larger society for reasons that initially appear irrational or simply based on blind resistance to anything that differs from what people are accustomed to. Three-quarters of people who actually purchased New Coke reported that they liked the new flavor better than the old, while even many active protesters admitted preferring the taste of New Coke. In a blind taste test, the leader of one major protest group actually chose New Coke over Old Coke and Pepsi. Thus, the rejection of New Coke did not reflect rejection of the product at all but

[5] However, the enormous bursts of innovation following dramatic paradigm changes such as the introduction of production-line manufacturing methods or digital technology show that the clogging effects may not immediately be apparent or may perhaps take many years to manifest themselves.

was based on the desire for things to remain as they have been – rejection of change itself.

In the South, many drinkers of Coke had a sentimental attachment to Old Coke, which they regarded as part of their regional identity as Southerners. Ceasing to manufacture Old Coke was perceived as robbing them of their birthright (the way things had always been) and as involving a new variant of the War between the States, with the Yankees once again overthrowing the Southern way. The result was anger and alienation, and the fact that most people actually liked the new flavor better quickly became irrelevant. As this example demonstrates, acceptance of innovation by the community at large can depend more on psychological reactions to change than on the actual properties of the innovative product.

THE ORGANIZATIONAL PARADOXES

About two decades ago, Staw (1995) pointed out that "firms tend to back away from [creativity]," and added rather ominously "perhaps with just cause" (p. 161).[6] DeFillippi, Grabher, and Jones (2007) discussed the paradoxical role of creativity in business and organizations, where it is simultaneously desired and rejected. The evidence is that some organizations routinely reject creative ideas even while espousing innovation as an important goal. For example, Ford and Gioia (2000) discussed resistance to innovation in management decision making, and West (2002) focused on resistance to generation and implementation of ideas in teams.

Reference has already been made to institutional sclerosis. Organizations become so committed to existing technologies and business practices that they are unable to change. The sclerosis may be worse when the existing and now outmoded way of doing things was once a great innovation. Some individual organizations have even preferred death (in the metaphorical sense) to implementing radical effective novelty. The examples of Smith-Corona and Polaroid have already been mentioned, as was the fate of Nokia when it refused to recognize that mobile phones are now part of the fashion industry and insisted on building technologically advanced mobile phones rather than devices that satisfied the desire of their customers for ever smaller, more streamlined fashion statements.

[6] What the just cause may be is discussed in a later section of this chapter.

Innovation Creates Problems in Organizations

Staw (1995) listed more specific and concrete reasons why organizations reject innovation:

(1) Innovation requires surplus personnel who are not fully occupied with specific activities that directly contribute to the current bottom line (an aspect of work organization).
(2) Innovation depends on disagreement and disobedience (personal properties of innovatively creative workers).
(3) It makes it necessary to take a chance instead of sticking to the tried and trusted (motivation).
(4) It threatens existing power hierarchies (social factors).

Baucus, Norton, Baucus, and Human (2008) also drew attention to four inherent aspects of the creative process that cause particular problems for organizations: (a) breaking rules and diverging from standard operating procedures; (b) challenging authority and defying tradition; (c) creating conflict, competition, and stress; and (d) exposing organizations to risks.

Benner and Tushman (2003) made the paradoxical nature of the situation at the level of the organization clear. A firm's survival requires not only that it develops new capabilities (i.e., innovates) but also that it preserves and extends its existing competencies. The total quality management movement of the 1990s and first decade of the 2000s often leads to managerial activity focused on standardization and optimization of what an organization already does, that is, to a focus on preserving and extending its existing competencies. In a plain-speaking discussion, Levitt (2002) made this state of affairs clear in down-to-earth terms. He stressed that the fundamental function of organizations is to "achieve order" (p. 143), not to overthrow order by generating novelty. In fact, an organization is a "vast machinery" for imposing order on looming chaos. The essence of order is "conformity and rigidity," and its natural enemy is novelty and change. And yet novelty and change are now widely accepted as not just the friend of organizations but as vital for their survival. Thus, in addition to fulfilling their fundamental task of imposing conformity in order to avoid death, organizations must somehow simultaneously foster change. In a sense then, innovation involves imposing disorder in an environment dedicated to the maintenance of order. *Thus, the fundamental organizational paradox is that disorder must be achieved in an orderly way.*

THE PERSONAL PARADOXES

At the level of the individual person too, innovation is not the unalloyed blessing it is often regarded as being. Innovators may go as far as openly defying the norms of society. Sternberg and Lubart (1995, p. 41) referred to the personal disposition underlying willingness to swim against the social current as contrarianism (although they were writing about giftedness in general and not specifically about innovation). Indeed, as was mentioned but not pursued in Chapter 4, the personal properties of innovative individuals include aspects that would usually be regarded as undesirable. Thus, at the meta-level and in the social and organizational environments, as well as in the individual environment, the generation of effective novelty has not only a good side, as depicted in Table 4.2, but a bad side as well. This paradox will be discussed in more detail in the following section.

Negative Properties of Innovative Individuals

D. H. Cropley, Cropley, Kaufman, and Runco (2010) pointed out that, despite the tendency in the creativity literature and in public understanding to regard creativity as always good and, in keeping with this, to assume that it involves only admirable personal characteristics, creativity has its dark side. Indeed, some studies have reported that undesirable personal attributes are associated with creativity, such as self-centeredness, self-righteousness, lack of feelings or willingness to hurt other people's feelings, arrogance, dishonesty, willingness to lie and skill at doing it, hostility, and destructiveness (e.g., D. H. Cropley, Cropley, Kaufman, & Runco, 2010; Gino & Ariely, 2012; Nebel, 1988; Silvia, Kaufman, Reiter-Palmon. & Wigert, 2011). Other studies have shown that creative people are more likely to manipulate test results (Gino & Ariely, 2012), tell more different kinds of creative lies than less creative people (Walczyk, Runco, Tripp, & Smith, 2008), deceive during conflict negotiation (De Dreu & Nijstad, 2008), and demonstrate less integrity (Beaussart, Andrews, & Kaufman, 2013). People who make greater use of creativity to inflict deliberate harm on other people are more likely to be physically aggressive (Lee & Dow, 2011) and have lower emotional intelligence (Harris, Reiter-Palmon, & Kaufman, 2013).

Consequently, harnessing creativity for the purposes of innovation requires more than balancing it with appropriate caution and reality checks.[7]

[7] There is some disagreement, however, about the negative personal characteristics. For instance, Silvia, Kaufman, Reiter-Palmon, and Weigert (2011) carried out a highly

TABLE 6.2. *The Down Side of the Innovative Person in an Organization*

Psychological Domain	Attribute
Motivation	• Unwillingness to carry out orders • Desire to do things differently • Self-centered desire for acclaim • Impatience to make changes for their own sake • Stubbornness
Social	• Lack of concern about others • Deceptiveness • Hostility • Disagreeableness • Pretentiousness • Willingness to be disrespectful to authority • Willingness to risk hurting people's feelings • Social divisiveness • Physical aggressiveness
Personal properties	• Arrogance • Self-centeredness • Self-righteousness • Uncritically positive self-image • Dishonesty • Willingness to lie • Hostility • Lower emotional intelligence

Some of the major psychological attributes defining the down side of the personal properties of innovative people from an organizational point of view are listed in Table 6.2.

The Phases of Creativity

The paradoxes of innovation as summarized, for example, in Tables 4.2, 6.1 and 6.2, and the need for innovative products to both challenge what already exists and yet fit in with the status quo (to impose disorder in an orderly way), mean that mutually contradictory processes, personal

differentiated analysis in which they were at pains to avoid conflating disagreeableness and hostility, and concluded that low agreeableness has often been mistaken for hostility. They argued that creative people are often not even disagreeable but simply pretentious (see the discussion of quasi-creativity in Chapter 2!

motives, personal dispositions, and feelings may be of equal importance in innovation. Particular factors may foster innovation but also block it. For instance, the personal tendency to behave in a nonconforming way or to engage in unfettered thinking may foster generation of novelty but inhibit painstaking verification of the value of ideas or effective communication in situations where the novelty must be linked to the requirements of the real world. This raises considerable conceptual difficulties.

The solution is provided by a phase approach: Contradictory poles of the paradoxes are both of central importance, but at different points in the process of generating and implementing effective novelty (e.g., Csikszentmihalyi, 2006). These points are referred to in the remainder of this book as phases. The classical phase approach in psychological research on creativity is that of Wallas (1926), who originally proposed seven phases in the development of a creative product, although over the years they were reduced to four: preparation, incubation, illumination, and verification. A. J. Cropley and Cropley (2009) pointed out that the phase approach is not without its critics. Nonetheless, it is now widely accepted that novel products do not appear out of the blue, although there is a tension between the step-by-step model of continuous innovation and the sudden breakthrough approach that emphasizes the sudden emergence of a well-advanced solution (e.g., Dasgupta, 2004; Simonton, 1999).

The four-phase model attributed to Wallas may be appropriate for discussions of generation of novelty. However, the phase approach must be extended if it is to encompass innovation, which requires that novelty must not merely be generated but must also be useful for some practical purpose and must be implemented, as was strongly emphasized in Chapter 2 (the usefulness imperative). Thus, innovation requires going beyond mere generation of novelty to encompass (a) a phase of communication to users (in the case of innovation, this most commonly means customers), and (b) acceptance of the novelty by these people. In this book, this final step (acceptance by users) is referred to as involving validation. Communication and validation are absolutely necessary for implementation; both communication to customers and acceptance by them is essential (see the discussion of Christensen [2013] and of Besemer [2006] in Chapter 3).

One further differentiation of the Wallas approach is also needed. In a meta-analysis of research findings, Davis (2009) reviewed the extensive discussion of the nature of creativity and concluded that it can be viewed as having three controlling components, the first of which is problem finding (p. 26). This conclusion is consistent with emphasis on sensitivity to problems and problem finding going back to Guilford (1950) and Torrance (1963). Mumford and Moertl (2003) described a case study of innovation in management practice and concluded that innovation was activated by intense dissatisfaction with the status quo (p. 262). In this book, recognition that there is a problem and a resulting urge to do something about it will be referred to from this point as involving activation. However, the following question arises: What activates innovative behavior? Problem awareness does not come out of the blue: You cannot see problems in and be dissatisfied with situations – and thus be activated to do something – you do not know anything about, as was emphasized in the discussion of expertise in Chapter 4. Thus, the generation of novelty commences with acquisition of knowledge in an area, in a phase referred to here as preparation.

These considerations lead to an extended, seven-phase framework involving preparation, activation, generation, illumination, verification, communication, and validation. The extended-phase model is shown in Figure 6.1. In the context of the present discussion, the principal difference between this phase structure and the commonly cited four-phase Wallas approach is that, in organizational terms, the expanded-phase model incorporates phases involving linking the generation of novelty to the requirements of the commercial world (i.e., preparation, communication, validation), whereas the Wallas model focuses on mere generation of novelty (i.e., activation, generation, illumination, verification). The phases do not necessarily form a lock-step progression of completely distinct stages, as was emphasized in Chapter 2.

There may well be interactions, false starts, restarts, early break-offs, and the like. Haner (2005, p. 289) summarized the relevant literature as showing that the phases of creativity are "iterative and non-sequential," and occur in a recurring "nonlinear cycle." Writing from the point of view of organizational psychology, Gupta, Smith, and Shalley (2006, p. 693) contrasted sequential or lock-step generation of effective novelty in an organization ("punctuated equilibrium") with nonlinear development ("institutional ambidexterity").

THE CONSEQUENCES OF THE PARADOXES FOR MANAGERS

From the point of view of managers, the paradoxes mean that, although innovation is hailed as undeniably good, *there is a price to pay for promoting innovation* in an organization – the price of uncertainty. Innovation brings surprises, and this means of necessity not knowing what is coming

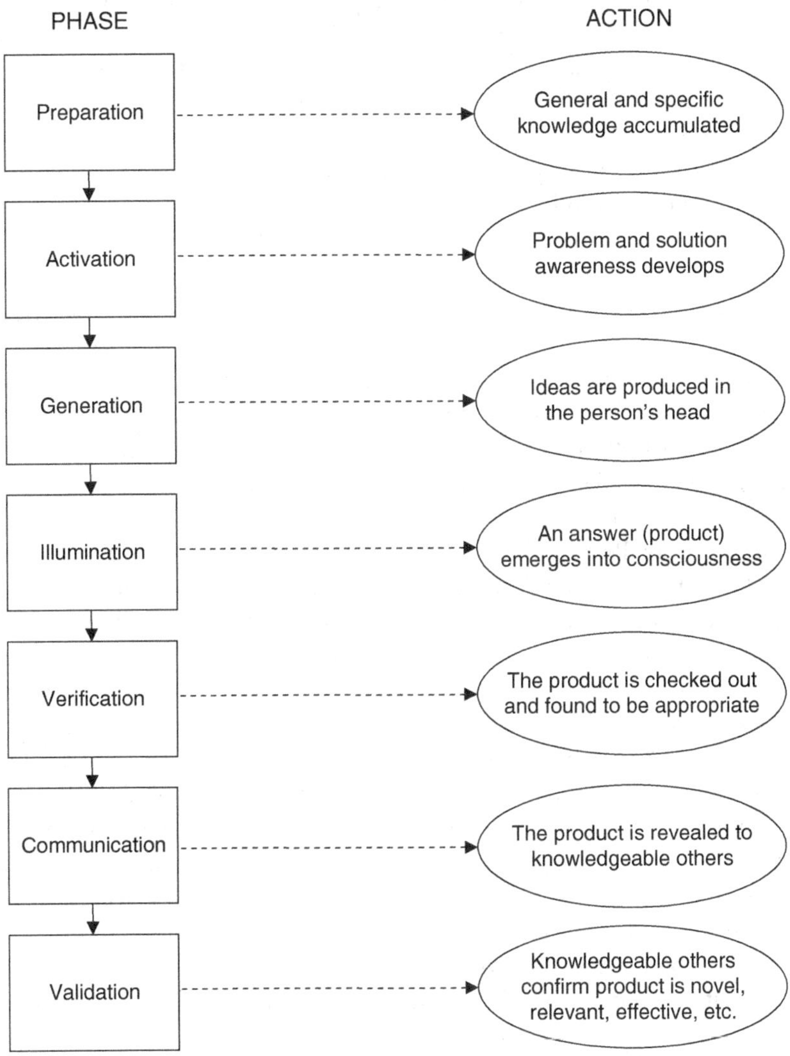

FIGURE 6.1. The Extended-Phase Model of Innovation[a]
[a] *Adapted from A. J. Cropley and Cropley, 2008.*

next. However, managers are required to specify what is coming next; that is their job. Innovation thus places their stock-in-trade in question and casts doubt on their knowledge and authority, and challenges their self-concept. Mainemelis (2010, p. 559) gave the concrete example of "creative *deviance*" (emphasis added) and discussed examples of an extreme form in organizational settings involving direct defiance of specific instructions from managers that in some cases eventually led – possibly to the discomfort of the managers in question – to acclaimed innovations. He gave the example of LED bright light technology, which was developed by a scientist who repeatedly ignored orders to abandon the project.

Under such circumstances, managers find their knowledge about how to run an organization, how to manage production processes, how to make decisions, or what constitutes a good product (to give a few examples) subjected to challenge. According to Levitt (2002, p. 142), managers have achieved success in their organization by virtue of "a lifetime of *judicious* executive behavior" (emphasis added), and so they *know* the answers to the questions mentioned here; however, innovation often means placing all that in doubt, thus threatening authority, certainty about what is right, feelings of self-efficacy, feelings of control, faith in what the organization is doing, and the like. Psychological research (e.g., Heimberg, Turk, and Mennin, 2004) has shown that people can tolerate only a limited amount of uncertainty. Beyond the critical level, it may disrupt clarity and logic of thinking, make information processing fixated on a narrow range of issues, generate feelings of anxiety, or even cause anxiety disorders ranging from worrying a lot to actual pathological anxiety states. These can cause behavior to become rigid and repetitive, even sometimes to the point of obsessive-compulsive behavior patterns.

Consequently, when dealing with innovative creativity, managers may find themselves forced into a position where they spend their time defending themselves against defiance and criticism, calming outrage at the violation of norms, clearing up damage, restoring order, quieting fears, and the like. The psychological challenge to managers is discomforting not only for the managers themselves but also for other employees, who may be happy with existing roles, expectations, patterns of power distribution, and the like (the devil they know). Even customers/consumers may prefer the way things are at present (see the New Coke example in Chapter 3).[8] Thus, a further task for innovation management involves dealing with possible (and conceivably not entirely unjustified) hostility to innovative individuals within organizations, both the hostility of the managers themselves and also that of the innovative individuals' colleagues. This psychological challenge to managers becomes particularly

[8] Reference has already been made to Besemer's dictum: Customers don't like too many surprises.

apparent in examples such as the LED case study already mentioned, where direct instructions were disobeyed.

A New Perspective on Management Styles

Levitt (2002) discussed in effect openness of executives to novelty and came to a conclusion that is of considerable importance for the present discussion: "Everybody knows some bosses are more receptive to new ideas than others" (p. 142). Chapter 5 proposed a 2 × 2 classification matrix as a mechanism for classifying examples of innovation in particular social settings (see Table 5.1). Although he was not writing specifically about innovation in organizations, A. J. Cropley (2009)[9] adopted a similar approach in speculating about possible individual differences in receptivity to new ideas among people in positions of authority (such as managers). As in Chapter 5, his analysis focused on (a) the amount of novelty they can tolerate (dichotomized as high versus low) and (b) the kind of novelty they are most comfortable with (dichotomized as radical versus orthodox). This categorization is extended here by adding a third dimension: (c) their focus of interest (dichotomized as involving either products or processes). Managers with different combinations of amount of novelty, kind of novelty, and focus are expected to be favorably inclined to or averse to different kinds of novelty production. A. J. Cropley (2009, p. 90) used rather colorful language to distinguish among, for instance, avant-gardists, Bohemians, sticklers, or conservers. These categorizations make it possible to refer in a systematic way to differences among managers in the way they react to generation of novelty. Table 6.3 is a modified version of the original table in A. J. Cropley (2009).

It must be admitted that the categories of manager given here (for example, avant-gardist, stickler, etc.) are purely intuitive; that is, their existence has not yet been demonstrated empirically on the basis of, for instance, observation of management behavior. Nonetheless, the idea of a systematic interaction among amount of novelty, kind of novelty, focus of interest, and reactions of managers offers a novel way of looking at familiar topics in the organizational literature, such as leadership (for a more traditional discussion, for instance, see Kouzes & Pozner, 2012), management style (more traditionally discussed, for instance, by Schermerhorn, 2012), and the like. This approach offers insights into the paradox of why

[9] He was writing about teachers.

TABLE 6.3. *Different Kinds of Manager and Generation of Novelty*

Amount of Novelty Tolerated/Encouraged	Kind of Novelty Tolerated/Encouraged	Orientation	Focus	Label
High	Radical	Product	Paradigm-breaking products	Innovator
High	Radical	Process	Doing things in a unique and novel way	Individualist
High	Orthodox	Product	Products that greatly extend what already exists in a known direction	Adapter
High	Orthodox	Process	Extending existing ways of doing things	Pathfinder
Low	Radical	Product	Products that are surprising, even if not very novel	Avant-gardist
Low	Radical	Process	Behaviors that are surprising, even if not very novel	Bohemian
Low	Orthodox	Product	Products that extend the known a little in a known direction	Conserver
Low	Orthodox	Process	Doing things in ways based on the tried and trusted	Traditionalist

managers simultaneously call for and yet reject innovation. To take an example, while enthusiastically endorsing innovation as a general phenomenon, an adapter, as defined in Table 6.3, is likely to reject introducing fundamentally new ways of doing things, preferring instead to build on and improve what already exists, whereas an individualist would welcome such an innovation.[10]

The categories in the right-hand column of Table 6.3 also seem capable of being applied to organizations themselves. For instance, the case study of Kodak that follows can be seen as an example of an organization that was a traditionalist adapter and consequently made entirely predictable errors in dealing with introduction of novelty. Barabba (2011) described how, since 2012, Kodak has virtually ceased to exist as a photographic company despite its long history of success with innovative film-based imaging techniques. This success was largely, although not entirely, based on their mastery of the chemical-based film and paper business. When confronted with the rise of digital photography, the company persisted in sticking with film despite the fact that its laboratories had invented the first megapixel camera. Its substantial digital know-how was applied to developing the Advantix film system, which made it possible for users to preview photos before deciding which ones to print. Unfortunately for Kodak, consumers rejected the system, which essentially involved making digital images, selecting the preferred ones, then printing them more or less in the traditional (photochemical) way.

The company did not reject innovation but went about it in a way that was doomed because it was an adapter competing with innovative individualists. It reacted to digital technology by perceiving it as a way of improving the revered existing photochemical technology based on film and paper (in a process referred to in Chapter 1 as incremental innovation) rather than as an entirely new way of capturing and viewing images that would ultimately replace chemical film entirely (see the discussion of disruptive innovation in Chapter 1). The revolutionary new possibilities of digital technology were obscured by the past success of the photochemical approach, which became a clog on progress. Sheer improvement in

[10] The analysis of person in Chapter 4 offers a psychological explanation of the source of the differences encapsulated in the labels in the right-hand column of Table 6.3 (adapter, individualist, and so on). For instance, an individualist would be open, a risk taker, and experience positive feelings about change, whereas a conserver would be closed, a risk avoider, and experience negative feelings about change.

the technology was not enough by a large margin; what was needed was a new paradigm.

OVERVIEW AND OUTLOOK

The very essence of creativity involves two elements that are inherently problematic and paradoxical. It overthrows existing orthodoxy, to be sure, but then sets up a new orthodoxy that itself can hamper further change, at the very least in a specific organization because that organization may become almost obsessed or fixated by enthusiasm for what was once the new way of doing things and is now unable to change. The eventually fatal influence of the Land camera on Polaroid is an example. At the broader societal level too, a successful innovation may close off all other lines of development; for example, the success of the internal combustion automobile has ended further development of the steam-driven car despite spasmodic attempts to revive steamers (with occasional reports of successes, such as the flash boiler, which eliminates the long firing-up phase with the steam engine).

At the level of the individual, innovation requires challenging what already exists, questioning the way things are currently done or the way the world is conceptualized. In doing so, it may create uncertainty in the minds of managers and colleagues, and uncertainty is experienced as stressful. Thus, innovative creativity is a challenge for managers, and it may generate hostility and resentment, distrust, a perception of disloyalty, or a desire to make the generator of novelty fall into line. Understanding of the paradoxes of innovation helps to build a framework for working out principles for promoting innovation in organizations, and the discussion now moves to more practical considerations of how this is to be done.

7

Measuring the Building Blocks of Innovation

Part 1 of this book presented a framework of four building blocks – person, product, process, and press – that together, as a system, are necessary for innovation. The role that each of these plays in the generation and exploitation of ideas was explained along with some of the challenges that they present to managers seeking to steer their innovation process to a successful outcome. To realize the full value and potential of innovation in organizational settings, however, it is necessary to be able to answer not just subjective, qualitative questions about the people involved, the products developed, the processes used, or the settings in which these are located. Managing and controlling innovation in an organizational context also raises objective, quantitative questions.

It is easy to see why this issue – measurement – is so important to successful innovation. It is one thing for a manager to demand more creative products, but deciding how much more requires a degree of objectivity, rigor, and repeatability. Decision-making processes – one of the convergent aspects of innovation (see Chapter 3) – cannot proceed effectively without an objective basis for selecting product A over product B. Continuous improvement and the ability to learn from mistakes are also harder if organizations cannot reflect on a failed innovation and understand if the product was, for example, too novel or perhaps not effective enough. By the same token, as managers seek to improve their organization's capacity for innovation, they cannot proceed in forming effective teams if they know nothing about the people who make up those teams. If team innovation, for instance, is facilitated by a diverse mix of people who are highly open to experience, excellent convergent thinkers, or willing to take risks, the ability to measure these aspects of the person would be helpful.

The same is true of the processes used to generate novel ideas and the environment in which innovation takes place. The successful management of innovation is built on a foundation of objective measurement of the person, product, process, and press. This chapter addresses the question of measurement for each of the building blocks. Creative products feed the innovation process, so how is product creativity measured? People possess a constellation of psychological resources – personal dispositions, motivation, feelings – that can help or hinder their ability to generate ideas, so how are these things measured? A key to idea generation is the divergent thinking process, so how does a manager know if this is working effectively? Both the organizational and social environments have an impact on the production and exploitation of effective novelty. Therefore, how is a manager to know when he or she has got it right?

This chapter discusses the steps for measuring for each of the building blocks of innovation, outlining some of the methods and instruments that are available to quantify these building blocks of innovation. As D. H. Cropley (1997, 1998a, 1998b) demonstrated, there is no fundamental impediment to rigorous, objective measurement, even for properties that appear qualitative in nature.

MEASURING PRODUCT CREATIVITY

Innovation begins with the generation of ideas. Those ideas (see Chapter 2) must be, at a minimum, new and effective. Once novel and effective ideas have been generated, they must be turned into viable, value-adding outputs. The measurement of product creativity is by no means a new problem in creativity research. Extensive studies show how to measure creativity in its broadest sense. O'Quin and Besemer (1999) describe three common approaches used to measure product creativity: indirect measurement, global judgment, and criterion-based measurement. These approaches have been developed in both a domain-general and a domain-specific context (for a more detailed discussion of domains and creativity, see Baer [2010]). Some of the possible solutions that span these different approaches include the use of expert raters (Amabile, 1996), divergent thinking–based scoring of creative products for originality or fluency (Reiter-Palmon, Illies, Cross, Buboltz, & Nimps, 2009), and assessment of a product's historical impact (Simonton, 2009).

Horn and Salvendy (2006) compared various product creativity measurement tools, including rating scales and subjective assessments. The former include Besemer and O'Quin's (1987, 1999) Creative Product Semantic Scale

(CPSS) and Reis and Renzulli's (1991) Student Product Assessment Form; the latter concentrated on Amabile's (1983, 1996) Consensual Assessment Technique (CAT). Horn and Salvendy (2006) also reported on the range of different domains to which rating scales have been applied, including artwork, cartoons, chairs, advertisements, scientific and creative writing, audio-visual products, and social studies. The CAT, by contrast, has been applied to stories, art, poetry, and other aesthetic products. The assessment of aesthetic works (such as paintings or poems) has, in fact, been extensively investigated for nearly a century (Baer, Kaufman, & Gentile, 2004; Cattell, Glascock, & Washburn, 1918; Child & Iwao, 1968).

However, surprisingly few studies assess the creativity of products in the sense of tangible, scientific, or technological products – for example, engineered artifacts or manufactured consumer goods. Studies that do examine such products do so primarily in connection with related concepts, such as usability (see, for example, Han, Hwan Yun, Kim, & Kwahk [2000]). In one such domain (mathematics), Mann (2009) argues that many of the current assessments are time-consuming to score; they also tend to be separate instruments designed to measure the specific domains. As a result, most of the work on mathematical creativity assessment cannot be applied easily to related domains (such as consumer products). What is needed is a universal aesthetic of creativity – a set of indicators that "can be recognized with a substantial level of agreement by different observers, and can be used to judge both amount and kind of creativity" (D. H. Cropley & Cropley, 2008, p. 155). Table 7.1 suggests what these might look like.

TABLE 7.1. *The Criteria of Creativity in a Solution (Product)*

Kind of Criterion	Level of Creativity	Kind of Creativity
External	• Differs from what already exists • Leads to surprise • Is generalizable • Is seminal • Is germinal	• Relevant • Valuable • Effective • Useful
Internal	• Generates many ideas • Leads to substantial reformulation of ideas • Opens up new principles	• Logical • Elegant • Understandable • Well crafted • Harmonious • Complex

Consensual Assessment

The most straightforward way of determining the creativity of a product is to ask people who know about such things whether it is creative. This sensible idea is at the heart of the method of consensual assessment (for a summary, see Hennessey & Amabile [1999]). Amabile and her colleagues have developed and refined this approach, and the Consensual Assessment Technique (CAT) is now relatively well known among creativity researchers. The method typically involves recruiting a panel of judges, often experts in the field to which the product belongs, to rate the creativity of a product. There is evidence, however, that even people without deep, expert knowledge of a field are capable of identifying creativity when they see it (Kaufman, Baer, Cropley, Reiter-Palmon, & Sinnett, 2013), particularly when given a set of guidelines to assist them. Judges' ratings, whether they are experts or not, seem to relate to genuine differences between products (i.e., they are valid), and they have been shown to be reliable in a statistical sense.

Although it involves assessing the creativity of products, the CAT is most widely used paradoxically as an instrument for identifying creative people. The CAT is often used by giving all members of a group – a class of students, for example – the same standardized task leading to a closely specified product (e.g., a collage made from an egg carton, a sheet of writing paper, a paper clip, and string). Judges then rate each person's product in order to identify the more (or less) creative members of the group. Subsequently, the people may be divided into subgroups on the basis of the score received by their product (e.g., the most creative third, the least creative third, and the people in the middle). The CAT popularized an important principle for assessing the creativity of products: agreement among observers. It is easy to see that the use of such a method has practical limitations in organizational settings – it is time-consuming and expensive to assemble a panel of experts every time the creativity of a design needs to be assessed.

Rating Scales

A more attractive proposition for measuring creativity in a variety of contexts – for example, product design – is the rating scale. Psychologists have developed instruments based on observers' ratings that allow for the systematic determination of the creativity of product. An early example was Taylor's (1975) Creative Product Inventory, which measures the dimensions of generation, reformulation, originality, relevancy, hedonics, complexity, and condensation. The criterion of hedonics raises an interesting issue: It is reminiscent of Jackson and Messick's (1965) very early distinction between external criteria of the effectiveness of a novel product (i.e., does it work?) and internal criteria such as logic, harmony among the elements of the product, and pleasingness (i.e., is it beautiful?). Taylor thus reinforces the importance of both functional criteria and aesthetic criteria in the measurement of product creativity.

Besemer and O'Quin (1999) developed the Creative Product Semantic Scale (CPSS), based on three dimensions: novelty (the product is original, surprising, and germinal), resolution (the product is valuable, logical, useful, and understandable), and elaboration and synthesis (the product is organic, elegant, complex, and well crafted). These criteria are assessed by asking raters to rate a product on bipolar dimensions (e.g., surprising – unsurprising, logical – illogical, elegant – inelegant). The raters' task is to indicate how close the object being rated is to one or the other pole of each bipolar dimension.

Criteria such as surprisingness, complexity, or germinality may appear to be highly subjective, but psychological research has shown that even untrained judges, working without knowledge of what other judges are saying, can reach much the same conclusions as the other judges about the prominence of many of the criteria in a solution. This means that the method has good inter-rater reliability and consistency (i.e., scale reliability) and also satisfactory test-retest reliability (similar ratings are given if raters are asked to re-rate the same products at a later date).[1] Indeed, various studies such as Hennessey (1994) and Vosburg (1998) have shown that different people seem to have a common and reliable understanding of novelty, complexity, elegance, and the like; can recognize them when they see them; and can express their judgments of the level of the characteristics in a quantifiable way. *This strongly suggests that trained managers could be expected to be able to make the same consistent ratings of creativity in organizational innovation settings using this type of rating scale.*

Baer, Kaufman, and Gentile (2004) extended such findings by looking at products that were *not* based on a narrowly defined task for each person. They gave thirteen raters personal narratives, stories, and poems written by schoolchildren in different classrooms, under different conditions, and

[1] A general word about measurement: Some readers may be unfamiliar with the methods and statistical techniques described here. For a good overview of the concepts of psychometric approaches to measurement and the statistical techniques used, see (DeVellis, 2012).

with varying instructions, that is, under diverse conditions. Their findings suggested that people who have experience and knowledge of a field of activity – presumably this would include professionals in a variety of organizational contexts – can agree on the creativity of domain-relevant products of different kinds and produced under varying conditions. The question is, can this be improved on? Can a rating scale be developed that does not require deep domain expertise or deep knowledge of creativity but yields valid and reliable measures of product creativity? Can this then be used to diagnose and improve creativity in a wide range of settings by nonexperts or quasi-experts?

The Creative Solution Diagnosis Scale (CSDS)

By combining the indicators of creativity of the type used in the scales presented in the preceding section with the four criteria of functional creativity already outlined, for instance, in Chapter 2 (relevance and effectiveness, novelty, elegance, genesis), D. H. Cropley and Cropley (2005) created a more detailed scale for the measurement of product creativity: the Creative Solution Diagnosis Scale (CSDS). The CSDS combines:

- Principles of creativity (relevance and effectiveness, novelty, elegance, genesis)
- Criteria of the principles (possession and use of knowledge, problematization, adding to existing knowledge, going beyond existing knowledge, external elegance, internal elegance, going beyond the immediate problem)
- Indicators of the presence of the criteria (e.g., diagnosis, prescription, redefinition, reconstruction, convincingness, completeness, germinality, seminality, etc.).

The scale was developed to facilitate the assessment (or diagnosis) both of the amount (or level) of creativity and the kind of creativity of products, including but not limited to tangible artifacts, systems, processes, and services. The scale expands on the four basic criteria of creativity with indicators that represent observable characteristics of a creative product. It is intended as a general diagnostic instrument for managers to use in the evaluation of products (and product concepts) and as a tool to drive the enhancement of creativity in those products.

The observable characteristics, or indicators, represent the operationalization of the abstract criteria of creativity. In other words, novelty is an extremely broad and abstract concept that characterizes a creative product, but diagnosis, prescription, prognosis, and so on, can be observed in the product and quantified by a judge – they are manifest.

Subsequent research (D. H. Cropley & Cropley, 2008) proposed a refinement of the original CSDS with the addition of an intermediate layer of descriptors linking the four latent criteria to the manifest indicators. Further recent research with the scale (D. H. Cropley & Kaufman, 2012, 2013; D. H. Cropley, Kaufman, & Cropley, 2011; Haller, Courvoisier, & Cropley, 2011; Haller & Cropley, 2010; Kaufman, Baer, Cropley, Reiter-Palmon, Sinnett, 2013) has demonstrated that the CSDS can be used, for example, by engineers and visual artists with high reliability to rate the creativity of manufactured products and artifacts, and also by teachers to assess the creativity of classroom artifacts such as student assignments (A. J. Cropley & Cropley, 2007). Analysis of the data collected in these empirical studies has established a five-factor structure of functional, or product, creativity. These factors are broadly similar to the original four criteria (relevance and effectiveness, novelty, elegance, and genesis) with the exception that novelty is better represented by two distinct factors: problematization and propulsion. The factor structure of the CSDS is shown in Table 7.2.

To evaluate the creativity of a product using the CSDS, raters apply each of the twenty-seven indicators listed in Table 7.2 using a five-point Likert scale, with values ranging from "not at all" (0 points) through "somewhat" (2 points), to "very much" (4 points). In other words, a given product might be evaluated for the indicator of performance (factor: relevance and effectiveness), as scoring 2 points.[2] Scores for factors (e.g., problematization) are determined by averaging scores for individual indicators and scaling those to a score out of 20 for each factor, for an overall product score out of 100. A maximum score of 100 therefore indicates that the product is highly creative, while a score of zero indicates that it is not creative at all. The research cited also shows that the CSDS can be used by professionals in a given domain (engineers, in this case), of varying levels of expertise, to make accurate and consistent judgments of product creativity.

With a reliable product creativity measurement scale now available to innovation managers, it is possible to make more differentiated judgments and comparisons. Imagine two hypothetical products (or design concepts): Product A and Product B. Each scores 70/100 on the CSDS (see Table 7.3).

[2] Descriptions of each indicator are given in D. H. Cropley, Kaufman, and Cropley (2011). For example, performance assesses the extent to which the solution does what it is supposed to do.

TABLE 7.2. *Indicators of Product Creativity in the CSDS*

	Factor				
	Relevance and Effectiveness	Problematization	Propulsion	Elegance	Genesis
Indicator	Performance	Prescription	Redefinition	Pleasingness	Vision
	Appropriateness	Prognosis	Reinitiation	Completeness	Transferability
	Correctness	Diagnosis	Generation	Sustainability	Seminality
	Operability		Redirection	Gracefulness	Path-finding
	Durability		Reconstruction	Convincingness	Germinality
	Safety			Harmoniousness	Foundationality
				Recognition	

TABLE 7.3. *Hypothetical Product Creativity Scores*

Creativity Factor	Product A	Product B
Relevance and effectiveness	18/20	15/20
Problematization	12/20	15/20
Propulsion	18/20	10/20
Elegance	10/20	20/20
Genesis	12/20	10/20
Total	**70/100**	**70/100**

Not only do these ratings tell a manager something about the nature of the products and their overall creativity, they also allow the manager to diagnose what is contributing to that creativity and thus what might be done to improve or enhance it. To generate this sort of judgment, the manager would turn to the indicators and drill down into each factor score to see where weaknesses, if any, lie. Product A, for example, scores well for effectiveness (18/20); it does what it is supposed to do. However, there is still some room for improvement and, by examining the individual indicators linked to effectiveness (Table 7.2), it might transpire that the design is assessed as slightly deficient in performance. This knowledge can then inform the design process. Product B, by comparison, scores only 10/20 for propulsion. An examination of the specific indicators of propulsion might show that it is deficient, for example, in generation because it does not offer a fundamentally new perspective on possible solutions. This also provides useful information that can be incorporated into the design process in an effort to improve product creativity. Product B is pleasing and neat in the way it works and how it looks, whereas Product A, although it works better than Product B, does not delight beholders or users. Such information can be incorporated into the design process in an effort to improve products: For example, Product A needs more work by design engineers to improve its elegance, whereas Product B needs to introduce some features that fall outside the box. In this way, detailed, quantifiable understanding of product creativity can feed directly into the innovation process.

MEASURING PROCESS: DIVERGENT THINKING

The dominant approach in creativity measurement has involved tests of divergent thinking. Such tests emphasize the underlying cognitive processes thought to be involved in production of novelty. The tests are interesting because they represent cognitive phenomena thought to be connected with creativity in concrete tasks. This means that they offer what is, in effect, an operational definition of creative thinking and give hints on how to recognize latent creativity. Research on the reliability (stability of scores) and validity (link between test scores and actual creativity) of the tests provides a degree of empirical support for the view that their representation of creative thought is useful.

Many of the tests are based on Guilford's original concept of divergent thinking, which has already been introduced in Chapter 3. Tests of divergent thinking typically require respondents to generate multiple answers to open-ended questions. There are no correct answers, and there may be many equally good answers to the same test question. The answers are sometimes unknown until the people being tested give them. Examples of items from divergent thinking tests are as follows:

- "Write down as many interesting and unusual uses as you can think of for a shoe."
- "What would be the consequences if gravity was half as strong as it is now?"
- "What problems can you imagine in connection with birds nesting in a tree in your garden?"

There are also nonverbal tests asking for unusual titles for pictures, completion of partially completed drawings, or interpretation of schematic drawings, to give a few examples. The people taking the tests are encouraged to give as many answers as possible (referred to as fluency) and different types of answers (flexibility), and to try to produce unusual or unexpected answers (originality) and develop these (elaboration).

The best known and most widely used of the tests based on Guilford's concept of divergent thinking are the Torrance Tests of Creative Thinking (TTCT). These tests were originally published in 1966 and have since been revised several times (e.g., Torrance, 2007). They are described in detail by Kim (2006), who subjected them to an extensive evaluation of their reliability and validity. Perhaps the most convenient test of creative thinking ability is the Test of Creative Thinking – Drawing Production (TCT-DP) (Urban & Jellen, 2010). The name of this test suggests that it is a divergent thinking test, and its acronym (TCT-DP) makes it easy to confuse with Torrance's TTCT. However, it is based on a Gestalt-psychology[3] theory of

[3] Gestalt psychology looks at the mind and behavior in holistic terms. In contrast, a behaviorist approach attempts to understand cognitive processes in a reductionist fashion.

creativity, which differs substantially from divergent thinking (Torrance) or divergent production (Guilford). The test has two forms, A and B, on each of which respondents are presented with a single sheet of paper containing a set of incomplete figures (a dot, a semicircle, a wavy line, a dotted line, a right angle) that supposedly are part of an artist's unfinished drawing. The respondents' task is to complete the drawing containing the fragments in any way they wish. Scoring assesses what the test authors call image production: Respondents' drawings (productions) are rated *not* according to statistical infrequency of occurrence but according to dimensions such as boundary breaking, new elements, and humor and affectivity. These are properties of a particular test answer sheet and do not depend on other people's drawings for their points tally. The test can thus be given to an individual person if desired.

Tests Based on Problem Solving

Runco, Plucker, and Lim (2001) argued that ideas are, in effect, products yielded by creative thinking. In the wider context of innovation, this might seem self-evident; however, in the narrower context of creativity, idea-as-product may be less obvious. Thinking of creativity in this way has the beneficial effect of drawing greater attention to the end goal of exploitation and therefore stresses the role of creativity as a driver of innovation (D. H. Cropley, 2006). Runco and his collaborators went on to suggest that it should be possible to specify observable, relatively objective behaviors that indicate the extent to which a person gets ideas and infer from these the presence of creative thinking. In other words, they aimed at measuring the effects, or output, of creative thinking compared to the thinking itself. They argued that such a test would provide a criterion against which to validate tests based on assessing thinking (in other words, their test would make it possible to show that the cognitive tests discussed earlier in this chapter are in fact measuring creativity). The result was the Runco Ideational Behavior Scale (RIBS).

This test has twenty-three items such as "I often have trouble sleeping at night because so many ideas keep popping into my head" (i.e., large number of ideas), "I am good at combining ideas in ways that others have not" (i.e., unusual combinations of idea), or "My ideas are often considered impractical or even wild" (i.e., unexpected ideas). The reliability of the scale was .91 and .92 in two college student samples. Its factor structure suggested that it measures one or two dimensions. Test scores correlated scarcely at all with grade point average (GPA), indicating that production of ideas is not related to academic achievement. Mumford, Baughman, Threlfall, Supinski, and Costanza (1996) and Mumford, Baughman, Maher, Costanza, and Supinski (1996) focused on problem solving. They developed tests of problem construction, information encoding, category selection, and category combination and reorganization.

MEASURING PERSONAL RESOURCES

The principal difficulty in tackling measurement and assessment of creativity and the person is deciding what aspects to include. A theme of Chapter 4 and indeed Part 1 of this book has been that the creative person possesses a constellation of psychological resources spanning feelings, personal properties, and motivation. Logic dictates that an examination of measurement and the person follow the same pattern. However, even focusing on how these properties are measured risks overlooking other aspects of the person that are relevant to creativity. For example, what about past creative behavior? For a manager to understand a person's potential to be creative so that it can be developed and fostered, it would be useful to know not just how motivated that person is or how positive he or she feels about creativity, but also if the person has been highly creative in the past.

Plucker and Makel (2010) give a very useful overview of approaches to the assessment of creativity in the person (and also in relation to product, process, and press). They divide the assessment of the person into three categories:

- Personality scales – that is, personality factors like openness, introversion, self-confidence, impulsivity
- Activity checklists – that is, biographical inventories, past creative achievement
- Attitudes – that is, beliefs about the importance of creativity, self-efficacy

Helson (1999) was also aware of the difficulty in deciding where to place the boundary when considering assessment of the person. She resolved this by differentiating between creative productivity and creative potential. In general, psychological tests, especially personality tests, measure only the latter. Consequently a number of authors (e.g., Helson, 1999; Kitto, Lok, & Rudowicz, 1994) have suggested that creativity tests are best thought of as

TABLE 7.4. *Possible Combinations of Psychological Prerequisites for Creativity*

	Person			Process	
	Personality Scales	Activity Checklists	Attitudes	Thinking Skills	Knowledge
Creative potential	✓		✓	✓	✓
Creative productivity		✓		✓	✓

tests of creative potential not of creativity. In recent years, this view has been presented with considerable force by Proctor and Burnett (2004). Productivity, in contrast, is perhaps more the domain of process (see Chapter 3 and earlier in this chapter) through things like divergent thinking tests as well as activity checklists. Nevertheless, all these factors relate to the person in some fashion, so none will be dismissed regardless of the general focus taken.

Another perspective on this comes from Proctor and Burnett (2004), who stressed that there is widespread (though not universal) agreement that measuring creativity requires more than simply testing thinking. Among other things, they quoted Sternberg's (1985, p. 126) conclusion that thinking tests (especially tests of divergent thinking) run the risk of measuring only "trivial forms of creativity," and they emphasized the need to take account of other aspects of the person in addition to cognitive processes. Table 7.4 attempts to clarify the situation. In the case of measurement, both person and process give us tools to assess both potential and productivity. Furthermore, process is something executed or utilized by the person.

Personal Resources and Potential

A procedure that has achieved considerable popularity in business circles in recent years is the Myers-Briggs Type Indicator (MBTI; Myers-Briggs & McCaulley, 1992). This test measures four dichotomous personality types:

- Extraversion (E) versus introversion (I)
- Sensing (S) versus intuiting (N)
- Thinking (T) versus feeling (F)
- Judging (J) versus perceiving (P)

A dimension, for example, sensing versus intuiting, is a dichotomous scale on which some individual people are rated as falling at one pole (sensing) and some at the other (intuiting). In the context of the discussions of creativity and personality so far, extraversion corresponds to being more attentive to external stimuli, while introversion corresponds to attending more to internal information. Sensing involves focusing on information delivered by the senses, whereas intuiting involves internal hunches and the like. Thinking focuses more on thinking about evidence, whereas feeling gives greater weight to things feeling right. Judging involves weighing and evaluating, whereas perception leads to proceeding on the basis of the way things look.

Individuals are rated on each dimension of the MBTI according to the pole to which they are closer. The four dichotomous dimensions produce sixteen possible combinations or types, which are represented by both their letter description – e.g., I-N-T-J – and their given descriptive archetypes, such as pedagogue, field marshal, inventor, or administrator. Of the various possible combinations, some are of particular interest to creativity. The profile I-N-F-P, for example, involves looking into oneself and not constantly checking what others are thinking or doing; playing hunches, and the like; being open to what feels right regardless of logic; and taking in all available information without censoring any of it. This profile is referred to as the questor archetype and is thought to be most favorable for production of variability. Conversely, the profile I-S-T-J (the trustee) involves being dominated by the way things are always done, looking to others for information and feedback, concentrating on hard information and knowledge, and puzzling things over and intellectualizing; it favors the production of orthodoxy or singularity.

A number of experts have suggested that creativity is particularly related to the sensing (S) – intuiting (N) dimension, with creative people very frequently being intuiters (N). However, it has also been shown (Walk, 1996) that creative graduate students showed a strong tendency toward the intuiting (N) – perceiving (P) combination (i.e., open for uncensored information *and* inclined to interpret it in terms of intuitions) compared to the sensing (S) – judging (J) combination (i.e., inclined to focus on concrete information and process it on the basis of strict logic, correctness, and the like). Although sometimes criticized as a research tool because of, for example, variable statistical properties (Michael, 2003), the MBTI can be a powerful adjunct for the innovation manager seeking to fit team members to particular stages of innovation.

Activity and Productivity

This category of assessment of the person is based on a widely held concept – that "the best predictor of future creative behavior may be past creative behavior" (Colangelo, Kerr, Hallowell, Huesman, & Gaeth, 1992, p. 158). There are a number of options for this category. Csikszentmihalyi, Rathunde, and Whalen (1993), for example, showed in a five-year longitudinal study of adolescents that early absorption and fascination with an area successfully predicted later adult creativity. Milgram and Hong (1999) conducted fifteen-year and eighteen-year longitudinal studies of the potency of predictors of later creativity and showed that teenage leisure activities predicted adult creativity much better than IQ or school achievement, although the latter were good predictors of undergraduate grades. Numbers of similar studies exist (see A. J. Cropley, 2001). Indeed, this approach traces its origins back to the earliest days of the modern creativity era (Buel, 1960, 1965; Buel & Bachner, 1961; Buel, Albright, & Glennon, 1966). On the basis of this connection between life circumstances, interests, hobbies, and adult creativity, a number of procedures have been developed for assessing such factors.

Michael and Colson (1979) developed the Life Experience Inventory (LEI) for assessing potential creativity on the basis of early life experiences. The 100-item inventory concentrates on factual information (e.g., number of changes of address in childhood, composition of family, education, hobbies, and recreation). As the authors pointed out, this approach enhances reliability. In an initial study of 100 electrical engineers who had also been classified as creative or noncreative on the basis of whether or not they held patents, forty-nine items differentiated between creative and noncreative participants. An intuitive grouping of these items by the authors indicated that they cover four areas:

- Self-striving or self-improvement (e.g., enjoying competition, displaying curiosity, being committed to an area of interest)
- Parental striving (parental emphasis on getting ahead, perceived need to do well in order to satisfy parents)
- Social participation and social experience (membership in organizations, helping other students with their schoolwork)
- Independence training (being allowed as children to choose their own friends, being allowed to set their own standards in judging their own accomplishments)

A different approach to the study of the creative person involves identifying personal characteristics (in contrast to cognitive processes, i.e., thinking), whose presence is thought to increase the likelihood of creativity or even to be essential for its appearance. This explains the comments made regarding the boundary between process and person in relation to assessment. The Creativity Checklist (CCL; Johnson, 1979) can be used for rating people at all age levels, including adults in work settings. On a 5-point scale ranging from "never" to "consistently," observers rate the behavior of the people being assessed on eight dimensions: In addition to the by now familiar cognitive dimensions of fluency, flexibility, and constructional skills, personal properties such as ingenuity, resourcefulness, independence, positive self-referencing, and preference for complexity are assessed.

Colangelo, Kerr, Hallowell, Huesman, and Gaeth's (1992) developed the Iowa Inventiveness Inventory initially by studying inventors who held industrial or agricultural patents. The final instrument consists of sixty-one statements (e.g., "Whenever I look at a machine, I can see how to change it") with which respondents indicate level of agreement on a 5-point scale. The inventory distinguished significantly between acknowledged creative individuals and other people, for instance, sorting into the expected order: (a) acknowledged inventors, (b) young inventors rated as inventive by teachers, and (c) noninventive academically talented adolescents. The Creatrix Inventory (C&RT; Byrd, 1986) is of considerable interest because it integrates both cognitive (thinking) and noncognitive (motivation) dimensions of creativity. It is based on the concept of idea production (the ability to produce unconventional ideas), with creativity being regarded as the result of an interaction between creative thinking and the motivational dimension of risk taking. The test consists of two blocks of twenty-eight self-rating or attitude statements; one block measures creative thinking, the other risk taking. These are answered using a 9-point scale ranging from complete disagreement to complete agreement (e.g., "I often see the humorous side when others do not," "Daydreaming is a useful activity"). Scores on the items of each dimension are summed and the total score for the dimension is rated as high, medium, or low. Each person's scores are then plotted on a two-dimensional matrix (creativity versus risk taking – hence the *C&RT* acronym), and the person is assigned to one of eight styles: reproducer, modifier, challenger, practicalizer, innovator, synthesizer, dreamer, and planner. The innovator is high both on creative thinking and risk taking, the reproducer is low on both, the challenger is high on risk taking but not creativity, the dreamer is high on creativity but not risk taking, and so on. Byrd reported a one-week test-retest reliability of .72 for this scale. He argued that the scale possesses face validity but provided no data on other forms.

More recently, two approaches to the assessment of creative production have emerged and both attempt to tackle a wide range of domains. The Creative Achievement Questionnaire (CAQ; Carson, Peterson, & Higgins, 2005) measures creativity in ten domains, including science and invention, with a series of self-rating items concerning past achievements. The instrument has demonstrated good reliability and evidence that it can differentiate between respondents who would be expected to be different (i.e., concurrent validity). In their own research, Carson, Perterson, and Higgins found also that the CAQ was related (statistically) to other measures of creative personality and showed a good relationship – predictive validity – to divergent thinking tests. The RIBS (Runco, Plucker, and Lim, 2001) also now includes subscales appropriate to specific domains, such as engineering. Studies have also established a relationship between RIBS and other personal resources, such as openness (Batey, Chamorro-Premuzic, & Furnham, 2010).

Attitude and Potential

Basadur and Hausdorf (1996) emphasized a somewhat different aspect of the personal correlates of creativity: attitudes favorable to creativity (e.g., placing a high value on new ideas, believing that creative thinking is not bizarre). The twenty-four-item Basadur Preference Scale consists of statements with which respondents express their degree of agreement/disagreement on a 5-point scale ranging from strong agreement to strong disagreement. Items include "Creative people generally seem to have scrambled minds," "New ideas seldom work out," and "Ideas are only important if they impact on major projects." Factor analysis has yielded three dimensions when the scale was administered to university students and young adults working in business settings: valuing new ideas, creative individual stereotypes, and too busy for new ideas.

Kirton's (1989) Adaptation–Innovation Inventory (KAI) distinguishes between people who solve problems by using what they already know and can do (adapters) and people who try to reorganize and restructure the problem (innovators). Kirton's view is that both adapting and innovating are involved in generating novelty, but the innovative style (which is accompanied by greater motivation to be creative, higher levels of risk taking, and greater self-confidence) leads to higher productivity. The scale consists of thirty-two items (e.g., "Will always think of something when stuck," "Is methodical and systematic," "Often risks doing things differently") on which respondents rate themselves by indicating how difficult it would be for them to be like the characteristic mentioned in each item on a 5-point scale ("very easy"—"very hard"). The procedure yields an overall score and scores on three subscales: originality, conformity, and efficiency. Various researchers have reported that the scale is reliable and valid (e.g., Kirton, 1989; Puccio, Treffinger, & Talbot, 1995).

A more recent development in the area of attitude and creative potential is the concept of creative self-efficacy. This addresses people's beliefs about their own capacity for creativity. Studies have shown that the construct can be measured with acceptable reliability and validity using items such as (Beghetto, 2006):

- I am good at coming up with new ideas,
- I have a lot of good ideas,
- I have a good imagination.

More recently, researchers such as Tierney and Farmer (2011) have been able to show that increases in creative self-efficacy correspond to increases in creative work performance in a professional work setting. Equally important, they were able to show that creative expectations from supervisors contributed to this effect.

Multifaceted Approaches to Diagnosing Creativity

Many instruments available for diagnosing creativity have been criticized for their poor predictive validity – that is, the extent to which the instrument is found to predict a future outcome. However, Milgram and Hong (1999) and Plucker (1999) concluded that creativity test scores are better predictors of creative life achievements than IQs or school grades. Plucker (1999) used sophisticated statistical procedures to reanalyze twenty-year longitudinal data on predictive validity originally collected by Torrance. He concluded that composite verbal (but not figural) creativity scores on the TTCT (obtained by averaging scores on three testings) accounted for about 50 percent of the variance of scores on the criterion of publicly recognized creative achievements and participation in creative activities obtained several years later, and predicted about three times as much of the criterion variance as IQs. This corresponds to a predictive validity coefficient of about .7. More recently, Plucker and Makel (2010), in their analysis of the various categories of assessment, and specific instruments, report many examples of at least satisfactory validity of various types.

Helson's (1996, 1999) studies are also informative here. Her findings are particularly important because:

- They are longitudinal, stretching over more than thirty years.
- They use a criterion of creativity derived from real-life behavior, indeed behavior related to earning a living rather than another creativity test or self- or observer ratings.

Helson showed that almost all creativity scores obtained from female college students age twenty-one at the time of testing correlated with ratings of the degree of creativity of their occupations at age fifty-two.

One of the difficulties with predicting creativity is that actual creative achievement, as has been suggested, requires more than simply the cognitive potential. The very fact that creativity is a blend – a system – of process (cognitive factors), person (personal resources), and press factors (an idea explored in Chapter 5 and again in Chapter 8) means that any attempt to examine predictive validity in a piecemeal fashion (i.e., by looking at only a single tested dimension and future outcomes) is likely to miss the complexities of what actually leads to creative performance. Of course, statistical techniques can help unravel these complexities; however, both the range of contributing factors and their subtle interactions may still make the task of predicting creativity inherently difficult.

More systems-level research is needed to understand better the interactions not only among process, press, and person, but also within these categories. It is well known that a range of factors play a major role when it comes to real-life achievements in creativity. Some of them are psychological (mental health and ego strength, diligence, technical skill, or knowledge of a field, presumably acquired via convergent thinking). Some are as mundane as luck or opportunity, or even something as apparently simple as good timing. It is also clear that a major psychological moderator of real-life creative achievement is noncognitive factors such as personality. Helson (1999) showed that youthful openness and unconventionality (typical characteristics emphasized in creativity tests) predict adult creative achievement only when they are associated with depth, commitment, and self-discipline. When accompanied by unresolved identity problems, lack of persistence, and self-defeating behavior, they do not. This finding brings out once again the need for psychological approaches to creativity to be multidimensional and differentiated in nature – in other words, the systems approach introduced earlier in this chapter.

Using Assessment of Personal Creativity

A theme of this book is the use of a deep knowledge of the building blocks of creativity and innovation to manage and improve organizational innovation. The current focus on aspects of personality and creativity should therefore be directed toward how this knowledge is used – not merely to identify individual differences but to drive change and improvement. Managers in organizations must use this knowledge to develop strategies and actions that boost the positive, creativity-enhancing aspects of personality while minimizing those aspects that inhibit creativity. An example of how creativity assessments can be used in an educational setting to provide creativity counseling is given in D. H. Cropley and Cropley (2000). This particular study first involved discussing with students in a university engineering class the Four Ps of creativity and how these influence the production of effective novelty. Students' scores on the TCT-DP were then used to construct a personal profile for each student. The students in this class were then individually counseled about their strengths and weaknesses in areas thought to be of relevance to creativity. The focus of the counseling was on identifying for the students what they could do to improve their creativity – for example, "you gave lots of ideas here (high fluency), but they were all generally the same (low flexibility)" and "when you solve a problem, try to think up lots of different kinds of ideas and not just variations on the same theme." As part of their course, students undertook a creative design task, which was an opportunity to put the counseling advice into practice. As part of their assessment, they were also asked to comment on social (press) factors in the groups in which they worked as well as describe the project outputs in terms of the characteristics of creative products.

Creativity counseling, of course, presupposes the ability to differentiate personal properties relevant to creativity in different people. The creativity tests described in this chapter provide the means for doing this, making it possible to construct individualized programs for fostering creativity. A number of important personal resources can be strengthened in different individuals, and these can be identified with tests. Table 7.5 summarizes these characteristics.

MEASURING THE ORGANIZATIONAL PRESS

Tests of Organizational Conditions

Mathisen and Einarsen (2004) reviewed several organizational climate inventories and summarized their psychometric properties. This section

TABLE 7.5. *Test-Defined Characteristics of the Person That Are Favorable to Creativity*

Motivation	Personality
• Goal-directedness	• Active imagination
• Fascination for a task or area	• Flexibility
• Resistance to premature closure	• Curiosity
• Risk taking	• Independence
• Preference for asymmetry	• Acceptance of own differentness
• Preference for complexity	• Tolerance for ambiguity
• Willingness to ask many (unusual) questions	• Trust in own senses
	• Openness to subconscious material
• Willingness to display results	• Ability to work on several ideas simultaneously
• Willingness to consult other people (but not simply to carry out orders)	• Ability to restructure problems
• Desire to go beyond the conventional	• Ability to abstract from the concrete

contains an overview of their findings, which is expanded by the addition of material on the Organizational Achieving Style Inventory (Lipman-Blumen, 1991).

KEYS: Assessing the Work Environment for Creativity (Amabile, Conti, Coon, Lazenby, & Herron, 1996) has been used in organizations in many fields, including electronics, high-tech, pharmaceuticals, manufacturing, and banking. It consists of seventy-eight statements about the organization such as "The tasks in my work are challenging," " I feel challenged by the work I am currently doing," "A great deal of creativity is called for in my daily work," and "I believe that I am currently very creative in my work." Respondents rate their own organization by answering "never or almost never in this organization," "sometimes," "often," "always or almost always." The scale rates the organization on ten dimensions: organizational encouragement, supervisory encouragement, work group support, sufficient resources, challenging work, freedom, organizational impediments, workload pressure, creativity, and productivity. The subscales have reliabilities (alpha coefficient) around .70 to .85, and their validity is supported by factor-analytic studies as well as some applications in real organizations.

The Situational Outlook Questionnaire (Isaksen, 2007) is in essence an English-language version of a rating scale originally published in Sweden. It consists of fifty statements about the organization. People rating the organization agree or disagree with these statements on a on a 4-point scale from "not at all applicable" to "applicable to a high extent." The scale has been applied mainly in scientific and engineering organizations as well as large manufacturing and business firms. It yields scores for the organization on nine scales: challenge, freedom, idea support, trust/openness, playfulness/humor, debates, conflicts, risk taking, and time for ideas. Alpha coefficients of .62 to .90 are reported for the various subscales, with most of them being above .80. Factor analytic studies have confirmed that the scale measures nine dimensions.

The Siegel Support for Innovation Scale (Siegel & Kaemmerer, 1978) consists of sixty-one items with which respondents agree or disagree on a 6-point Likert scale ranging from "strongly agree" (1 point) to "strongly disagree" (4 points). It has been used in schools, engineering firms, and a university school of nursing, among other organizations. It assesses five dimensions of the organization: leadership (support of ideas, diffusion of power, support of workers' individual development), ownership (of ideas, procedures, and processes), norms for diversity (being different is accepted, workers choose ways to solve problems, creativity is rewarded), continuous development (fundamental assumptions of the organization are constantly questioned, its goals and its methods change), and consistency (people work together toward common goals).

The Team Climate Inventory (Anderson & West, 1994) has been used to assess health services, university staff members, oil companies, and a TV production company, among others. It consists of about forty items, depending on the version being used. On some items the people rating the organization respond on 7-point scales ranging from "not at all" to "completely" or on 5-point scales from "strongly disagree" to "strongly agree." This scale yields scores on four dimensions: vision (the organization has clearly defined goals, shared goals, and attainable goals), participative safety (it is safe to present new ideas), task orientation (members of the organization have a shared concern with excellence), and support for innovation (within the organization there is approval and practical support of attempts to introduce novelty).

The Achieving Styles Questionnaire (Lipman-Blumen, 1991) specifically incorporates the idea of achieving a good fit between the characteristics of the people in an organization and the psychological characteristics of the organization, which has already been mentioned in the section titled Using Assessment of Personal Creativity. The questionnaire has two versions, one for organizations and one for individual people. The two forms can be administered and then used to make a diagnosis based, in essence, on goodness of fit. The individual version consists of forty-five statements

TABLE 7.6. *Overview of Tests of the Workplace Environment*

Test	Number of Items	Level	Aspects Tested
Situational Outlook Questionnaire (English language version of Creativity Climate Questionnaire – Swedish) (Isaksen, Lauer, Ekvall, & Britz, 2001)	Fifty statements: participants agree/disagree on a 4-point scale from "not at all applicable" to "applicable to a high extent"	Engineers and scientists	**Nine scales**: challenge, freedom, idea support, trust/openness, playfulness/humor, debates, conflicts; risk taking, time for ideas
KEYS: Assessing the Work Environment for Creativity (Amabile & Gryskiewicz, 1989)	Seventy-eight statements: participants respond on a 4-point scale from "never or almost never in this organization" to "sometimes," to "often," to "always or almost always"	Many organizations including electronics, high tech, pharmaceuticals, manufacturing, and banking	**Ten scales**: organizational encouragement, supervisory encouragement, work group supports, sufficient resources, challenging work, freedom, organizational impediments, workload pressure, creativity, productivity
Siegel Support for Innovation Scale (Siegel & Kaemmerer, 1978)	Sixty-one items: participants respond on 6-point Likert scale: "strongly agree" to "strongly disagree"	Schools, engineering firms, university school of nursing	**Five dimensions**: leadership (support of ideas, diffusion of power, support of workers' individual development), ownership (of ideas, procedures, and processes), norms for diversity (being different is accepted, workers choose ways to solve problems, creativity is rewarded), continuous development (fundamental assumptions of the organization are constantly questioned, its goals change, and its methods change), consistency (people work together toward goals)

(continued)

TABLE 7.6. *(continued)*

Test	Number of Items	Level	Aspects Tested
Team Climate Inventory (Anderson & West, 1994)	Thirty-eight items: sometimes responses made on 7-point Likert scale from "not at all" to "completely," sometimes on a 5-point scale from "strongly disagree" to "strongly agree"	Health services, university staff, oil companies, TV production company	**Four dimensions**: vision (clearly defined goals, shared goals, attainable), participative safety (safe to present new ideas), task orientation (shared concern with excellence), support for innovation (approval and practical support of attempt to introduce novelty)
Lipman-Blumen Organizational Achieving Style Inventory (Lipman-Blumen, 1991)	Forty-five items: participants respond on 7-point Likert items from "never" to "always."	Many different organizations	**Three broad domains**, each with three specific styles (nine styles in all): relational style (vicarious, contributory, collaborative), direct style (intrinsic, competitive, power), instrumental style (entrusting, social, personal) Can be administered to assess organization and individuals, and assess the degree of match between relational styles of individual people and those of the organization

(e.g., "Faced with a task I prefer a team approach to an individual one" or "I achieve by guiding others towards their goals") to which participants respond on a 7-point Likert-type scale ranging from "never" to "always." These define nine achieving styles such as "collaborative," "competitive," "vicarious," or "personal." Lipman-Blumen reported reliabilities (alpha coefficients) ranging from .82 to .91 for the nine subscales, while construct validity was demonstrated by means of factor analytic studies as well as correlations with data on variables like task accomplishment, gender roles, or leadership style. Puccio and Cabra (2010) review a wider range of studies of this scale spanning nine different studies and many dimensions. An overview of these scales appears in Table 7.6.

OVERVIEW AND OUTLOOK

William Thomson (also known as Lord Kelvin) noted that "when you can measure what you are speaking about, and express it in numbers, you know something about it; but when you cannot measure it, when you cannot express it in numbers, your knowledge is of a meager and unsatisfactory kind" (Thomson, 1889). A first step toward managing innovation is the ability to measure the building blocks – the Four Ps that affect innovation in organizations. Product, process, person, and press can be measured objectively and rigorously. The innovation manager has a suite of instruments that can be used to quantify these building blocks of innovation. While each of these can be measured separately in a satisfactory way, the real task for the innovation manager is orchestrating their collective contribution to the process of innovation in organizations. This requires a shift in focus – indeed a paradigm shift – from a reductionist, componential view of the building blocks of innovation to a holistic, systems view of innovation and the measurement of outcomes. The next two chapters address this paradigm shift and propose both a theoretical framework and an instrument for measuring innovation in organizations.

8

Innovation and Organizational Performance

In the previous chapter, the measurement of the building blocks of innovation – person, product, process, and press – was discussed. To understand innovation as a systems phenomenon – an emergent property of a set of interacting components – it will be clear that the building blocks cannot simply be assessed separately and individually in order to gain insights into the resultant organizational outcomes. Innovation managers also need to move beyond understanding outcome in the narrow, proximate sense of the ideas generated and instead examine outcomes in their broader, business context, consistent with a focus on organizational innovation. To do this it is logical to ask, What are the visible, external, and measurable signs of successful innovation? How does a manager know when creative individuals are working effectively together, in a favorable setting, to develop novel and useful products that form the basis of a business enterprise? What is the effect, in the broadest sense, that results from the interaction of the person, product, process, and press?

Part of this shift in scale and focus is a shift away from the relatively simple realm of smaller numbers of observable variables, and relationships among those variables, to the more complex interaction of larger numbers of latent variables, with multiple predictive relationships and associations, and competing models. To assist in understanding the relationships between the independent and dependent variables that define the innovation process, this chapter uses path diagrams and concepts from structural equation modeling (SEM). For a more detailed discussion of this methodology, see Grace, Schoolmaster, Guntenspergen, Little, Mitchell, Miller, and Schweiger (2012).

Studying the effect of innovation in an organizational context means studying organizational performance. In the literature of organizations and innovation, the popular term that describes this is firm performance. It is axiomatic, in studying organizational innovation, that "all the innovative activities must result in better firm performance compared to companies that do not innovate" (Kemp, Folkeringa, De Jong, & Wubben, 2003, p. 18). However, the task is not simply to survey the different ways that firm performance is measured in practice; rather, it is to take a step back to a more theoretical foundation and question what managers should be measuring.

Aside from the theoretical imperative, there is a more practical reason for asking what should be measured in an attempt to assess the effect of innovation in an organizational context. Davila, Epstein, and Shelton (2012, p. 145) explain that "what gets measured gets done." If innovation is defined, for example, in terms of a specific output, such as the number of new products introduced, then it must be demonstrated that this parameter does indeed tap into the underlying construct (innovation). A better example of the perils of getting this wrong is cited by Davila, Epstein, and Shelton (2012) as a measure of ideation, itself part of process. They describe conference attendance (p. 162) as one way to quantify ideation! Without a theoretical framework that explains the rationale for the relationship between conference attendance and innovation, and without empirical evidence to support this, an organization may invest a great deal of time and money sending staff members to conferences for no tangible benefit – "what gets measured gets done." In terms that are more formal, this is a reminder that correlation does not imply causation. Just because two variables appear to be related does not mean that one is the cause of the other. More important, the first step in establishing if an apparent relationship is in fact causal is to have a sound theoretical model of the phenomenon in question.

So measurement in this context begins with a premise – innovation causes better firm performance (Figure 8.1). From this starting point, the discussion will return to first principles and examine the models and evidence linking predictors and outcomes.

By building a measurement model founded on a rigorous theoretical framework, managers are better placed to judge the efficacy of current measures of innovation and organizational performance, and to construct new measures that help with understanding how entrepreneurs turn creativity into business value. The first step in decoding the relationship between innovation and organizational performance is to map out a very general measurement model that links cause (predictor) and effect (outcome). Vincent, Bharadwaj, and Challagalla (2004, p. 13) remind readers

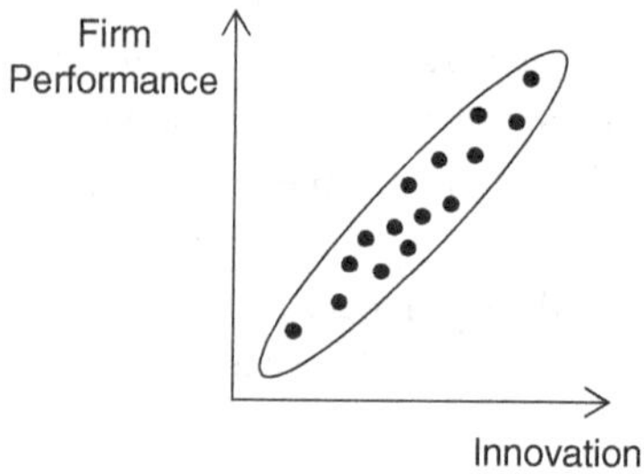

FIGURE 8.1. The Positive Relationship between Innovation and Firm Performance

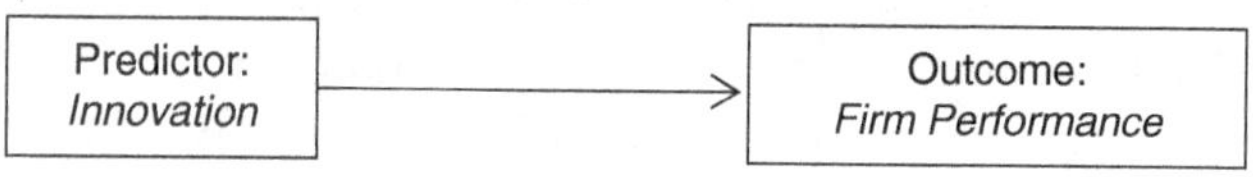

FIGURE 8.2. Path Diagram: Innovation and Firm Performance

that "[p]ast research has demonstrated that there is a direct, robust relationship between organizational innovation and performance." Figure 8.2 illustrates this using widely accepted conventions for manifest (directly observable) and latent (indirectly observable) variables, and path diagrams (see, for example DeVellis, 2012; Frazier, Tix, & Barron, 2004; Sekaran, 2006).

This diagram, while conceptually helpful, immediately gives rise to further questions. A variable is, by definition (Creswell, 2005, p. 118), "a characteristic or attribute of an individual or an organization that (1) researchers can measure or observe and (2) varies among individuals or organizations studied." How is innovation measured? How is firm performance measured?

What is readily apparent is that neither innovation nor firm performance can be observed directly. They are accessible only through their effect on other observable and relevant characteristics or attributes and are thus latent. Consequently, a more appropriate path diagram of the relationship in question distinguishes between the latent predictor – innovation – and the latent outcome – firm performance – and their respective observable indicator variables (see Figure 8.3).

At this point in the development of a measurement model, a manager may feel reasonably confident that she knows what the observable indicators of innovation are – indeed, that is the point of much of what has been discussed in preceding chapters! As indicated at the start of this chapter,

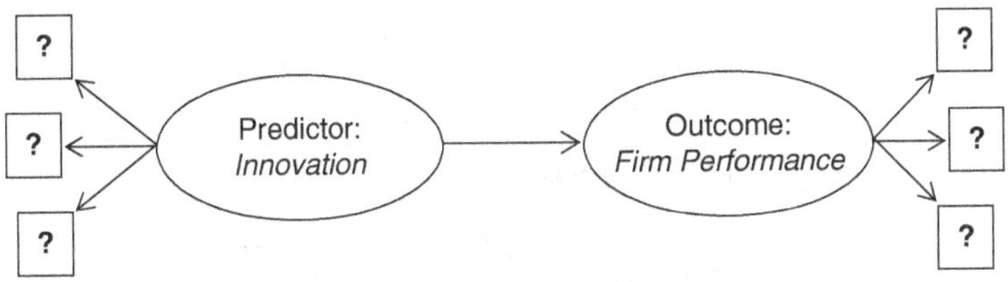

FIGURE 8.3. Latent and Observed Variables: Innovation and Firm Performance

however, no account has yet be taken for the variety of issues that emerge only when these indicators – the Four Ps – are considered as a system of interacting variables. At the other end of the relationship represented in Figure 8.3 is the measurement of firm performance. How is that variable measured, what are the observable indicators, and is the causal relationship between innovation and firm performance as simple as depicted? It is not hard to imagine that there is considerable uncertainty surrounding the question "What influences what?" in organizational innovation. Far from being a technical, statistical matter, constructing and understanding a model of the relationship among independent (or predictor) variables, dependent (or outcome) variables, and the factors that influence this relationship is a key to innovation research. The discussion will begin by picking out the details of the latent variable innovation.

MEASURING INNOVATION

Vincent, Bharadwaj, and Challagalla (2004) examined a total of eighty-three empirical studies of organizational innovation and found that typical measures of innovation – indicators that are candidates for operationalizing the latent variable (Figure 8.4) – fall into one of the following categories:

- Frequency counts – a sum of all innovations adopted in an organization
- Dichotomous, adoption/nonadoption measures
- R&D intensity measures
- Implementation scales (process)
- innovation radicalness scales (i.e. product novelty).

Hülsheger, Anderson, and Salgado (2009), in contrast, found that many studies also use a variety of subjective ratings of innovation, including self, peer, supervisor, and subject matter expert ratings. Both Vincent, Bharadwaj, and Challagalla (2004) and Hülsheger, Anderson, and

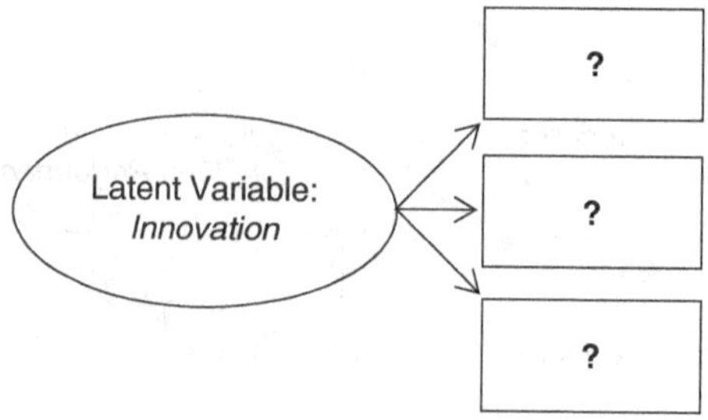

FIGURE 8.4. Defining the Latent Variable of Innovation

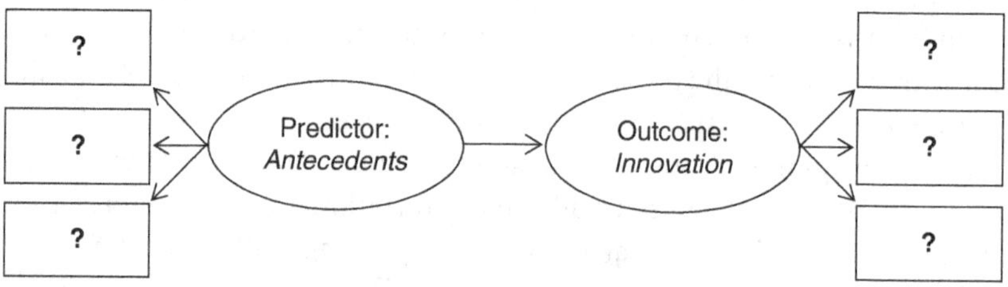

FIGURE 8.5. Defining Antecedents and Innovation

Salgado (2009) make it clear that the measurement of the latent construct, innovation, is more complex than that depicted in Figure 8.4. Not only do the different measurement approaches – subjective and objective – exhibit only modest correlations, but research must also take into account a suite of antecedent variables that serve as predictors of the outcome variable innovation (see Figure 8.5).

The antecedents to innovation may be grouped according to the level at which measurement and analysis occurs. Vincent, Bharadwaj, and Challagalla (2004), for example, study organizational-level antecedents: (a) organizational capabilities, (b) organizational demographics, (c) organizational structures, and (d) environmental factors.

A BUSINESS MODEL OF INNOVATION

Davila, Epstein, and Shelton (2012) address the challenge of measuring innovation and describing the causal relationships involved in somewhat different terms, with a business model of innovation. They define a more dynamic view of input, process, output, and outcome as follows:

- **Inputs** define what the organization starts with and include a range of resources, both tangible (e.g. money, time) and intangible (e.g. motivation, culture), as well as other resources such as corporate strategy, venture capital, suppliers, and training systems.
- **Processes** define how the organization executes innovation – they represent the dynamic innovation effort. According to Davila, Epstein, and Shelton (2012) these include the creative process, the project management process, and the corporate business processes that manage a portfolio of innovation projects.
- **Outputs** define "what the innovation efforts have delivered" (Davila, Epstein, & Shelton, 2012, p. 151) within the organization – new products introduced, improved customer loyalty, increased market share (i.e., what Vincent, Bharadwaj, and Challagalla [2004] called "innovation").
- **Outcomes**, by contrast, define the end result in terms of firm performance – for example, profitability, share price, sales growth.

A key feature of this model concept is that inputs are "leading measures of success" (p. 152); processes represent "real-time measures" (p. 147), and outputs are "lagging measures because they inform after the fact" (p. 153). This has three consequences for innovation. First, leading measures imply that these factors (e.g., motivation, culture) are static, at least in the time frame of a single project. Second, leading measures also imply that the impact of these factors is uniform across a project; culture, for example, affects a project in the same way at the beginning of the project as it does in the middle or at the end. Third, the lagging measures imply that these factors are accessible only after a project has finished, perhaps influenced by the static nature of the leading measures. In other words, there is a presumption that a large part of the innovation process is mechanistic and predetermined. It is wound up and set it in motion, and the manager waits to see what happens, with the outcome largely determined by the fixed inputs. Although the processes imply a more dynamic, real-time monitoring and control, the crucial point is that a business model of innovation based on a concept of static, leading indicators and, to a lesser extent, wholly dependent lagging output measures fails to capture the much more dynamic nature not only of the processes but of the input, outputs and outcomes.

Davila, Epstein, and Shelton (2012) describe specific measures for each "perspective" (input, process, output, and outcome). Their antecedent, leading, or input measures include the time dedicated to innovation, the percentage of the budget allocated to innovation efforts, the number of strategic alliances, the number of experienced team members, the perception of brand, the clear articulation of objectives, the quality of information technology infrastructure, and the level of empowerment of functional units and managers. Real-time measures of the process of innovation, as distinct from innovation as an outcome variable, include time, budget, and product performance; development time and cost; R&D productivity; and product and process quality. Davila et al. (2012) also distinguish between a strategic level for measurement, and a project level, and what is measured at these levels differs somewhat. For example, they identify "ideation" at a strategic, organizational level as a case of leveraging "the human capital of the organization" (p. 160). Within this category, they include culture but also "objective measures like employee turnover" (p. 161).

Perhaps the most important consequence of the Davila, Epstein, and Shelton (2012) business model of innovation is that it draws attention to two different aspects of outcome in the sense of dependent variables. In the narrower, more tactical sense, there are lagging measures of the output of a given innovation process. These measures are contrasted with the broader, more strategic, lagging measures that capture the impact of the innovation on the organization, that is, firm performance. This highlights an important fact for the measurement model: Innovation is both an outcome variable (predicted by various antecedents) and a predictor variable (of the outcome firm performance). This can be illustrated as shown in Figure 8.6, and has some important consequences for the measurement model that will be developed after discussing measures of firm performance.

MEASURING "FIRM PERFORMANCE"

What is it that a manager wants to know? In the context of innovation, she wants to know if her organization is succeeding or failing in this activity. If her business is to generate novel and effective ideas and to turn those into commercially viable solutions to problems, then how does she

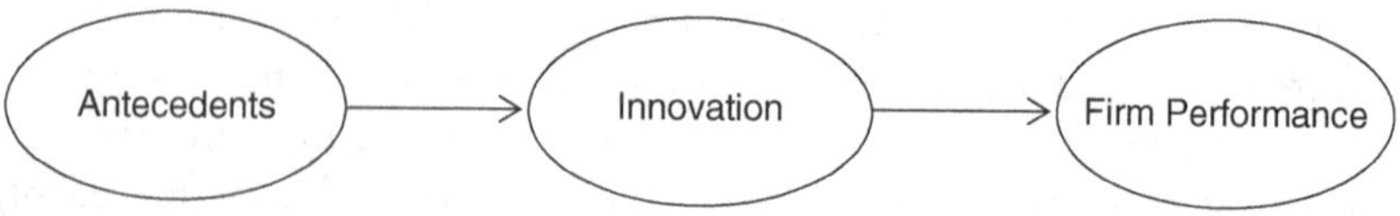

FIGURE 8.6. The Relationship among Antecedent, Innovation, and Firm Performance

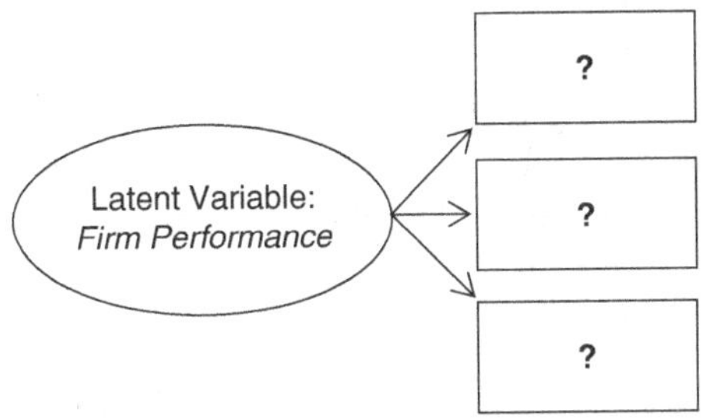

FIGURE 8.7. Defining Firm Performance

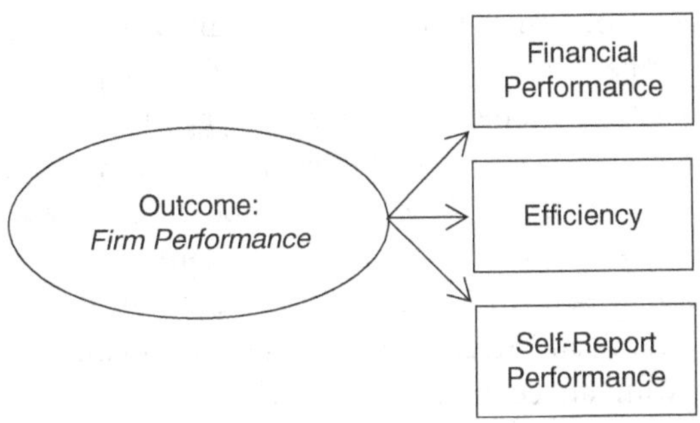

FIGURE 8.8. Operationalizing Firm Performance: Finances

know when she is doing well? How exactly does she measure this strategic outcome (see Figure 8.7)?

Vincent, Bharadwaj, and Challagalla (2004) identified three types of consequence (firm performance) of innovation: "(1) financial performance, (2) efficiency gains, and (3) self-report subjective measures of innovation performance" (p. 6). Of these three, financial performance and efficiency gains (Figure 8.8) make sense because not only are they readily measureable but they also fit the context of entrepreneurial creativity (innovation) directed to a business activity or outcome. If the point of innovation is to achieve better performance than companies that are not innovating (Kemp, Folkeringa, De Jong, & Wubben, 2003), then what better way to measure this than with profitability and share price?

Davila, Epstein, and Shelton (2012), although differentiating between the outputs of innovation (i.e., performance) and the outcomes for the whole enterprise (i.e., the value added), nevertheless still define predominantly financial measures of firm performance, albeit in two categories (p. 173):

- Long-term corporate profitability:
  - Stock price
  - Projected sales growth
  - Projected residual income
- Short-term corporate profitability:
  - Residual income growth
  - Sales growth
  - Return on equity
  - Percentage of sales from new products

Koellinger (2008) looked in particular at the role of Internet-based technologies as enablers of product and process innovation and measured firm performance in terms of profitability, financial turnover, and employment levels. While this remained anchored in a for-profit, financial context, he also posited a model that places the type of innovation (process or product/service), as a mediator of the relationship between technology and firm performance, with resource factors moderating these relationships. This chapter's discussion will return to the question of mediators and moderators of the basic predictor-outcome relationship shortly.

Bowen, Rostami, and Steel (2010) stay tied to a financial concept of firm performance with an economic rent-seeking view of performance. In simple terms, this views innovation as a driver of the generation of new, valuable, and unique resources that confer a competitive advantage on the firm in question. However, they also note an important qualifier of the innovation-firm performance relationship – namely, the temporal sequence (does past firm performance drive current innovation; does present innovation drive improved future performance?). They also noted that performance may be classified in terms of "market measures" or "accounting measures" (p. 1181), the former being leading indicators, the latter are lagging indicators.

Most recently, Dul and Ceylan (2014, p. 1) considered firm performance in terms of new product productivity ("the extent to which the firm introduced new products to the market") and new product success ("the percentage of the firm's sales from new products"). These are based on measures defined by Hansen (1992). While still predominantly financial in focus, these measures introduce a more nuanced relationship between predictors and outcomes. Dul and Ceylan (2014) were examining the relationship between a creativity-supporting work environment (independent variable) and new product success (dependent variable) but conceived of new product productivity as an intervening or mediator variable.

An important question now emerges. If measures of firm performance – the outcome of innovation – are predominantly financial in nature, then how is the effect of innovation assessed in sectors of the economy in which profitability, share price, and sales are meaningless, for example, in non-profit organizations? Kaplan (2001), writing on the application of the balanced scorecard concept (Kaplan & Norton, 1992) in the nonprofit sector, takes an approach that moves beyond the narrow focus on financial performance. Kaplan (2001, p. 354) noted that "[e]ven for-profit companies have recently recognized that financial measurements by themselves are inadequate for measuring and managing their performance." He drew attention to the fact that "[f]inancial reports measure past performance but communicate little about long-term value creation" (p. 354), noting that "[s]uccess for non-profits should be measured by how effectively and efficiently they meet the needs of their constituencies" (p. 353).

Regardless of the popularity or otherwise of the balanced scorecard approach, the underlying concept – that firm performance cannot be described only in terms of financial performance – is highly relevant to the analysis of the outcomes of innovation. Without meaningful and relevant measures of firm performance, organizations have "no way to distinguish whether their strategy [is] succeeding or failing" (Kaplan, 2001, p. 354). At the highest level of abstraction, therefore, we can operationalize firm performance (Figure 8.9) as a function of both financial performance (e.g., share price, profit), and nonfinancial performance.

The latter will include, but not be limited to, what Kaplan (2001) describes as the customer perspective. Firm performance as an outcome of innovation is then addressed by two questions: "How do we create value for our customers (nonfinancial performance)"? and "If we succeed, how will we look to our stakeholders (financial performance)"?. The former is Kaplan's (2001) characterization of customer perspective (p. 355), but the latter makes one important change to how he operationalizes the financial

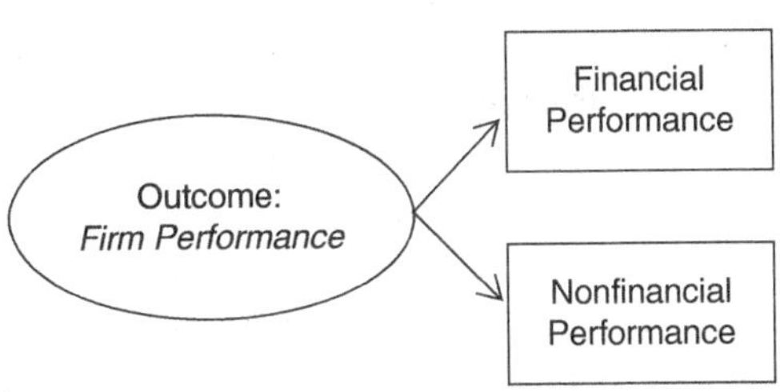

FIGURE 8.9. Operationalizing Firm Performance: Balanced Approach

perspective. Instead of shareholder, the present discussion will use the term *stakeholder*. This allows the argument to incorporate financial elements of firm performance that apply both to for-profit and nonprofit organizations. A financial stakeholder might be, for example, a government body funding a charity. They have a financial interest in the performance of the organization, but they are not shareholders in the for-profit sense of the word.

THE RELATIONSHIP BETWEEN INNOVATION AND FIRM PERFORMANCE

In Figure 8.6, it was noted that innovation in fact sits between the antecedent predictor variables and the outcome variable firm performance. This suggests that innovation, however measured, is a mediator of the relationships between the antecedents and firm performance Frazier, Tix, and Barron (2004) state that "mediators establish 'how' or 'why' one variable predicts or causes an outcome variable. "More specifically, a *mediator* is defined as a variable that explains the relation between a predictor and an outcome" (p. 116). The possibility that innovation mediates the relationship between antecedents and firm performance also raises the prospect that, if it is not a mediator, it is at least a moderator of the relationship. In fact, Vincent, Bharadwaj, and Challagalla (2004) considered both of these possibilities as they attempted to address "a lack of understanding surrounding the relationship between the antecedents of innovation, innovation itself, and organizational performance outcomes" (p. 13).

Considering innovation as a moderator (Figure 8.10) of the relationship between predictor variable(s) (i.e., organizational/environmental antecedents) and outcome variable (firm performance) highlights the fact that a moderator variable, in general "alters the direction or strength of the relation between a predictor and an outcome" (Frazier, Tix, & Barron, 2004, 116). Frazier, Tix, and Barron (2004) make the further point that "a moderator is nothing more than an interaction whereby the effect of one variable depends on the level of another" (p. 116). This implies that the effect of, for example, organizational demographics on firm performance depends on the level of the measure of innovation (e.g., R&D intensity). This seems intuitively unsatisfactory because it relegates innovation to a secondary role. Previous arguments, not least the relationship implied by Davila, Epstein, and Shelton (2012), and the considerable body of evidence in support of a direct, causal relationship between innovation and firm performance suggests that innovation plays a more central role. The primary goal of Vincent, Bharadwaj, and Challagalla (2004) was to test

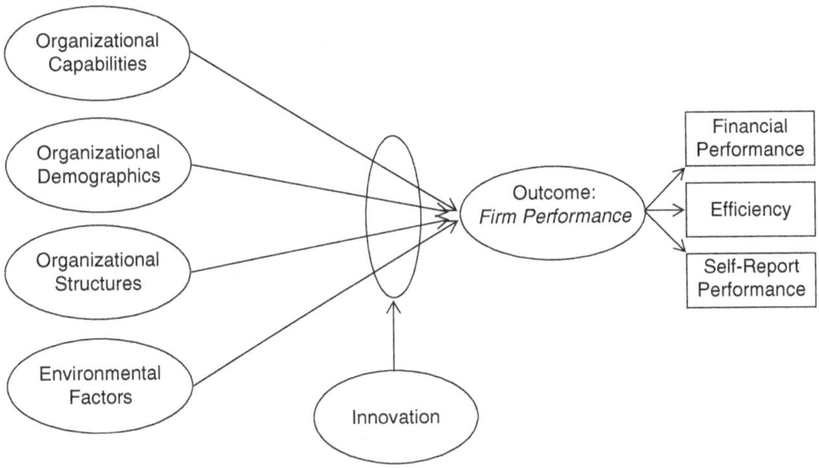

FIGURE 8.10. Innovation as Moderator of the Antecedent–Firm Performance Relationship

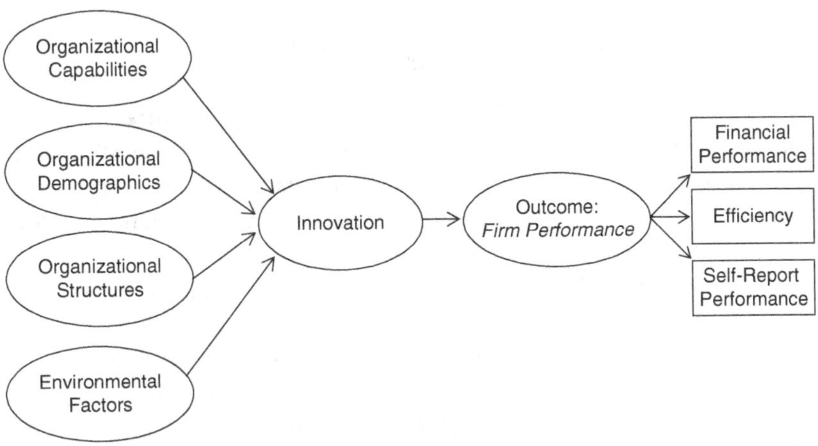

FIGURE 8.11. Innovation as Mediator of the Antecedent–Firm Performance Relationship

this assertion with a meta-analysis of eighty-three empirical studies of organizational innovation, subjecting three models of innovation as mediator to analysis using SEM. In general terms, their proposition was that innovation mediates the relationship between antecedents and firm performance, as shown in Figure 8.11. The results of the analysis by Vincent,

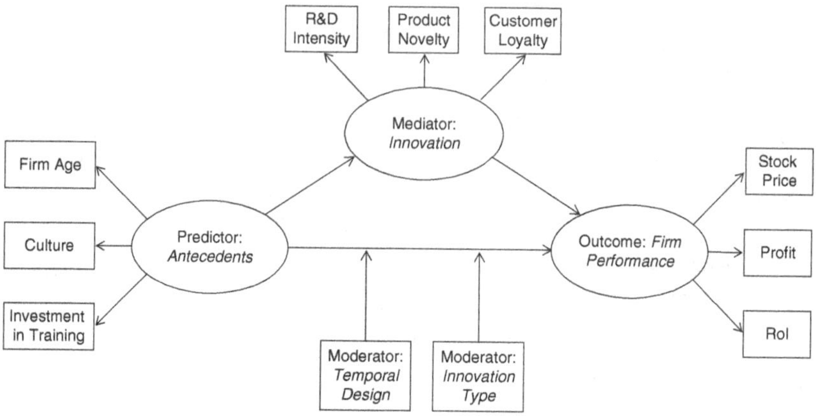

FIGURE 8.12. Innovation as a Partial Mediator of the Antecedent–Firm Performance Relationship

Bharadwaj, and Challagalla (2004) in fact supported a model of innovation as a partial mediator of the antecedent–firm performance relationship (see Figure 8.12).

Vincent, Bharadwaj, and Challagalla (2004) also noted the presence of two moderators of the direct path from antecedents to firm performance: temporal design and innovation type. Temporal design captures the notion of studying the predictor-outcome relationship in unique slices with respect to time – i.e., taking a snapshot at a particular moment in time. Given that a mediator intervenes in the relationship between the time that the predictor variable operates to influence the outcome variable and the actual impact on the outcome variable, it is not hard to hypothesize that a cross-sectional study might fail to coincide with the influence of the mediator. It is sufficient to summarize this as follows: Time makes a difference when the impact of innovation on firm performance is studied. Innovation type highlights the fact that the predictor-outcome relationship, still mediated by innovation, is subtly different for a product innovation compared, for example, to a process or service innovation. Table 8.1 shows a broad correspondence between the business model of innovation (Davila, Epstein, & Shelton, 2012) and the causal relationships expressed by Vincent, Bharadwaj, and Challagalla (2004).

The model of innovation as a partial mediator sheds considerable light on the relationships among antecedents, innovation, and the organizational outcomes. However, it is an exploratory model in the sense that it attempts to explain, ex post facto, the relationships embedded in empirical

TABLE 8.1. *Comparing Models of Innovation*

	Predictor Variable(s)	Mediator Variable(s)	Moderator Variable(s)	Outcome Variable(s)
Vincent, Bharadwaj, and Challagalla (2004)	Antecedents	Innovation	Temporal design Innovation type	Firm performance
Davila, Epstein, and Shelton (2012)	Inputs	Processes/outputs		Outcomes

data. This means it is constrained by the nature of the variables that were available in the empirical data. What is also needed to advance understanding of innovation is the ability to take a confirmatory approach – a means by which hypotheses about the relationships between variables in the domain of innovation can be constructed and a means by which theories can be tested. To do this two things are needed: a theoretical framework and a more general measurement model. These are addressed in the following sections.

A THEORETICAL FRAMEWORK FOR ORGANIZATIONAL INNOVATION

It will be clear to readers that to serve the purpose of guiding the construction of hypotheses and to aid in the development and testing of theories about organizational innovation, a theoretical framework must reflect accurately, and to the greatest extent possible, how innovation works in the real world. Writing in the context of business research, Sekaran (2006, p. 91) reminds readers that a theoretical framework is "a conceptual model of how one theorizes or makes logical sense of the relationships among the several factors that have been identified as important to the problem" and that it is "pivotal in developing a scientific basis for investigating the research problem."

In previous chapters, the case has been made – proceeding from a psychological foundation of creativity research – that understanding organizational innovation is a matter of understanding the interactions among person, product, process, and press. In Chapter 6, it was suggested that these variables interact in various ways across stages, or phases, in the process of organizational innovation. In Chapter 6, it was also suggested that paradoxes – seemingly contradictory states that appear simultaneously to both favor and hinder innovation – are embedded in the innovation process. In this chapter, empirical evidence in support of organizational innovation has been examined, and echoes of the following were found:

(1) The Four Ps – in the antecedents of innovation and firm performance
(2) Phases – in the moderating effect of the temporal design
(3) Paradoxes – in the model of organizational innovation as a partial mediator of the relationship between antecedents and firm performance

Is it possible to construct a theoretical framework that captures all these elements in combination and can then serve as the scientific basis for constructing hypotheses, and testing theories, about organizational innovation?

The motivation to find an appropriate theoretical framework is more than just a desire to formulate hypotheses. As Davila, Epstein, and Shelton (2012, p. 87) remind us, "many large firms have struggled and, by their own description, failed in the attempt to integrate innovation into their organization." The driver, therefore, is very practical and addresses the question that Davila, Epstein, and Shelton (2012, p. 87) ask, "[H]ow to structure a company for innovation?" In fact, Davila, Epstein, and Shelton (2012) provide further support for the role of phases in organizational innovation. They discuss balancing creativity with value creation (p. 89) in an organization. They describe the "internal marketplaces" (p. 89) in organizations that "weigh, select, and prioritize innovations for their creativity and inherent commercial value or worth to the company." Davila, Epstein, and Shelton (2012) reinforce the conflicting and paradoxical nature of these processes but imply, drawing on Shelton (2001), that the key to successful innovation is to balance these.

THE INNOVATION PHASE MODEL (IPM)

D. H. Cropley and Cropley (2008) first proposed a phase model of innovation that integrates the concepts described as necessary for a theoretical framework of organizational innovation – the innovation phase model (IPM). This model taps into the interaction of antecedent process, person, product, and press factors across a series of stages noting, as did Csikszentmihalyi (2006), that the creative process may include distinct phases that draw on different psychological resources. The interaction of the Four Ps with the phases of the innovation process resolves the paradoxical nature of organizational innovation. Whereas Davila, Epstein, and Shelton (2012) see the balance between creativity and value creation as one of compromise, the present model resolves the paradox – the conflicting needs of creativity and value creation – by noting that each must be applied in full, but at the right time in the process. In this way, the competing needs of creativity and value creation with respect to the process, person, product, and press can coexist, provided the organization understands when each takes precedence over the other.

In fact, Davila, Epstein, and Shelton (2012) hinted at this time-and-place resolution of the paradoxes of innovation in their discussion of the changing balance of creativity processes and value creation processes as organizations mature. Although making a somewhat different point, they arrive at the same conclusion as that embedded in the IPM – "In the earliest stages, a company is focused on creating new, improved products or services. At that point, the attention to maximizing the value capture . . . is relatively low" (p. 91). Conversely, they note, "In the later stages of growth and maturity, the singular drive to be creative usually decreases and is replaced by a shift to increasing value capture" (p. 92). Although they make their point relative to the maturity of the organization, their argument applies also to the innovation process. At certain stages of the innovation process, there is a "bias toward creativity," while at other stages there is a "focus on value capture" (p. 92). Davila, Epstein, and Shelton (2012) would argue that a balance of the two processes – creativity and value creation – is achieved when an organization is adept, in general, at both. This addresses "what" is required, in general terms, for successful organizational innovation. With the IPM (Table 8.2), this is taken a step further by showing both "when" and "why" those processes are required in order to succeed at innovation.

The IPM was first placed in the context of organizational innovation in D. H. Cropley (2009) and D. H. Cropley and Cropley (2010), and this was followed by further discussion in the same context in D. H. Cropley and Cropley (2011). Coupling the expanded Four Ps model of creativity outlined in Chapter 4 with the expanded phases of generation of effective novelty described in Chapter 6 (see Figure 6.1), the IPM creates a matrix of intersections of specific Ps with specific phases (e.g., the P of personal motivation in the phase of activation or the P of process in the phase of generation). The cells in this matrix are referred to as nodes.

TABLE 8.2. *The Innovation Phase Model (IPM)*

Building Blocks	Phase / Poles	Invention					Exploitation	
		Preparation Knowledge, problem recognition	**Activation** Problem definition, refinement	**Generation** Many candidate solutions	**Illumination** A few promising solutions	**Verification** A single optimal solution	**Communication** A working prototype	**Validation** A successful product
Process	Convergent versus Divergent	Convergent	Divergent	Divergent	Convergent	Convergent	Mixed	Convergent
Person (motivation)	Reactive versus Proactive	Mixed	Proactive	Proactive	Proactive	Mixed	Reactive	Reactive
Person (properties)	Adaptive versus Innovative	Adaptive	Innovative	Innovative	Innovative	Adaptive	Adaptive	Adaptive
Person (feelings)	Conserving versus Generative	Conserving	Generative	Generative	Generative	Conserving	Conserving	Conserving
Product	Routine versus Creative	Routine	Creative	Creative	Creative	Routine	Routine	Routine
Press	High Demand versus Low Demand	High	Low	Low	Low	High	High	High

The IPM model then describes each P in terms of a dichotomy bounded by two poles. Table 8.2 shows the poles that apply to each building block – the P of process, for example, is defined by divergent thinking at one pole and convergent thinking at the other, while personal motivation is extrinsic at one pole, intrinsic at the other. Any given node has a favorable pole of the P involved in that node (from the point of view of innovation). This is the pole of the P involved in the node in question that is most important for innovation in that phase. For example, in the phase generation, divergent thinking is the process most important for innovation because generation involves the production of ideas. Thus, in the node process/generation, divergent thinking is vital. Conversely, in the phase verification, convergent thinking is the process that is critical for innovation because in this phase ideas that have already been produced must be tested and evaluated. Thus, in the node process/verification, convergent thinking is required. As becomes apparent, what is good for innovation in one node – whether an aspect of process, product, person, or press – is not necessarily good in another node. The crucial thing is to know when and why each pole of each antecedent P is critical to innovation, and the IPM provides this information (see Table 8.2).

Equipped with the IPM as a theoretical framework, innovation managers are now in a better position both to make sense of empirical research, such as that of Vincent, Bharadwaj, and Challagalla (2004) and their model of innovation as a partial mediator of the antecedent–firm performance relationship, and to take a more proactive approach to specifying hypotheses and testing theories about the relationships between the full range of personal and organizational antecedents, and firm performance in its broadest sense.

MEASUREMENT MODELS OF ORGANIZATIONAL INNOVATION

The IPM (Table 8.2) emphasizes that organizational innovation is not a one-size-fits-all process. Can the models developed earlier in this chapter be refined to reflect more closely the differential impact of antecedents, the intermediate products of innovation, and the more strategic operationalization of firm performance that are suggested by the theoretical model?

Consistent with the theoretical model embodied in Table 8.2, Figure 8.13 now represents each innovation stage variable (the latent variables labeled 1, 2, etc.) both as an antecedent for the following stage and as an outcome for the current stage. For example, 1 is both the

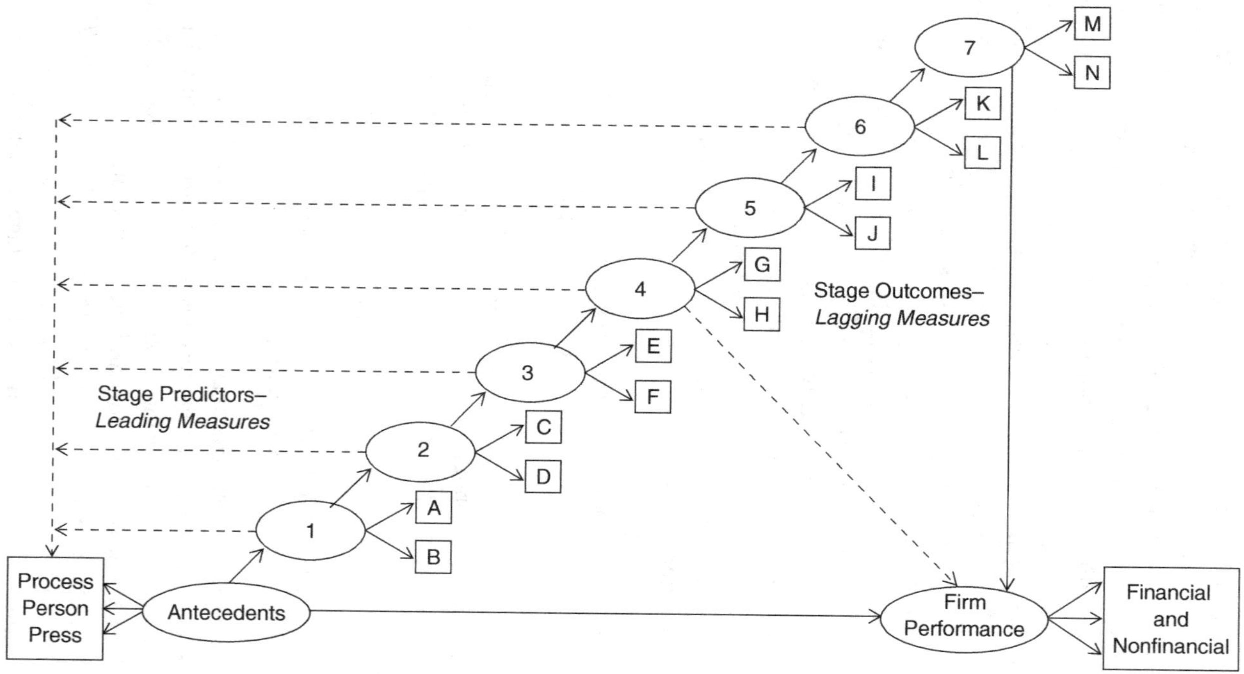

FIGURE 8.13. Path Diagram: Innovation and Firm Performance

outcome variable stage 1 innovation and the predictor variable stage 2 antecedent. This new model also highlights the fact that innovation at each stage/phase may be operationalized differently (represented in Figure 8.13 by variables A, B, C, etc.). As an output of stage 3 (generation), for example, innovation may be measured best through indicators such as the number of ideas generated, in contrast to stage 5 (verification), where the quality of a single solution becomes important. A further advantage of this improved model is that we can also examine the mediating effect of intermediate stages of innovation on firm performance (indicated by the dotted arrow from stage 4 to firm performance). This allows questions about the relative importance of different stages of innovation on overall performance to be examined.

In fact, Vincent, Bharadwaj, and Challagalla (2004, p. 20) anticipated the need for an improved model when they noted, "Further research should seek to utilize the measure of innovation best suited for the particular research question being addressed," making a more phase-specific model an imperative. The need for a more differentiated model is also supported by the statement that "the performance implications associated with innovation were significantly different based on the temporal nature of the research design" (p. 20). In other words, the stage, or phase, of innovation that is studied has an impact on the nature of, and relationship between, antecedents and outcomes.

The IPM (Table 8.2) and the improved measurement model based on it (Figure 8.13) help with understanding the complex network of relationships among antecedents, innovation, and firm performance. They allow innovation managers to drill down into the specifics of particular antecedents, particular stages of innovation, and particular outcomes. However, they also set the stage for another very important function – managing the paradoxes of organizational innovation in a collective and diagnostic sense, which will be explored next in Chapter 9.

OVERVIEW AND OUTLOOK

Successful innovation management is underpinned by the measurement of the building blocks (product, process, person, and press) discussed in Chapter 7. However, it is important to recognize that these are necessary but not sufficient for innovation management. Business models of innovation shift thinking from a reductionist mind-set, to a systems view of innovation that links the antecedent building blocks to innovation and firm performance outcomes.

This shift in focus also turns attention to the visible indicators of innovation and firm performance. What concrete, measurable outcomes define innovation? If innovation is measured, for example, in terms of product novelty, then there is a way to link a building block – product – to innovation. The innovation manager is then equipped not only to measure the outcome but also to make changes to the innovation process to lead to meaningful changes in product novelty. Linking the measurement of building blocks to the measurement of the innovation outcome supports causal models of innovation.

In fact, this process of joining causes with effects for effective innovation management goes a step further. Firm performance defines the external, business impact of the innovation process. The building blocks act together to drive the generation of novel, valuable products (innovation), which have measurable financial and nonfinancial effects on the business (firm performance) – that is, profit, sales growth, market share, customer value, customer loyalty, and so on.

To be fully effective as a guide for innovation managers, measurement models need to link not only the building blocks to innovation and firm performance but also must take into account the paradoxes (Chapter 6) that shape and constrain innovation. This is achieved with a measurement model developed around a framework that recognizes the influence of phases in the innovation process. The IPM presented in this chapter leads to the development of a measurement model that resolves the apparent paradoxes of innovation. The model explains when and why apparently exclusive states of the building blocks – convergent and divergent thinking, for example – contribute to innovation and firm performance. It gives the innovation manager the means to resolve these apparent paradoxes.

9

Managing the Paradoxes of Innovation

The innovation phase model (IPM) described in Chapter 8 provides a framework for understanding the contribution of the building blocks (person, process, product, and press) to innovation. The IPM also serves as a mechanism for understanding the paradoxes – in particular, the personal environment paradoxes – that were discussed in Chapter 6. In simple terms, the innovation manager is faced with a problem – how to use his or her knowledge of the six building blocks derived from the expanded Ps model, their contributions to innovation and firm performance, and the paradoxes they embody to improve innovation in an organization.

It would be reasonable to conclude, from the arguments and concepts presented so far in this book, that the right approach to managing innovation is to start from the bottom and work up. The antecedent building blocks drive innovation and firm performance (Figure 9.1).

The obvious conclusion is that the best approach would be to measure those antecedents, as described in Chapter 7; characterize the available innovation resources; and then fit the two together in the best way possible – align them to the favorable poles set out in the IPM – to improve the organization's capacity for innovation. For example, in a phase in which divergent thinking is most favorable to innovation, it makes sense to focus on individuals who have been identified as divergent thinkers. When risk aversion is favorable, it seems logical to insert the risk-averse individuals into the process.

Although this approach accounts for the IPM and the paradoxes within that model, its bottom-up nature has several weaknesses. It may make sense to allocate certain individuals to certain parts of the process based on their behavioral dispositions and the particular requirements of the part of the process in question, but how does the innovation manager deal with

FIGURE 9.1. Antecedents Drive Innovation and Firm Performance

the press in this bottom-up approach? If the organizational climate is characterized in a certain way and is static or fixed, then how is the innovation manager to fit that to the paradoxical nature of press described in the IPM? The weakness of this bottom-up approach is its static nature; it is an approach that is reminiscent of trait theories of individuals in psychology.

Trait theories of human behavior (e.g., Wortman, Loftus, & Marchall, 1985) focus on the consistency of broad and relatively stable aspects of personality. Guilford (1959), for example, defined traits in terms of enduring differences between individuals. Applied in the context of organizations, an approach based on this concept to managing the paradoxes of innovation adopts a goodness-of-fit paradigm. Innovation is improved and the paradoxes are managed by fitting individuals to those parts of the process that correspond to their natural traits. If an individual, for example, is assessed as strong in divergent thinking or is highly open to new ideas, then that person should be used in phases such as generation, where his or her natural strengths align with the needs of the innovation process as set out in the IPM (Table 8.2). While this might work for a collection of individuals, it is harder to see how a trait approach to press can accommodate one fixed and enduring organizational climate – it may align to some stages but almost certainly not to others.

By contrast, an approach based on the concept of behavioral dispositions (see, for example, the discussion of the personal environment in Chapter 4) asserts that individuals can learn how to respond to different situations in the most appropriate manner. This approach builds on Sternberg's (2007) conceptualization of creativity as a malleable habit that is developed through opportunity, recognition, and reward. The job of the innovation manager then is not simply a reactive and somewhat defeatist task of attempting to fit square pegs into square holes. Instead, it is a proactive, dynamic, and empowering assignment in which individuals exercise their capacity for lifelong learning to adapt their behavior to the requirements of the innovation process.

While it may be true that the former approach is capable of improving innovation – the right pegs in the right holes are surely better than the wrong pegs in the wrong holes – this reactive style takes a production-line approach to innovation. Like an assembly line, its premise is stability, uniformity, volume, and repeatability. However, innovation is, by its nature, unique and disorderly – an outcome suited not to an assembly-line approach but to a model of individual, unit production in which production resources must be flexible and adaptable.

The assembly-line model also represents an unsatisfactory way of dealing with deficiencies in the resources available. If the innovation manager has no divergent thinkers, for example, the only solution is to hire them. The latter paradigm, by contrast, seems inherently more flexible and efficient, and it addresses the same problem by teaching the existing personnel how to adapt their behavior and think divergently. The concept of behavioral dispositions also resolves the problem presented by the press. The organizational climate is no longer characterized as a fixed and enduring trait of the organization but as a flexible, adaptable organizational disposition that can be changed to suit the requirements of the innovation process.

THE TOP-DOWN APPROACH

The concept of behavioral dispositions embodies a fundamental shift from a bottom-up, trait approach – measure the building blocks and then fit those pegs into their holes – to a more flexible top-down approach (Figure 9.2) based on the organizational environment as the top. Under this new paradigm, the first measurement involves the organizational environment level (see Chapter 5) and identifies a constellation of behavioral dispositions that exist in the particular firm. In other words, this measurement establishes a pattern of dispositions across the entire innovation process, covering person, process, product, and press as they exist at the time of measurement (with the ultimate intention of modifying those dispositions where necessary in order to promote innovation).

In contrast to the static, bottom-up paradigm, which viewed these dispositions as fixed and enduring – i.e., as traits – the top-down paradigm recognizes that dispositions are flexible and adaptable. No individuals and no organizations are characterized by one inflexible pattern of traits; each one is a blend of different dispositions that become active at different times and under different conditions in the innovation process. By measuring this constellation of dispositions, the innovation manager can then

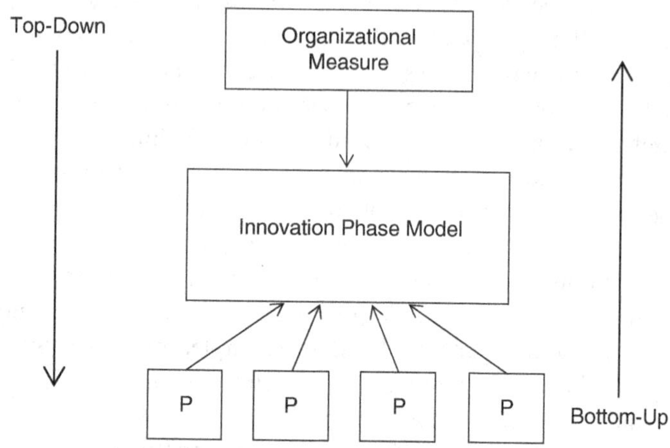

FIGURE 9.2. Bottom-Up and Top-Down: Managing Innovation

maximize the alignment of particular dispositions – in effect, teaching the individuals and, by extension, the organization, to behave in the manner most favorable for innovation at any given stage of the process. There is one obvious question, however, that emerges at this stage of the discussion: How can this constellation of dispositions be measured?

THE INNOVATION PHASE ASSESSMENT INSTRUMENT (IPAI)

To facilitate the top-down, dispositional approach to managing innovation and the paradoxes within that process, D.H. Cropley and Cropley (2010, 2011, 2012) and D. H. Cropley, Cropley, Chiera, and Kaufman (2013) developed the innovation phase assessment instrument (IPAI). This instrument is grounded in the theoretical framework represented by the IPM (Chapter 8).

D. H. Cropley and Cropley (2012) argued that the building blocks represented in the IPM (e.g., process, person [motivation], press; refer again to Table 8.2) are not unitary traits that are either present or absent (e.g., motivation is not either present or absent) but are dispositions of various kinds and with varying levels. Consistent with the concept of the paradoxical nature of innovation, they characterized these building blocks as dichotomies and gave labels to the contrasting poles of the dichotomies.[1]

[1] This dichotomization represents an oversimplification because the dispositions being discussed are not either/or propositions but are often continuous variables. Dichotomization is adopted here for simplicity of presentation.

Thus, the cognitive process may be convergent or divergent, person (motivation) may be proactive or reactive, press may be high demand or low demand, and so on (see Table 8.2). Both kinds of process (divergent and convergent thinking), both kinds of motivation (proactive and reactive), and both kinds of press (high demand and low demand) are important for innovation. However, the crucial point is that they are important in different phases of the overall process of innovation.[2] For instance, the process divergent thinking may be favorable for innovation in the phase of generation but unfavorable in the phase of verification. The vital issue is that each particular combination of a specific phase and a specific dimension requires a particular form of the building block. For example, in the phase of generation, the kind of process required is divergent thinking, whereas in the phase of verification the kind of process required is convergent thinking. This is the paradoxical nature of innovation.

Each specific combination of phase and building block is referred to as a node in the IPAI. The intersection of generation with process, for example, defines a node (referred to simply as generation/process), as does motivation during verification (defining the node as verification/motivation), and so on. These intersections yield $6 \times 7 = 42$ nodes, each node defined by a particular phase and building block (refer again to Table 8.2). In the node generation/process, for example, divergent thinking is favorable for innovation; in the node verification/motivation, proactive motivation is favorable; in the node communication/process, convergent thinking is favorable; and in the node communication/motivation, reactive motivation is what is needed to facilitate innovation. D. H. Cropley and Cropley (2012, p. 38) listed the crucial, or favorable, pole of each particular building block (such as proactive versus reactive motivation) for all forty-two nodes, and these are reproduced in Table 8.2.

As a result, an innovation manager needs to foster, for example, divergent thinking in some nodes but convergent thinking in others. This proactive and dynamic behavioral approach is built on an assumption that individuals in the organization can combine "tendencies of thought and action that in most people are segregated" (Csikszentmihalyi, 1996, p. 47); to "oscillate," as Martindale (1989, p. 228) put it; or to operate in "alternating psycho-behavioral waves" (Koberg & Bagnall,1991, p. 38) through what Bledow, Frese, Anderson, Erez, and Farr (2009b, p. 365) called "dynamic shifting." The purpose of the IPAI therefore is to diagnose

[2] For an overview of the phases, see Figure 6.1.

for a particular organization the nodes in which the individual and organizational behavioral dispositions are favorable for innovation and the nodes in which they are unfavorable so that the innovation manager can drive learning and adaptation to maximize the opportunity for successful innovation outcomes.

Items of the IPAI

The IPAI contains four items for each of the forty-two nodes represented by the intersection of a phase and a building block. This results in a total of 168 test items. Table 9.1 lists a sample of items from the scale for a selection of different building blocks in three of the seven phases: activation, illumination, and validation.

Each item consists of a dichotomous statement. All statements extend the common stem: "In this organization . . . ." Respondents are asked to indicate whether a statement is true or false with regard to their organization in the usual course of events. For example, the items for the node activation/process are:

- In this organization, staff help to define the goals of their work.
- In this organization, within broad guidelines, staff decide for themselves what they will focus on.

TABLE 9.1. *Examples of IPAI Items*

Phase	Sample Item (*"In this organization . . . "*)	Standard Answer
Activation	Staff do not analyze their own work. (process)	False
	Staff get a feeling of satisfaction out of dissecting what they do. (person – feelings)	True
Illumination	It is expected that progress will be made in small steps. (press)	False
	Early in a project, staff preserve a large set of candidate solutions. (product)	False
Validation	Staff want their ideas to be subjected to external scrutiny. (person – motivation)	True
	Staff become very nervous when their ideas go public. (person – properties)	False

- In this organization, right from the beginning, managers state clear criteria for recognizing solutions.
- In this organization, staff do not analyze their own work.

The four items relating to any particular node, such as those listed here, are not clustered in a single block in the instrument but are scattered randomly throughout the 168-item scale in order to reduce the likelihood of raters recognizing that certain items belong together and answering accordingly. In some cases, items are phrased positively (e.g., "Staff produce lots of ideas"); in others, they are phrased negatively (e.g., "Products are not released unless we are very confident that they will proceed").

Each item has a response that, according to the model (D. H. Cropley & Cropley, 2012. p. 38), represents the ideal behavioral disposition for a particular node. The ideal response, in other words, describes the behavioral disposition that is optimal for innovation in the particular combination of phase and building block. These ideal responses are referred to as standard answers in Table 9.1. The standard answer is sometimes true (e.g., "Staff want their ideas to be subjected to external scrutiny") and sometimes false (e.g., "Staff do not analyze their own work"). For example, in the case of the node generation/motivation, one item is, "In this organization staff prefer unambiguous information." According to the IPM (Table 8.2, Chapter 8), the underlying behavioral disposition that favors innovation in the generation phase is a high tolerance for ambiguity. Therefore, the standard answer to this statement (i.e., the answer indicating the behavioral disposition favorable to innovation) is false. The right-hand column of Table 9.1 indicates the standard answer for the sample items in the table.

Administering and Scoring the Scale

The scale is suitable for administration to individuals in a group setting. Respondents fill out the scale by answering true or false to each item. They are asked to respond in terms of their own understanding of what the item means and not to concern themselves with what the test constructors might have meant. They are reminded that they are describing their own organization as they perceive it, not giving their opinions about what a work environment ought to be like or the way they would like their organization to be. Their task is also to describe what is typical of the organization they are assessing even if there are occasional deviations or special situations where things are sometimes different. They are asked to respond according to what comes into their minds immediately when they read an item, not to think long and hard about, for instance, the exact percentage of the time their response actually applies to their organization or to check their responses to earlier items.

Responses of each individual filling out the scale are then scored by checking them against a key that specifies the standard answer for that item. A response that corresponds to the standard answer receives one point; a response that differs from the standard answer receives zero points. The number of items that are answered with the standard answer for the item in question is then aggregated to produce a score out of 168 for the organization. The closer this total score is to 168, the more the particular respondent has described the organization as being "aligned" to the constellation of behavioral dispositions that are favorable to innovation.[3]

Individual scores can also be calculated for each of the forty-two nodes by summing the number of standard or aligned answers given to the four items for each particular node. In the example already given for the node activation/process, the answers true, true, false, false would yield a score of 4 for the node in question because all four answers correspond to the pole of process favorable for innovation. Aligned answers can also be summed for each phase by adding scores across the six building blocks relating to that phase (twenty-four items for each phase) or for each building block by aggregating scores across the seven phases for that building block (twenty-eight items for each building block). In this way, several levels of analysis are possible. Table 9.2 shows hypothetical IPAI results for an organization.

Individual node scores range in value from 0 to 4. If aggregated responses to the four items for a given node indicate no alignment to the favorable behavioral dispositions, then the score for that node would be 0. Conversely, where aggregated responses indicate alignment for all four items, the score for the node would be 4. Similarly, aggregating node scores for a given building block across all seven phases results in a score ranging from 0 to 28. The higher the score, the more aligned are the behavioral dispositions of the organization for that building block, regardless of phase. The same approach can be taken for aggregating scores for each phase. In this case, scores range from 0 to 24 as node scores for a given phase are

[3] As a rule, an organization is rated by more than one respondent. In this case the scoring procedure is repeated for each rater, and the evaluation of the total group is obtained by averaging the scores of the group of raters for each node, phase, or building block.

TABLE 9.2. *Hypothetical IPAI Data*

Phase Building Block	Preparation	Activation	Generation	Illumination	Verification	Communica- tion	Validation	Building Block Score
Process	3	3	2	3	3	3	4	**21**
Personal motivation	3	4	3	4	4	4	4	**26**
Personal properties	3	3	4	3	2	4	4	**23**
Personal feelings	4	3	4	3	3	3	4	**24**
Product	4	2	2	3	3	4	1	**19**
Press	3	4	2	3	3	4	3	**22**
Phase Score	**20**	**19**	**17**	**19**	**18**	**22**	**20**	**135**

aggregated across the six building blocks. The higher the score, the more aligned are the behavioral dispositions for that phase.

Interpreting Scores

Consistent with the top-down proactive approach to innovation management described earlier in this chapter, in the section titled The Top-down Approach, the purpose of the IPAI is not simply to rate organizations as having (or lacking) the capacity to innovate successfully. Rather, the purpose of the instrument is to facilitate the diagnosis of an organization's strengths and weaknesses by identifying those nodes in which behavioral dispositions are already favorably aligned and those where they are not, and to formulate a plan for the optimal management of existing alignments and the development and promotion of required behavioral dispositions that are not currently well aligned.

One approach to the interpretation of IPAI data therefore is to focus on relative differences in scores at the level of phases, building blocks, and specific nodes. For instance, examining individual phases, an organization might have higher scores on preparation, verification, communication, and validation but lower scores on activation, generation, and illumination. Such an organization would be better at defining tasks; selecting promising solutions; presenting solutions to customers, consumers, and the like; and assessing the effectiveness of solutions or products. It would be weaker at encouraging staff members to build up wide-ranging knowledge of a field, identify and seek to solve problems, see alternative approaches to finding a solution, and so on. Such an organization would be more likely to continue producing routine products (recall the definition in Chapter 2), albeit in an efficient way, than it would be to innovate. The innovation manager seeking to enhance the organization's capacity to innovate would therefore formulate a strategy for developing the dispositions to search for and acquire a wide range of disparate information, identify problems or potential problems, or be open to "far out" solutions in order to promote favorable behaviors in the phases that are currently weaker.

To assist in the interpretation of IPAI data, scores are converted to percentages to indicate the degree to which individual nodes, phases, and building blocks align with the favorable dispositions that support successful innovation. To illustrate the process of interpreting the IPAI, the following section describes a case study of the application of the IPAI to a team of engineers in a large manufacturing firm.

Case Study: Manufacturer—Firm XYZ

Thirty-six engineers in one division of Organization XYZ (a manufacturing firm) completed the IPAI. Table 9.3 shows aggregate scores for each intersection (node) of innovation phase (preparation, activation, etc.) and each social-psychological building block (process, motivation, etc.). These aggregate scores represent a percentage alignment to the conditions that are ideal for organizational innovation. Thus, a figure of 87 indicates that, for the intersection in question (e.g., communication/motivation), the organization is 87 percent aligned to the conditions that are ideal for innovation, for that node. Referring to the IPM in Table 8.2, the favorable behavioral disposition is reactive motivation (for further discussion of personal resources, see Chapter 4). The data collected for Organization XYZ (Table 9.3) indicate a diverse range of strengths as well as areas for potential improvement.

Prior to undertaking the assessment of Organization XYZ, the IPAI consultant met with the sponsoring manager (the head of the division in question) to discuss her needs and objectives in relation to improving organizational innovation. This included an indication that her division's primary business focus was in the exploitation of ideas – in other words, the latter phases (verification, communication, and validation) of the innovation process – but that there was a growing move to undertake more design and concept generation activities, representing a move to undertake earlier phases of the innovation process as well. Thus, her expectation was to see relative strengths in the latter phases, and she hoped that the earlier phases would show good alignment, indicating a readiness in terms of behavioral dispositions, to undertake these new activities. The manager also indicated a general concern that staff members in the division were unmotivated but that the general organizational climate was positive and supportive of innovation. Depending on the results, her expectation was also to consolidate strengths in the latter phases and to target any particular weaknesses in earlier phases as a first step toward improving her division's capacity for the innovation in the earlier phases. It was agreed that this process would utilize at least two additional assessments with the IPAI, interspersed with specific development activities to address weaknesses in required behavioral dispositions.

Analysis

The analysis of IPAI data leads to results and feedback at four possible levels. First, the total aggregate alignment for the division of Organization XYZ was 64 percent. This indicates a generally positive position with respect to the

TABLE 9.3. *Aggregate IPAI Scores by Node for Organization XYZ*

Phase Building Block	Preparation	Activation	Generation	Illumination	Verification	Communication	Validation
Process	59	76	47	65	72	53	59
Motivation	60	72	62	85	88	87	47
Personal properties	68	49	57	58	56	78	65
Feelings	59	66	76	56	74	72	58
Products	63	60	58	61	69	83	47
Press	60	61	41	53	59	73	67

alignment of behavioral dispositions ideal for organizational innovation. At the most basic level, 64 percent of the 168 questions indicated alignment with favorable behavioral dispositions across all phases and building blocks.

The second level of analysis examines the results for Organization XYZ by phase. Aggregate scores for each phase of the innovation process (Table 9.4) indicate broad strengths and weaknesses across the stages of the innovation process. With respect to the stated needs and objectives of the division's manager, three items stand out in this analysis:

1. The division in question has relative strengths that broadly align with the focus of current work – that is, the latter stages of the innovation process.
2. There is, however, an identified weakness in the final phase (validation) relative to the preceding two phases, suggesting an avenue for improving the division's current work focus.
3. There is a foundation of positive alignment in the earlier stages of the innovation process on which the division's future goals can be built; however, there is room for these to be strengthened.

Table 9.4 shows the aggregate percentage scores for each phase as well as a shaded indication of relative strengths, weaknesses, opportunities, and threats (SWOT) in these phases. These categories are defined relative to the mean phase score and are defined as follows. Strengths are those phases for which the aggregate phase score is greater than 1 standard deviation above the mean. Opportunities and threats are those phase scores that are between ±1 standard deviation about the mean. Weaknesses are those phase scores that are less than 1 standard deviation below the mean. This SWOT analysis confirms that the division of Organization XYZ has a relative strength in the phases of verification and communication, and relative weaknesses in generation and validation.

The third level of analysis examines the results for Organization XYZ by building block – that is, the social/psychological parameters that characterize creativity and innovation. Aggregate scores for each building block (Table 9.5) once again indicate a range of strengths, weaknesses, opportunities, and threats that have been assessed in the same manner as for phases. With respect to the stated needs and objectives of the division's manager, three conclusions are evident:

1. Contrary to the manager's expectations, the motivation of staff members is reasonably well aligned to that required for innovation and is a relative strength of the division.

TABLE 9.4. *Aggregate IPAI Scores by Phase for Organization XYZ*

	Preparation	Activation	Generation	Illumination	Verification	Communication	Validation
Phase	61	64	57	63	70	74	57
Strengths					■	■	
Opportunities		■		■			
Threats	■						
Weaknesses			■				■

TABLE 9.5. *Aggregate IPAI Scores by Building Block for Organization XYZ*

Building Block		Strengths	Opportunities	Threats	Weaknesses
Process	62				
Personal motivation	71				
Personal properties	62				
Personal feelings	66				
Products	63				
Press	59				

2. Again, contrary to the manager's expectations, the general organizational climate (press) is a relative weakness. This is all the more interesting in light of the higher than expected motivation. It suggests that the positive motivation of staff members is unexploited due in part to a poor organizational climate.
3. There are several other relative threats and they represent building blocks that, if left unattended, risk becoming outright weaknesses. They may be preventing the organization from achieving its full potential with respect to innovation.

The fourth level of analysis returns to Table 9.3 in light of the identified phase and building block results. With a continued focus on the analysis in light of the manager's goals and expectations, this node analysis makes it possible to identify more specific areas of concern or interest. It is now clear that specific intersections of phase and building block (i.e., nodes) are creating weaknesses at the aggregated levels of phase and building block. For example, in the final phase of validation, there are particular issues with motivation (47 percent) and products (47 percent) that weaken this phase, while a notable point of weakness in the building block press occurs in the generation phase (41 percent).

Recommendations for Action

On the basis of these results, and building on the goals and aims of the division manager for Organization XYZ, the following recommendations for action were made. In this case, Organization XYZ was concerned about the impact of a wide-ranging program of change and intervention, and opted to implement a limited number of changes to those areas most in need; these would be followed by further IPAI assessment and monitoring:

1. To strengthen the division's core business (identified by the division manager as the latter stages of the process), attention was focused on the nodes communication/process (53 percent) and validation/motivation (47 percent).
2. To build capacity for successful innovation in the division's targeted activities in the earlier stages of innovation, attention was focused on the nodes generation/process (47 percent), activation/personal properties (49 percent) and generation/press (41 percent).
3. While other nodes could also be addressed, the recommendations were limited to those stated in order to allow for a cycle of action/measurement and to build the confidence of the staff members of the division.

A target agreed to by the manager of the division was to achieve a 10-point improvement in the five nodes in question after a period of training and staff development, followed by a period for changes to be consolidated. The target IPAI analysis is shown in Table 9.6 and should be compared to Table 9.3. If successful, these initial changes would also lead to an improvement in the overall total from approximately 63 percent to 65 percent.

Specific actions implemented by the IPAI consultant to bring about these desired improvements included the following:

1. **Awareness:** Staff training in understanding the stages of innovation and the differing factors that affect innovation. Developing an understanding, both in managers and staff members, of where the team is at any stage of the innovation process so that actions and building blocks can be tailored to the innovation process.
2. **Thinking:** Training in specific divergent thinking processes to address the weakness in the generation/process phase.
3. **Qualities:** Workshops to address weaknesses in personal properties that are blocking innovation, for example, assisting staff members in developing skills in identifying and assessing risks in order to facilitate informed risk taking, and workshops to develop tolerance for uncertainty and ambiguity. Both of these support improvements in the weakness identified in the node activation/personal properties.
4. **Support** – Working with staff members and the manager(s) to identify and address issues that are creating an unfavorable organizational press, in the node generation/press.

TABLE 9.6. *Initial Improvement Targets for Specific Nodes*

Phase Building Block	Preparation	Activation	Generation	Illumination	Verification	Communic- ation	Validation	Building Block Scores
Process	59	76	47 + 10	65	72	53 + 10	59	62 → 64
Motivation	60	72	62	85	88	87	47 + 10	71 → 73
Personal properties	68	49 + 10	57	58	56	78	65	62 → 63
Feelings	59	66	76	56	74	72	58	66
Products	63	60	58	61	69	83	47	63
Press	60	61	41 + 10	53	59	73	67	59 → 61
Phase scores	61	64 → 66	57 → 60	63	70	70 → 76	57 → 59	

The success of the suite of recommendations and actions depends on a close partnership among the IPAI consultant, the staff members in the organization, and the management of the organization.

Conclusion of the Case Study for Organization XYZ

Organization XYZ is undertaking a range of activities in partnership with the IPAI consultant over a period of approximately six months. The next step in this process is a reassessment of the division using the IPAI to assess the impact of the interventions and to reevaluate further actions. The general strategy is one of capacity building over time – improving areas of weakness, maintaining and consolidating strengths – in order to lift the organization's capacity for innovation higher and higher, consistent with their goals.

IMPROVEMENTS TO THE IPAI

D. H. Cropley, Cropley, Chiera, and Kaufman (2013) published results from a large study (n = 454) using the IPAI and established the instrument's reliability and validity. However, the original, 168-item instrument is limited by the dichotomous structure of the items, with the range and power of statistical analyses confined to weaker measures of central tendency, and nonparametric inferential statistics. While this limitation is not critical for the task of characterizing the alignment of behavioral dispositions using the IPAI, it becomes problematic if innovation managers wish to examine more sophisticated relationships among, for example, different groups.

A second factor that affects the use of the IPAI in practical, organizational settings is its length. While the individual questions require only a true-or-false answer, the fact that there are 168 of them means that the instrument takes between ten and twenty minutes to complete. It is therefore desirable to use the empirical evidence collected by D. H. Cropley, Cropley, Chiera, and Kaufman (2013) to create the shortest version of the IPAI possible that retains high levels of reliability and validity.

To this end, the authors have been driving a series of empirical studies with a range of different organizations, across both for-profit and nonprofit sectors, and spanning four different languages. Five versions of the IPAI are now under investigation, with each available in English, German, Norwegian. and Russian. The versions are shown in Table 9.7.

Preliminary analysis of data using the three-question/5-point Likert scale version of the IPAI indicates that both reliability and validity remain above acceptable thresholds and that statistically significant differences

TABLE 9.7. *IPAI Versions*[a]

Number of Questions Scale Type	4 Questions/ Node (Total 168)	3 Questions/Node (Total 126)	1 Question/ Node (Total 42)
Dichotomous (true/ false)	✓	✓	✓
5-point Likert scale		✓	
6-pPoint Likert scale			✓

[a] Further details of the tests can be obtained by contacting the author (david.cropley@unisa.edu.au).

between groups – for example, males and females – are discernible in the data. Demographic variables normally included in IPAI studies include gender, age, experience, level of education, and job role. Across all of these, preliminary analyses suggest significant differences in the mean scores for some individual IPAI test items. Identification of such group differences provides the innovation manager with useful supplementary information as strategies are formulated to address behavioral dispositions in the innovation process. The factors of gender and age hark back to discussions of group differences in Chapter 4.

OVERVIEW AND OUTLOOK

The IPAI is a response to the call for better integration and management of the range of paradoxical factors that influence the successful execution of the innovation process. Its purpose is not to classify organizations but to assist managers and employees in understanding how each of the building blocks affects the process of innovation. Its chief strength is that, unlike other instruments, it does not assume a one-size-fits-all approach to creativity and innovation. The IPAI is based on a theoretical model that acknowledges the paradoxes inherent in creativity and innovation. What is good for creativity in one phase, for example, may inhibit creativity in another phase. The IPAI helps managers to understand where they are in the process and whether their organization is aligned to the conditions needed for success in a particular phase.

10

General Conclusions

Although it was not directly inspired by him, this book has taken up an issue raised by Nussbaum (2013, p. 234) when he argued that "we need to switch from efficiency to *creativity* models" (emphasis added). In essence, this is what this book has done. It has drawn attention to a number of shortcomings or weaknesses in existing ways of conceptualizing innovation and has proposed a shift in focus to a more proactive and dynamic approach based on creativity theory. An overview of the kinds of shortcoming in current theorizing about innovation that are addressed in this book is presented in Table 10.1.

WHAT IS THE PRACTICAL PROBLEM?

The practical problem has been stated clearly by a number of authors. In a nutshell, overwhelming lip service is given to the importance of innovation summarized in Chapter 1 and the litany of benefits it is thought to bring (see, for example, Table 1.1), but as Nussbaum (2013, p. 234) put it, it is "shunted to the periphery." Such failure to innovate is now recognized as a matter of organizational life or death. The issue that thus arises is why firms choose to fiddle while Rome burns.

This book has shown that the problem has its roots in the three components of the system of which innovation is the outcome: the personal environment (see Chapter 4), the organizational environment, and the social environment (see Chapter 5). All three environments are marked by characteristics that support innovation, to be sure, but they are also marked by other characteristics that act as blockers of innovation (see Chapter 5). One blocker that cuts across environments is the absence of a clear understanding of the process of generation and implementation of

TABLE 10.1. *Examples of Often-Neglected Issues Addressed in This Book*

Domain	Issue	Source
Meta-issue	• The concept of innovation is diffuse. • There is a "lack of conceptual and theoretical coherence."	• Read (2000) • Smith and Lewis (2011, p. 382)
Paradoxes	• "People desire but reject creativity." • It is possible to have too much of a good thing. • Innovation involves both benefits and dangers. • Despite the benefits it brings, innovation is "shunted to the periphery."	• Mueller, Melwani, and Goncalo (2012, p. 13) • Gabora and Tseng (2014, p. 4) • Rosenbusch, Brinckmann, and Bausch (2011, p. 445) • Nussbaum (2013, p. 234)
Press	• Failure to understand that "innovation comes about as the result of the interaction among people, the processes they engage in, and the environment in which they work."	• Puccio and Cabra (2010, p. 149)
	• The belief that, metaphorically speaking, "all [managers] should be strangled on their sixtieth birthday."	• Huxley (1901, p. 101)
Product	• Persistence of the belief that "you don't have to make things in order to be creative."	• Rothman (2014)
	• Problem that "creativity is not enough."	• Levitt (2002, p. 137)
	• Problem that "consumers don't like too many surprises."	• Besemer (2006, p. 171)
Process	• Failure to understand that "the innovation process as it unfolds over time is messy, reiterative, and often involves two steps forwards for one step backwards plus several side-steps."	• Anderson, Potocnik and Zhou (2014, p. 5)

(*Continued*)

TABLE 10.1. *(continued)*

Domain	Issue	Source
	• Persistence of the romantic notion that creative thinking involves "waiting for the muse to strike."	• Kawenski (1991, p. 263)
Person	• Inadequate understanding of "how to select, develop, and motivate individuals."	• O'Shea and Buckley (2007, p. 102)
	• We "know very little about what makes one person more [innovative] than another."	• Dyer, Gregersen, and Christensen (2009, p. 60)
	• There is need for a solid body of widely accepted concepts for understanding the person in innovation.	• Rauch, Wiklund, Lumpkin, and Frese (2009)

effective novelty, for instance, equating the process with unfettered divergent thinking (see Chapter 2) or with something approaching divine inspiration. Another blocker is the inability of individual people, organizations, and societies to tolerate more than a limited amount of uncertainty or of risk (see Chapters 5 and 6, for example), whereas the essence of innovation is creating uncertainty, and one of its major drawbacks is that it is a risky business.

A third blocker is the conceptualization of innovation in reactive and static terms. For example, it is not infrequently assumed that individual people generate novelty only when they are forced to do so as a result of the status quo coming under threat and that just enough novelty is generated to cope with the threat (i.e., innovation is a reaction to external pressure and is controlled by such pressure). It is also not infrequently assumed that the factors in the personal environment (properties of individual people) that they employ as personal resources for creativity are, so to speak, in their DNA, thus a matter of biological endowment and therefore immutable. In a similar way, organizational properties such as, let us say, reward systems or information flows, are frequently treated as though their effects are fixed and have the same effects throughout the innovation process, from the first glimmer of a novel idea to the emergence of a finished marketable product (i.e., the interrelationship among organizational, social, and personal aspects of innovation is static).

In this book, by contrast, a proactive and dynamic approach has been adopted. This approach has been achieved by applying an individual, psychological filter to the lens through which the processes and properties of organizations are examined. The culmination of this approach has been a measuring instrument – the innovation phase assessment instrument (IPAI) – that integrates the paradoxical person, product, process, and press factors of innovation, and gives the innovation manager the means for checking the performance of the organization in its efforts to innovate. For any attempt to implement continuous improvement, whether focused on high-volume artifact production or on strategic processes such as innovation, the Deming cycle (e.g., Deming, 1986) of plan-do-check-act (PDCA) is a suitable framework into which the measurement processes can be inserted.

The following sections draw out the key concepts from the two major sections of this book. They culminate in a further discussion of the IPAI as the hub around which a Deming-style PDCA continuous improvement process might revolve as organizations seek to enhance their capacity for innovation.

PART 1: THE BASIC CONCEPTS OF INNOVATION

Innovation is universally acknowledged as a key to human development, well-being, and indeed survival. It is the mechanism by which societies and organizations respond to constant change. That change may be characterized as stemming from one of two drivers:

- Technology push – new devices, new drugs, and new processes, for example, generate implementation problems. How can these technologies be exploited?
- Market pull – new demands, new expectations, and new challenges create generation problems. What solutions will satisfy these needs?

Of these two problems, the former – implementation – may have dominated business-focused discussions of innovation and neglected somewhat the generation of the novel and effective ideas that are in fact the necessary driver of all innovation. Whereas the former is the focus of organizations, the latter – generation – is the primary concern of creative individuals. Innovation, in other words, is a combination of invention – creativity – and exploitation. To be fully effective at innovation, organizations therefore cannot neglect the individual creativity that results in exploitable effective novelty. While organizational factors – culture, workforce, organizational structures – remain important, these are underpinned by four factors that can be thought of as the building blocks of innovation – product, process, person, and press.

The product (see Chapter 2) is the exploitable idea that powers innovation processes. It encompasses four kinds of outputs:

- A tangible product – for example, the cell phone
- A process – for example, a way of managing patients in a healthcare system
- A system – in the sense of a network of interacting, interdependent parts, for example, a business information system
- A service – an intangible product such as a high-interest, low-fee savings account offered by a bank

Most important for innovation is the fact that these products arise as a response to change. Although they seem to represent technology push and a problem of implementation, that implementation is logically preceded by market pull and an underpinning need. In other words, change creates needs – economic change, health change, climate change, for example – and the needs require solutions. It is axiomatic that those new needs cannot be met with existing technology and therefore new solutions are needed. It is also self-evident that solutions must be not only novel but also effective – they must solve the problem.

- The key properties of the product in the innovation process are therefore novelty and effectiveness.

The process (see Chapter 3) addresses the cognitive – i.e., thinking – process that individuals draw on to generate ideas. Critical to the understanding of innovation is the recognition that there are two kinds of thinking – convergent thinking and divergent thinking – and they are qualitatively different.

Convergent thinking can be thought of as a family of cognitive processes directed at finding the single, correct answer to a problem. It is characterized by analysis, logic, knowledge, and expertise, and may even be thought of, broadly speaking, as a representation of so-called crystallized intelligence. Divergent thinking, in contrast, can be thought of as a process of finding many possible answers to a problem. It is more flexible and fluid, and draws on processes such as the ability to form remote associates and redefine problems.

Innovation uses both forms of thinking at different stages of the process. The generation of solution ideas, for example, may draw on divergent thinking. Once generated, however, those ideas must be evaluated and assessed (convergent thinking) in terms of their ability to meet the underpinning need. In fact, there is a complex interplay between the two, and both are necessary components of innovation.

- Process utilizes both convergent and divergent thinking to support the generation and evaluation of ideas during innovation.

The person (see Chapter 4) deals with the personal properties – resources – of the individual people who engage in generating exploitable, effective novelty. Traditionally, these resources have defined the relationships between:

- different forms of individual motivation – intrinsic and extrinsic – and how these help or hinder creativity and innovation
- different kinds of feelings and moods – for example, excitement and anxiety – and the impact that these have on idea generation and exploitation
- different attributes – risk taking versus risk aversion, for example – and why both are important to innovation

In addition to the personal resources that individuals draw on in the process of innovation, there are also fixed individual differences – age and gender, for instance – that must be managed across the innovation process.

- The person defines a constellation of behavioral dispositions, spanning motivation, feelings, and attributes, that have an impact on the innovation process in different ways, at different stages.

The press (see Chapter 5) describes both the wider social environment and the more proximate organizational environment within which individuals interact to engage in the process of innovation. As such, the press is the link between the individual – characterized by person and drawing on process – and organization as products are generated and exploited. The social and organizational environments define a wide range of parameters that affect innovation, including ethics, and the amount and kind of innovation that can be tolerated. Both environments also act to encourage or discourage innovation through mechanisms such as the emergence of assisters (champions) and resisters, and the nature and composition of teams.

- The press consists of both the wider social environment and the proximate organizational environment within which innovation takes place. Both environments may act to foster or block creativity and innovation.

PART 2: MEASURING FOR INNOVATION MANAGEMENT

The individual building blocks – product, process, person, and press – define, in effect, the antecedents of innovation. Managing organizational innovation may be characterized as a cyclical process of planning and implementing changes to these building blocks; checking the impact of those changes on the innovation process and on the organization; and taking appropriate action as a result – reinforcing positive change or rethinking negative change.

Deming's (1986) well-known PDCA cycle reflects the empirical, hypothesis-testing basis of the scientific method and fits well with a paradigm of continuous improvement that drives innovation management. However, the key to an effective improvement process is measurement. If the wrong things are measured or if the right measurements are interpreted incorrectly, then the attempts to improve organizational innovation will be, at best, misdirected and inefficient.

Critical to the process of interpretation, and therefore to continuous improvement, is the theoretical framework that describes the nature of the variables of interest to organizational innovation. Chapter 6 explains that, although a great deal of research has acknowledged the paradoxical nature of innovation (factors appear to be both good and bad for innovation), this apparent impasse can be resolved by drawing on psychological research and creativity theory. Understanding the paradoxes of innovation moves the manager away from a one-size-fits-all paradigm to a differentiated paradigm.

Equipped with the mind-set of a differentiated paradigm of organizational innovation, the innovation manager can now proceed to measurement, which occurs at two levels. In Chapter 7, measurement of the building blocks – the antecedents of organizational innovation – was described. A range of different measures of product, process, person, and press were discussed.

However, it is not until these are integrated into a system (see Chapter 8) that a resolution of the paradoxes of innovation becomes apparent. The innovation phase model (IPM) shows how it is possible for apparently exclusive states of any given antecedent to coexist in an organization. Convergent and divergent thinking, for example, seem to be opposites and yet both are necessary for innovation. The answer that the IPM presents is that different poles of each of the antecedents are active, and favorable to innovation, at different points in the process. Checking and acting, in the context of a PDCA improvement process, therefore take place relative to this framework. An organizational climate, for example, is no longer assessed as inherently good or inherently bad for innovation, and actions are no longer directed at fixing a problem. Instead, continuous improvement is a function of the organization's ability to do the right things at the right time. The primary measurement consideration is therefore one of the organization aligning with favorable conditions defined in the IPM, and the secondary measurement consideration is then one of understanding misalignments so that these can be aligned correctly when it is favorable to do so.

The IPAI described in Chapter 9 is the mechanism by which the innovation manager can establish the organization's pattern of alignment. Continuous improvement for organizational innovation can be modeled as four steps in the Deming cycle, as follows:

1. Plan – The process for improving organizational innovation is built on a foundation that links the antecedent product, process, person, and press to improved innovation, and innovation is the driver of firm performance. Weaknesses in these antecedents take the form of misalignments – if individuals, for example, are good at divergent thinking but poor at convergent thinking, then improvement will be based on applying strengths in divergent thinking at the appropriate stage of the innovation process and developing the necessary skills in convergent thinking to apply at the appropriate points in the process.
2. Do – Early in the improvement process, the focus will be on higher, meso-level measurement and the IPAI. Is the organization well-aligned with respect to the antecedents? What is the impact on firm performance? Once weaknesses have been identified, subsequent rounds of measurement then focus on monitoring changes in alignment and firm performance. Within this process, specific measurements may be required to understand the nature of weaknesses. For example, if the IPAI identifies a misalignment with regard to motivation in a particular phase, a specific measure of individual motivation can be used to diagnose the exact nature

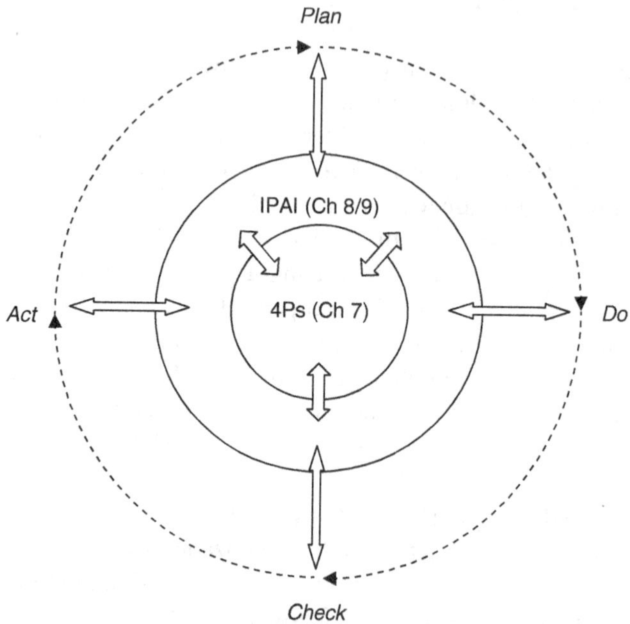

FIGURE 10.1. Measurement and the PDCA Cycle

of the misalignment and therefore the most appropriate actions for addressing it.

3. Check – This stage of the continuous improvement process assesses measurements against the theoretical framework. What does the pattern of alignment resulting from the IPAI tell the innovation manager about the organization? What do specific measures of antecedents tell the manager about behavioral dispositions?
4. Act – The actions resulting from the preceding stages are tailored to the theoretical framework. Actions are targeted to the specific active phase of the innovation process, and further cycles monitor performance and alignment in this same context.

FINAL THOUGHTS

There is no doubt that organizations of all kinds are acutely aware of the importance of innovation. A traditional focus of firm performance only on financial metrics may have led to an association between innovation and commercial considerations; however, innovation is much more than just a means to making a profit. Even organizations that exist ostensibly for commercial reasons innovate not so much to make money but as a response to change.

Change is found in every aspect of society and is as diverse as economic change, health change, and climate change. Innovation results from the way that societies respond to these changes. In simple terms, societies can choose to do nothing in response to the change – a path that seems likely to lead to stagnation and decay – or societies can choose to find new responses to the change. Thus, for example, climate change (e.g., global warming) and economic changes (e.g., the cost and availability of oil) have led to responses including the development of new forms of renewable energy (e.g., efficient, cost-effective solar panels) and new products that reduce fuel consumption (e.g., winglets on commercial aircraft). In many cases, these responses also create commercial opportunities for organizations. In the final analysis, however, the most important question is how organizations – commercial or nonprofit – coordinate and integrate the building blocks of innovation to deliver novel, value-adding outcomes to their stakeholders in response to the changes that are pervasive and inevitable.

The integrating theme of this book is that successful innovation is driven by a core of four building blocks – product, process, person, and press – and that psychological research has developed a framework to understand how these building blocks interact and can be managed to deliver novel, value-adding outcomes.

REFERENCES

Abra, J. (1994). Collaboration in creative work: An initiative for investigation. *Creativity Research Journal*, 7, 1–20.

Allport, G. W. (1961). *Pattern and growth in personality*. New York, NY: Holt, Rinehart, and Winston.

Altshuller, G. S. (1988). *Creativity as an exact science*. New York, NY: Gordon and Breach.

Amabile, T. M. (1983). *The social psychology of creativity*. New York, NY: Springer.

Amabile, T. M. (1996). *Creativity in context*. Boulder, CO: Westview Press.

Amabile, T. M. (1997). Innovative creativity through motivational synergy. *Journal of Creative Behavior*, 31, 18–26.

Amabile, T. M., Conti, R., Coon, H., Lazenby, J., & Herron, M. (1996). Assessing the work environment for creativity. *Academy of Management Journal*, 1154–1184.

Amabile, T. M., & Gryskiewicz, N. D. (1989). The creative environment scales: Work environment inventory. *Creativity Research Journal*, 2, 231–253.

Amabile, T. M., Schatzel, E. A., Moneta, G. B., & Kramer, S. J. (2004). Leader behaviors and the work environment for creativity: Perceived leader support. *The Leadership Quarterly*, 15, 5–32.

Amabile, T. M., & Tighe, E. (1993). Questions of creativity. In J. Brockman (Ed.), *Creativity: The reality club* (Vol. 4, pp. 7–27). New York, NY: Simon and Schuster.

Anderson, N., Potocnik, K., & Zhou, J. (2014). Innovation and creativity in organizations: A state-of-the-science review and prospective commentary. *Journal of Management*, 40, 1297–1333.

Anderson, N. R., & West, M. A. (1994). *The Team Climate Inventory: Manual and users' guide*. Windsor, UK: NFER-Nelson.

Andriopoulos, C. (2001). Determinants of organisational creativity: A literature review. *Management Decision*, 39, 834–841.

Anita Borg Institute. (2014). Innovation by design: The case for investing in women. Retrieved December 5, 2014, http://anitaborg.org.

Baas, M., De Dreu, C. K. W., & Nijstad, B. A. (2008). A meta-analysis of 25 years of mood–creativity research: Hedonic tone, activation, or regulatory focus? *Psychological Bulletin*, 134, 779–806.

Bacon, F. (1909). *Essays, civil and moral, and the new Atlantis [1627]*. New York, NY: Collier.

Baer, J. M. (2010). Is creativity domain specific? In J. C. Kaufman & R. J. Sternberg (Eds.), *The Cambridge handbook of creativity* (pp. 321–341). New York, NY: Cambridge University Press.

Baer, J. M., Kaufman, J. C., & Gentile, C. A. (2004). Extension of the consensual assessment technique to nonparallel creative products. *Creativity Research Journal*, 16, 113–117.

Baer, M., Oldham, G. R., Jacobsohn, G. C., & Hollingshead, A. B. (2008). The personality composition of teams and creativity: The moderating role of team creative confidence. *The Journal of Creative Behavior*, 42, 255–282.

Bailin, S. (1988). *Achieving extraordinary ends: An essay on creativity*. Dordrecht, Holland: Kluwer.

Baltes, P. B., & Smith, J. (1990). Towards a psychology of wisdom and its ontogenesis. In R. J. Sternberg (Ed.), *Wisdom—its nature, origins and development* (pp. 87–120). New York, NY: Cambridge University Press.

Barabba, V. (2011). *The decision looms: A design for interactive decision-making in organizations*. Axminster, UK: Triarchy Press.

Barker, J., 1993. *Paradigms: The business of discovering the future*. New York, NY: HarperBusiness.

Barreto, I. (2012). Solving the innovative puzzle: The role of innovative interpretation in opportunity formation and related processes. *Journal of Management Studies*, 49, 356–380.

Barron, F. X. (1955). The disposition toward originality. *The Journal of Abnormal and Social Psychology*, 51, 478.

Barron, F. X. (1969). *Creative person and creative process*. New York, NY: Holt, Rinehart & Winston.

Bartlett, F. C. (1932). *Remembering*. Cambridge, UK: Cambridge University Press.

Basadur, M., & Hausdorf, P. A. (1996). Measuring divergent thinking attitudes related to creative problem solving and innovation management. *Creativity Research Journal*, 9, 21–32.

Batey, M., Chamorro-Premuzic, T., & Furnham, A. (2010). Individual differences in ideational behavior: Can the big five and psychometric intelligence predict creativity scores? *Creativity Research Journal*, 22, 90–97.

Batey, M., & Furnham, A. (2006). Creativity, intelligence and personality: A critical review of the scattered literature. *Genetic, Social, and General Psychology Monographs*, 132, 355–429.

Baucus, M. S., Norton, W. I., Baucus, D. A., & Human, S. E. (2008). Fostering creativity and innovation without encouraging unethical behavior. *Journal of Business Ethics*, 81, 97–115.

Beaussart, M. L., Andrews, C. J., & Kaufman, J. C. (2013). Creative liars: The relationship between creativity and integrity. *Thinking Skills and Creativity*, 9, 129–134.

Beghetto, R. A. (2006). Creative self-efficacy: Correlates in middle and secondary students. *Creativity Research Journal*, 18, 447–457.

Beghetto, R. A., & Kaufman, J. C. (2007). Toward a broader conception of creativity: A case for" mini-c" creativity. *Psychology of Aesthetics, Creativity, and the Arts*, 1, 73–79.

Benner, M. J., & Tushman, M. (2003). Exploitation, exploration, and process management: The productivity dilemma revisited. *Academy of Management Review*, 27, 238–256.

Berlyne, D. E. (1962). *Conflict, arousal and curiosity*. New York, NY: McGraw Hill.

Besemer, S. P. (2006). *Creating products in the Age of Design*. Stillwater, OK: New Forums Press.

Besemer, S. P., & O'Quin, K. (1987). Creative product analysis: Testing a model by developing a judging instrument. In S. G. Isaksen (Ed.), *Frontiers of creativity research: Beyond the basics* (pp. 367–389). Buffalo, NY: Brady.

Besemer, S. P., & O'Quin, K. (1999). Confirming the three-factor creative product analysis matrix model in an American sample. *Creativity Research Journal*, 12, 287–296.

Bharadwaj, S., & Menon, A. (2000). Making innovation happen in organizations: Individual creativity. *Journal of Product Innovation Management*, 17, 424–434.

Birren, J. E., & Fisher, L. M. (1990). The elements of wisdom: Overview and integration. In R. J. Sternberg (Ed.), *Wisdom—its nature, origins and development* (pp. 317–322). New York, NY: Cambridge University Press.

Blackburn, R., & Kovalainen, A. (2009). Researching small firms and entrepreneurship: Past, present and future. *International Journal of Management Reviews*, 11, 127–148.

Blanchard, B. S., & Fabrycky, W. J. (2006). *Systems engineering and analysis* (4th ed.). Upper Saddle River, NJ: Pearson Prentice Hall.

Bledow, R., Frese, M., Anderson, N., Erez, M., & Farr, J. (2009a). A dialectic perspective on innovation: Conflicting demands, multiple pathways, and ambidexterity. *Industrial and Organizational Psychology*, 2, 305–337.

Bledow, R., Frese, M., Anderson, N., Erez, M., & Farr, J. (2009b). Extending and refining the dialectic perspective on innovation: There is nothing as practical as a good theory; nothing as theoretical as a good practice. *Industrial and Organizational Psychology*, 2, 363–373.

Bloom, B. S., & Sosniak, L. A. (1985). *Developing talent in young people*. New York, NY: Ballantine Books.

Boden, M. A. (1996a). Introduction. In M. A. Boden (Ed.), *Dimensions of creativity* (pp. 1–8). Cambridge, MA: MIT Press.

Boden, M. A. (1996b). What is creativity? In M. A. Boden (Ed.), *Dimensions of creativity* (pp. 75–118). Cambridge, MA: MIT Press.

Bowen, F. E., Rostami, M., & Steel, P. (2010). Timing is everything: a meta-analysis of the relationships between organizational performance and innovation. *Journal of Business Research*, 63, 1179–1185.

Brophy, D. R. (1998). Understanding, measuring and enhancing individual creative problem-solving efforts. *Creativity Research Journal*, 11, 123–150.

Bruner, J. S. (1962). The conditions of creativity. In H. Gruber, G. Terrell & M. Wertheimer (Eds.), *Contemporary approaches to cognition* (pp. 1–30). New York, NY: Atherton Press.

Buel, W. D. (1960). The validity of behavioral rating scale items for the assessment of individual creativity. *Journal of Applied Psychology*, 44, 407–412.

Buel, W. D. (1965). Biographical data and the identification of creative research personnel. *Journal of Applied Psychology*, 49, 318–321.

Buel, W. D., Albright, L. E., & Glennon, J. R. (1966). A note on the generality and cross-validity of personal history for identifying creative research scientists. *Journal of Applied Psychology*, 50, 217–219.

Buel, W. D., & Bachner, V. M. (1961). The assessment of creativity in a research setting. *Journal of Applied Psychology*, 45, 353–358.

Burgelman, R. A. (2002). Strategy as vector and the inertia of coevolutionary lock-in. *Administrative Science Quarterly*, 47, 325–357.

Burghardt, M. D. (1995). *Introduction to the engineering profession* (2nd ed.). New York, NY: HarperCollins College Publishers.

Burkhardt, H. (1985). *Gleichheitswahn, Parteienwahn: Massenpsychosen der Gegenwart*. Tűbingen, Germany: Hohenrain-Verlag.

Burston, D. (1991). *The legacy of Erich Fromm*. Boston, MA: Harvard University Press.

Buzan, A. (2007). Foreword. In S. C. Lundin & J. Tan (Eds.), *CATS: The nine lives of innovation* (pp. iv–viii). Spring Hill, Queensland: Management Press.

Byrd, R. E. (1986). *Creativity and risk-taking*. San Diego, CA: Pfeiffer International Publishers.

Canadian Intellectual Property Office. (2015). What can you patent? Retrieved March 28, 2015, from http://www.ic.gc.ca/eic/site/cipointernet-internetopic.nsf/eng/h_wr03652.html?Open&wt_src=cipo-patent-main&wt_cxt=learn

Carson, S. H., Peterson, J. B., & Higgins, D. M. (2005). Reliability, validity, and factor structure of the Creative Achievement Questionnaire. *Creativity Research Journal*, 17, 37–50.

Cattell, J., Glascock, J., & Washburn, M. F. (1918). Experiments on a possible test of aesthetic judgment of pictures. *The American Journal of Psychology*, 29, 333–336.

Chan, J., & Thomas, K. (2013). Introduction to the chapters. In K. Thomas & J. Chan (Eds.), *Handbook of research on creativity* (pp. 1–10). Cheltenham, UK: Edward Elgar.

Chang, L., & Burkitt, B. (2005). Managing intellectual capital in a professional service firm: Exploring the creativity-productivity paradox. *Management Accounting Research*, 15, 7–31.

Child, I. L., & Iwao, S. (1968). Personality and esthetic sensitivity: Extension of findings to younger age and to different culture. *Journal of Personality and Social Psychology*, 8, 308–312.

Christensen, C. M. (1997). *The innovator's dilemma*. Boston, MA: Harvard Business School Press.

Christensen, C. M. (2013). *The innovator's dilemma: When new technologies cause great firms to fail*. Boston, MA: Harvard Business School Press.

Christensen, C. M., Anthony, S. D., & Roth, E. A. (2004). *Seeing what's next: Using the theories of innovation to predict industry change*. Boston, MA: Harvard Business Press.

Cohen, L. Y. (2010). 10 Reasons Why We Need Innovation. Retrieved July 29, 2013, from http://www.amcreativityassoc.org/Articles/CohenTOP%2010%20Reasons%20Why%20We%20Need%20INNOVATION.pdf

Colangelo, N., Kerr, B., Hallowell, K., Huesman, R., & Gaeth, J. (1992). The Iowa Inventiveness Inventory: Toward a measure of mechanical inventiveness. *Creativity Research Journal*, 5, 157–163.

Collis, J. (2010). *Innovate or die: Outside the square business thinking*. New York, NY: HarperCollins.

Crant, J. M. (2000). Proactive behavior in organizations. *Journal of Management*, 26, 435–462.

Creswell, J. W. (2005). *Educational research: Planning, conducting, and evaluating quantitative and qualitative research* (2nd ed.). Upper Saddle River, NJ: Pearson Education.

Cropley, A. J. (1967). *Creativity*. London, UK: Longman.

Cropley, A. J. (1969). Creativity, intelligence and intellectual style. *Australian Journal of Education*, 13, 3–7.

Cropley, A. J. (1995). Creative performance in older adults. In W. Bos & R. Lehmann (Eds.), *Reflections on educational achievement. Papers in honour of T. Neville Postlethwaite* (pp.75–87). Münster, Germany: Waxmann.

Cropley, A. J. (1999). Creativity and cognition: Producing effective novelty. *Roeper Review*, 21, 253–260.

Cropley, A. J. (2001). *Creativity in education and learning: A guide for teachers and educators*. London, UK: Kogan Page.

Cropley, A. J. (2002). Creativity and innovation: Men's business or women's work? *Baltic Journal of Psychology*, 3, 77–88.

Cropley, A. J. (2006). In praise of convergent thinking. *Creativity Research Journal*, 18, 391–404.

Cropley, A. J. (2009). Teachers' antipathy to creative students: Some implications for teacher training. *Baltic Journal of Psychology*, 10, 86–93.

Cropley, A. J. (2012). Creativity and education: An Australian perspective. *International Journal of Creativity and Problem Solving*, 22, 9–25.

Cropley, A. J., & Cropley, D. H. (2007). Using assessment to foster creativity. In A.-G. Tan (Ed.), *Creativity: A handbook for teachers* (pp. 209–230). Singapore: World Scientific.

Cropley, A. J., & Cropley, D. H. (2008). Resolving the paradoxes of creativity: An extended phase model. *Cambridge Journal of Education*, 38, 355–373.

Cropley, A. J., & Cropley, D. H. (2009). *Fostering creativity: A diagnostic approach for education and organizations*. Cresskill, NJ: Hampton Press.

Cropley, A. J., & Field, T. W. (1968). Intellectual style and high school science. *Nature*, 217, 1211–1212.

Cropley, D. H. (1997). "Information and semiotics in measurement." PhD diss., University of South Australia, Adelaide, South Australia.

Cropley, D. H. (1998a). Towards formulating a semiotic theory of measurement information–Part 1: Fundamental concepts and measurement theory. *Measurement*, 24, 237–248.

Cropley, D. H. (1998b). Towards formulating a semiotic theory of measurement information–Part 2: Semiotics and related concepts. *Measurement*, 24, 249–262.

Cropley, D. H. (2005). *Eleven principles of creativity and terrorism*. Paper presented at the Fourth Homeland Security Summit and Exposition, Canberra, Australia.

Cropley, D. H. (2006). *The role of creativity as a driver of innovation.* Paper presented at the IEEE International Conference on the Management of Information Technology, Singapore.

Cropley, D. H. (2009). Fostering and measuring creativity and innovation: Individuals, organisations and products in measuring creativity. *Proceedings for the conference Can Creativity Be Measured?* (pp. 257–278). Brussels, May 2009.

Cropley, D. H. (2010). Malevolent innovation: Opposing the dark side of creativity. In D. H. Cropley, A. J. Cropley, J. C. Kaufman, & M. A. Runco (Eds.), *The dark side of creativity* (pp. 339–359). New York, NY: Cambridge University Press.

Cropley, D. H. (2014a). Engineering, ethics and creativity: N'er the twain shall meet? In S. Moran, D. H. Cropley, & J. C. Kaufman (Eds.), *The ethics of creativity* (pp. 152–169). Basingstoke, UK: Palgrave MacMillan Ltd.

Cropley, D. H. (2015). *Creativity in engineering: Novel solutions to complex problems.* San Diego, CA: Academic Press.

Cropley, D. H., & Cropley, A. J. (2000). Fostering creativity in engineering undergraduates. *High Ability Studies*, 11, 207–219.

Cropley, D. H., & Cropley, A. J. (2005). Engineering creativity: A systems concept of functional creativity. In J. C. Kaufman & J. Baer (Eds.), *Faces of the muse: How people think, work and act creatively in diverse domains* (pp. 169–185). Hillsdale: NJ: Lawrence Erlbaum.

Cropley, D. H., & Cropley, A. J. (2008). Elements of a universal aesthetic of creativity. *Psychology of Aesthetics, Creativity, and the Arts*, 2, 155–161.

Cropley, D. H., & Cropley, A. J. (2010). Understanding the innovation-friendly institutional environment: A psychological framework. *Baltic Journal of Psychology*, 11, 73–87.

Cropley, D. H., & Cropley, A. J. (2011). Understanding value innovation in organizations: A psychological framework. *International Journal of Creativity and Problem Solving*, 21, 17–36.

Cropley, D. H., & Cropley, A. J. (2012). A psychological taxonomy of organizational innovation: Resolving the paradoxes. *Creativity Research Journal*, 24, 29–40.

Cropley, D. H., & Cropley, A. J. (2013). *Creativity and crime: A psychological approach.* Cambridge, UK: Cambridge University Press.

Cropley, D. H., & Cropley, A. J. (2014). Managing entrepreneurship for innovation: A psychological analysis. In R. Sternberg & G. Krauss (Eds.), *Handbook of research on entrepreneurship and creativity* (pp. 21–59). Cheltenham, UK: Edward Elgar Publishing.

Cropley, D. H., Cropley, A. J., Chiera, B. A., & Kaufman, J. C. (2013). Diagnosing organizational innovation: Measuring the capacity for innovation. *Creativity Research Journal*, 25, 388–396.

Cropley, D. H., Cropley, A. J., Kaufman. J. C., & Runco, M. A. (Eds.) (2010). *The dark side of creativity*, New York, NY: Cambridge University Press.

Cropley, D. H., & Kaufman, J. C. (2012). Measuring functional creativity: Non-expert raters and the Creative Solution Diagnosis Scale. *The Journal of Creative Behavior*, 46, 119–137.

Cropley, D. H., & Kaufman, J. C. (2013). Rating the creativity of products. In K. Thomas & J. Chan (Eds.), *Handbook of research on creativity* (pp. 196–211). Cheltenham, UK: Edward Elgar Publishing.

Cropley, D. H., Kaufman, J. C., & Cropley, A. J. (2008). Malevolent creativity: A functional model of creativity in terrorism and crime. *Creativity Research Journal*, 20, 105–115.

Cropley, D. H., Kaufman, J. C., & Cropley, A. J. (2011). Measuring creativity for innovation management. *Journal of Technology Management & Innovation*, 6, 13–30.

Crozier, W. R. (1999). Age and individual differences in artistic productivity: Trends within a sample of British novelists. *Creativity Research Journal*, 12, 197–204.

Csikszentmihalyi, M. (1988). Society, culture, and person: A systems view of creativity. In R. J. Sternberg (Ed.), *The nature of creativity* (pp. 325–339). New York, NY: Cambridge University Press.

Csikszentmihalyi, M. (1996). *Creativity: Flow and the psychology of discovery and invention*. New York, NY: HarperCollins.

Csikszentmihalyi, M. (1999). Implications of a systems perspective for the study of creativity. In R. J. Sternberg (Ed.), *Handbook of creativity* (pp. 313–335). Cambridge, UK: Cambridge University Press.

Csikszentmihalyi, M. (2006). Foreword: Developing creativity. In N. Jackson, M. Oliver, M. Shaw, & J. Wisdom (Eds.), *Developing creativity in higher education: An imaginative curriculum* (pp. xviii–xx). London, UK: Routledge.

Csikszentmihalyi, M., Rathunde, K. R., & Whalen, S. (1993). *Talented teenagers: The roots of success and failure*. New York, NY: Cambridge University Press.

Damanpour, F. (1991). Organizational innovations: A meta-analysis of effects, of determinants and moderators. *Academy of Management Journal*, 34, 555–590.

Dasgupta, S. (2004). Is creativity a Darwinian process? *Creativity Research Journal*, 16, 403–414.

Davila, T., Epstein, M. J., & Shelton, R. (2012). *Making innovation work: How to manage it, measure it, and profit from it*. Upper Saddle River, NJ: FT Press.

Davis, M. A. (2009). Understanding the relationship between mood and creativity: A meta-analysis. *Organizational Behavior and Human Decision Processes*, 108, 25–38.

de Bono, E. (1993). *Water logic*. New York, NY: Viking Penguin.

De Dreu, C. K., & Nijstad, B. A. (2008). Mental set and creative thought in social conflict: Threat rigidity versus motivated focus. *Journal of Personality and Social Psychology*, 95(3), 648–661.

DeFillippi, R., Grabher, G., & Jones, C. (2007) Introduction to paradoxes of creativity: Managerial and organizational challenges in the cultural economy. *Journal of Organizational Behavior*, 28, 511–521.

Deming, W. E. (1986). *Out of the crisis*. Cambridge, MA: Massachusetts Institute of Technology.

Dennis, W. (1973). *Children of the crèche*. New York, NY: Appleton Century Crofts.

Descartes, R. (1991 [1644]). *Principles of philosophy*. (V. R. Miller & R. P. Miller, Trans.). Boston, MA: Kluwer.

DeVellis, R. F. (2012). *Scale development: Theory and applications*. Thousand Oaks, CA: Sage Publications.

Dillon, J. T. (1982). Problem finding and solving, *Journal of Creative Behavior*, 16, 97–111.

Dillon, T. A., Lee, R. K., & Matheson, D. (2005). Value innovation: Passport to wealth creation. *Research-Technology Management*, 48, 22–36.

Dul, J., & Ceylan, C. (2014). The impact of a creativity-supporting work environment on a firm's product innovation performance. *Journal of Product Innovation Management*, 31, 1254–1267.

Dul, J., Ceylan, C., & Jaspers, F. (2011). Knowledge workers' creativity and the role of the physical work environment. *Human Resource Management*, 50, 715–734.

Dyer, J. H., Gregersen, H., & Christensen, C. M. (2009). The innovator's DNA. *Harvard Business Review*, 87, 60–67, 128.

Ehrlinger, J., & Dunning, D. (2003). How chronic self-views influence (and potentially mislead) estimates of performance. *Journal of Personality and Social Psychology*, 84, 5–17.

Eisenman, R. (1999). Creative prisoners: Do they exist? *Creativity Research Journal*, 12, 205–210.

Ekvall, G. (1996). Organizational climate for creativity and innovation. *European Journal of Work and Organizational Psychology*, 5, 105–123.

Ericsson, K. A., & Lehmann, A. C. (1999). Expertise. In M. A. Runco & S. R. Pritzker (Eds.), *Encyclopedia of creativity* (pp. 695–707). San Diego, CA: Academic Press.

Eysenck, H. J. (1952). *The scientific study of personality*. London, UK: Routledge and Kegan Paul.

Facaoaru, C. (1985). *Kreativität in Wissenschaft und Technik* [Creativity in science and technology]. Bern, Switzerland: Huber.

Feldhusen, J. F. (1995). Creativity: A knowledge base, metacognitive skills, and personality factors. *Journal of Creative Behavior*, 29, 255–268.

Finke, R. A., Ward, T. B., & Smith, S. M. (1992). *Creative cognition*. Boston, MA: MIT Press.

Flavell, J. H. (1976). Metacognitive aspects of problem solving. In L. B. Resnick (Ed.), *The nature of intelligence* (pp. 231–236). Hillsdale, NJ: Erlbaum.

Florida, R. (2004). America's looming creativity crisis. *Harvard Business Review*, 82, 122–136.

Florida, R. (2011). *The great reset*. New York, NY: HarperBusiness.

Ford, C. M., & Gioia, D. A. (2000). Factors influencing creativity in the domain of managerial decision making. *Journal of Management*, 26, 705–732.

Frängsmyr, T. (1997). *Les prix nobel* [The Nobel Prizes 1996]. Stockholm, Sweden: Nobel Foundation.

Franses, P. H. (2013). When do painters make their best work? *Creativity Research Journal*, 25, 472–473.

Franses, P. H. (2014). When did Nobel Prize laureates in literature make their best work? *Creativity Research Journal*, 26, 372–374.

Frazier, P. A., Tix, A. P., & Barron, K. E. (2004). Testing moderator and mediator effects in counseling psychology research. *Journal of Counseling Psychology*, 51, 115–134.

Freeman, C., & Soete, L. (1997). *The economics of industrial innovation* (3rd ed.). Boston, MA: MIT Press.

Frese, M., & Fay, D. (2001). Personal initiative: An active performance concept for work in the 21st century. *Research in Organizational Behavior*, 23, 133–187.

Fromm, E. (1980). *Greatness and limitations of Freud's thought*. New York, NY: New American Library.

Gabora, L., & Tseng, S. (2014). Computational evidence that self-regulation of creativity is good for society. Retrieved August 21, 2014, from arXiv:1408.2512 [cs.CY]

Galenson, G. W. (2009). Old masters and young geniuses: The two life cycles of human creativity. *Journal of Applied Economics*, 12, 1–9.

Gardner, H. (1983). *Frames of mind: The theory of multiple intelligences*. New York, NY: Basic Books.

Gersick, C. J. G. (1991). Revolutionary change theories: A multilevel exploration of the punctuated equilibrium paradigm. *Academy of Management Review*, 16, 10–36.

Gertner, J. (2012). *The idea factory: Bell Labs and the great age of American innovation*. London, UK: The Penguin Press.

Getzels, J. W., & Jackson, P. W. (1962). *Creativity and intelligence*. New York, NY: Wiley.

Gino, F., & Ariely, D. (2012). The dark side of creativity: Original thinkers can be more dishonest. *Journal of Personality and Social Psychology*, 102, 445–459.

Glover, J. A., Ronning, R. R., & Reynolds, C. R. (Eds.). (1989). *Handbook of creativity*. New York, NY: Plenum.

Glück, J., Ernst, R., & Unger, F. (2002). How creatives define creativity: Definitions reflect different types of creativity. *Communication Research Journal*, 14, 55–67.

Goncalo, J. A., Vincent, L. C., & Audia, P. G. (2010). Early creativity as a constraint on future achievement. In D. H. Cropley, A. J. Cropley, J. C. Kaufman, & M. A. Runco (Eds.), *The dark side of creativity* (pp. 114–133). New York, NY: Cambridge University Press.

Gordon, W. J. (1961). *Synectics*. New York, NY: Harper.

Grace, J. B., Schoolmaster, D. R., Jr., Guntenspergen, G. R., Little, A. M., Mitchell, B. R., Miller, K. M., & Schweiger, E. W. (2012). Guidelines for a graph-theoretic implementation of structural equation modeling. Retrieved March 28, 2015, from http://dx.doi.org/10.1890/ES12-00048.1

Gribov, I. A. (1989). Psychological and educational conditions of development of creative self-expression of students and teachers. *Voprosy-Psikhologii*, 2, 75–82.

Gruber, H. E. (1993). Creativity in the moral domain: Ought implies can implies create. *Creativity Research Journal*, 6, 3–15.

Guilford, J. P. (1950). Creativity. *American Psychologist*, 5, 444–454.

Guilford, J. P. (1959). *Personality*. New York, NY: McGraw-Hill.

Gupta, A. K., Smith, K. G., & Shalley, C. E. (2006). The interplay between exploration and exploitation. *Academy of Management Journal*, 49, 693–706.

Haller, C. S., Courvoisier, D. S., & Cropley, D. H. (2010). Correlates of creativity among visual art students. *The International Journal of Creativity and Problem Solving*, 20, 53–71.

Haller, C. S., Courvoisier, D. S., & Cropley, D. H. (2011). Perhaps there is accounting for taste: Evaluating the creativity of products. *Creativity Research Journal*, 23, 99–109.

Hamel, G. (1996). Strategy as revolution. *Harvard Business Review*, 75, 69–82.

Han, S. H., Hwan Yun, M., Kim, K.-J., & Kwahk, J. (2000). Evaluation of product usability: Development and validation of usability dimensions and design elements based on empirical models. *International Journal of Industrial Ergonomics*, 26, 477–488.

Haner, U.-E. (2005). Spaces for creativity and innovation in two established organizations. *Creativity and Innovation Management*, 14, 288–298.

Hansen, J. A. (1992). Innovation, firm size, and firm age. *Small Business Economics*, 4, 37–44.

Harrington, D. M. (1999). Conditions and settings/environment. In M. A. Runco & S. R. Pritzker (Eds.), *Encyclopedia of creativity* (Vol. 1, pp. 323–340). San Diego, CA: Academic Press.

Harris, D. J., Reiter-Palmon, R., & Kaufman, J. C. (2013). The effect of emotional intelligence and task type on malevolent creativity. *Psychology of Aesthetics, Creativity, and the Arts*, 7, 237–244.

Hausman, C. R. (1984). *A discourse on novelty and creation*. Albany, NY: State University of New York Press.

Heimberg, C. L., Turk, D. S., & Mennin, R. G. (2004). *Generalized anxiety disorder: Advances in research and practice*. New York, NY: Guilford Press.

Helson, R. (1996). In search of the creative personality. *Creativity Research Journal*, 9, 295–306.

Helson, R. (1999). A longitudinal study of creative personality in women. *Creativity Research Journal*, 12, 89–101.

Hennessey, B. A. (1994). The consensual assessment technique: An examination of the relationship between ratings of product and process creativity. *Creativity Research Journal*, 7, 193–208.

Hennessey, B. A., & Amabile, T. (1999). Consensual assessment. In M. A. Runco & S. R. Pritzker (Eds.), *Encyclopedia of creativity* (pp. 347–359). San Diego, CA: Academic Press.

Hennessey, B. A., & Amabile, T. M. (2010). Creativity. *Annual Review of Psychology*, 61, 569–598.

Heron, W. (1957). The pathology of boredom. *Scientific American*, 52–56.

Herzog, P. (2008). *Open and closed innovation*. Wiesbaden, Germany: Gabler.

Higgins, J. M. (1995). *Innovate or evaporate: Test & improve your organization's IQ, its innovation quotient*. Winter Park, FL: The New Management Publishing Company.

Horenstein, M. N. (2002). *Design concepts for engineers* (2nd ed.). Upper Saddle River, NJ: Prentice-Hall.

Horibe, F. (2009). *Creating the innovation culture: Leveraging visionaries, dissenters and other useful troublemakers*. New York, NY: John Wiley & Sons.

Horn, D., & Salvendy, G. (2006). Consumer-based assessment of product creativity: A review and reappraisal. *Human Factors and Ergonomics in Manufacturing & Service Industries*, 16, 155–175.

Hudson, L. (1967). *Contrary imaginations: A psychological study of the English schoolboy*. Harmondsworth, UK: Penguin.

Hull, D. L., Tessner, P. D., & Diamond, A. M. (1978). Planck's principle. *Science*, 202, 717–723.

Hülsheger, U. R., Anderson, N., & Salgado, J. F. (2009). Team-level predictors of innovation at work: A comprehensive meta-analysis spanning three decades of research. *Journal of Applied Psychology*, 94, 1128–1145.

Hunter, S. T., Bedell, K. E., & Mumford, M. D. (2007). Climate for creativity: A quantitative review. *Creativity Research Journal*, 19, 69–90.
Huxley, L. (1901). *Life and letters of Thomas Henry Huxley* (Vol. 2). New York, NY: Appleton.
IBM. (2010). *Capitalizing on complexity: Insights from the Global Chief Executive Officer Study*. Somers, NY: IBM Global Business Services.
Isaksen, S. G. (2007). The Situational Outlook Questionnaire: Assessing the context for change. *Psychological Reports*, 100, 455–466.
Isaksen, S. G., Lauer, K. J., Ekvall, G., & Britz, A. (2001). Perceptions of the best and worst climates for creativity: Preliminary validation evidence for the situational outlook questionnaire. *Creativity Research Journal*, 13, 171–184.
Jackson, P. W., & Messick, S. (1965). The person, the product, and the response: Conceptual problems in the assessment of creativity. *Journal of Personality*, 33, 1122–1131.
Jay, E. S. & Perkins, D. N. (1997). Problem finding: The search for mechanisms. In M. A. Runco (Ed.), *The creativity research handbook* (Vol. 1, pp. 257–294). Cresskill, NJ: Hampton Press.
Johnson, D. L. (1979). *The creativity checklist*. Wood Dale, IL: Stoelting.
Josephson, M. (1959). *Edison: A biography*. New York, NY: Wiley.
Kampylis, P. G., & Valtanen, J. (2010). Redefining creativity: Analyzing definitions, collocations, and consequences. *Journal of Creative Behavior*, 44, 191–214.
Kanazawa, S. (2003). Why productivity fades with age: The crime-genius connection. *Journal of Research in Personality*, 37, 257–252.
Kaplan, R. S. (2001). Strategic performance measurement and management in nonprofit organizations. *Nonprofit Management and Leadership*, 11, 353–370.
Kaplan, R. S., & Norton, D. P. (1992). The Balanced Scorecard: Measures that drive performance. *Harvard Business Review*, 71–79.
Katz, D., & Kahn, R. L. (1978). *The social psychology of organizations* (2nd ed.). New York, NY: Wiley.
Kaufman, J. C., Baer, J., Cropley, D. H., Reiter-Palmon, R., & Sinnett, S. (2013). Furious activity vs. understanding: How much expertise is needed to evaluate creative work? *Psychology of Aesthetics, Creativity, and the Arts*, 7, 332–340.
Kaufman, G. (2003). Expanding the mood-creativity equation. *Creativity Research Journal*, 15, 131–135.
Kawenski, M. (1991). Encouraging creativity in design. *The Journal of Creative Behavior*, 25, 263–266.
Kemp, R. G. M., Folkeringa, M., De Jong, J. P. J., & Wubben, E. F. M. (2003). *Innovation and firm performance*. Zoetermeer, Netherlands: EIM Business & Policy Research.
Kim, J., & Han, S. H. (2008). A methodology for developing a usability index of consumer electronic products. *International Journal of Industrial Ergonomics*, 38, 333–345.
Kim, K. H. (2006). Can we trust creativity tests? A review of the Torrance Tests of Creative Thinking (TTCT). *Creativity Research Journal*, 18, 3–14.
Kim, K. H. (2011). The creativity crisis: The decrease in creative thinking scores on the Torrance Tests of Creative Thinking. *Creativity Research Journal*, 23, 285–295.

Kim, W. C., & Mauborgne, R. (2004). Value innovation: The strategic logic of high growth. *Harvard Business Review*, 82, 172–180.

King, N. (1992). Modelling the innovation process: An empirical comparison of approaches. *Journal of Occupational and Organizational Psychology*, 65, 89–100.

Kirton, M. (1989). *Adaptors and innovators: Styles of creativity and problem solving.* London, UK: Routledge.

Kitto, J., Lok, D., & Rudowicz, E. (1994). Measuring creative thinking: An activity-based approach. *Creativity Research Journal*, 7, 59–69.

Kleinknecht, A., & Mohnen, P. A. (Eds.). (2001). *Innovation and firm performance.* London, UK: Palgrave Macmillan.

Knapper, C., & Cropley, A. J. (2000). *Lifelong learning and higher education.* London, UK: Kogan Page.

Koberg, D., & Bagnall, J. (1991). *The all new universal traveler: A soft-systems guide to creativity, problem-solving, and the process of reaching goals.* Los Altos, CA: William Kaufmann, Inc.

Koellinger, P. (2008). The relationship between technology, innovation, and firm performance: Empirical evidence from e-business in Europe. *Research Policy*, 37, 1317–1328.

Kouzes, J. M., & Pozner, B. Z. (2012). *The leadership challenge* (5th ed.). San Francisco, CA: Jossey Bass.

Kozbelt, A., & Meredith, D. (2011). Composer age and melodic originality: A hierarchical linear modeling approach. *International Journal of Creativity and Problem Solving*, 21, 63–79.

Kriekels, J. (2013). *Innovate or die.* New York, NY: Lannoo Publishers.

Larey, T. S., & Paulus, P. B. (1999). Group preference and convergent tendencies in small groups: A content analysis of group brainstorming performance. *Creativity Research Journal*, 12, 175–184.

Lee, S., & Dow, G. T. (2011). Malevolent creativity: Does personality influence malicious divergent thinking? *Creativity Research Journal*, 23, 73–82.

Lehman, H. C. (1953). *Age and achievement.* Princeton, NJ: Princeton University Press.

Leifer, R., McDermott, C. M., O'Connor, G. C., & Peters, L. S. (2000). *Radical innovation: How mature companies can outsmart upstarts.* Boston, MA: Harvard Business Press.

Levitt, T. (2002, August). Creativity is not enough. *Harvard Business Review*, 80, 137–144.

Liedtka, J. (1998). Strategic thinking: Can it be taught? *Long Range Planning*, 31, 120–129.

Light, P. C. (1998). *Sustaining innovation: Creating non-profit and government organizations that innovate naturally.* San Diego, CA: Jossey Bass.

Lipman-Blumen, J. (1991). *Individual and organizational achieving styles: A handbook for researchers and human resource professionals* (4th ed.). Claremont, CA: Achieving Styles Institute.

Lipman-Blumen, J. (1996). *Women in corporate leadership: Reviewing a decade's research.* Wellesley, MA: Wellesley College Center for Research on Women.

Litwin, G., & Stringer, R. (1968). *Motivation and organizational climate.* Boston, MA: Harvard University Press.

Lonergan, D. C., Scott, G. M., & Mumford, M. D. (2004). Evaluative aspects of creative thought: Effects of appraisal and revision standards. *Creativity Research Journal*, 16, 231–246.

Luecke, R., & Katz, R. (2003). *Managing creativity and innovation*. Boston, MA: Harvard Business School Press.

Lynch, P., Walsh, M. M., & Harrington, D. (2010). *Defining and dimensionalizing organizational innovativeness*. Paper presented at the International CHRIE Conference, San Juan, Puerto Rico.

Mainemelis, C. (2010). Stealing fire: Creative deviance in the evolution of new ideas. *Academy of Management Review*, 35, 558–578.

Mann, E. L. (2009). The search for mathematical creativity: Identifying creative potential in middle school students. *Creativity Research Journal*, 21, 338–348.

Martindale, C. (1989). Personality, situation, and creativity. In J. A. Glover, R. R. Ronning, & C. R. Reynolds (Eds.), *Handbook of creativity* (pp. 211–228). New York, NY: Plenum.

Martindale, C. (1990). *The clockwork muse*. New York, NY: Basic Books.

Martinsen, O. L. (2011). The creative person: A synthesis and development of the creative person profile. *Creativity Research Journal*, 23, 185–202.

Mascitelli, R. (2000). From experience: Harnessing tacit knowledge to achieve breakthrough innovation. *Journal of Product Innovation Management*, 17, 179–193.

Maslow, A. H. (1973). Creativity in self-actualizing people. In A. Rothenberg & C. R. Hausman (Eds.), *The creative question* (pp. 86–92). Durham, NC: Duke University Press.

Mathisen, G. E., & Einarsen, S. (2004). A review of instruments assessing creative and innovative environments within organizations. *Creativity Research Journal*, 16, 119–140.

May, R. (1976). *The courage to create*. New York, NY: Bantam.

McLaren, R. B. (1993). The dark side of creativity. *Creativity Research Journal*, 6, 137–144.

McMullen, J. S., & Shepherd, D. A. (2006). Entrepreneurial action and the role of uncertainty in the theory of the entrepreneur. *Academy of Management Review*, 31, 132–152.

Michael, J. (2003). Using the Myers-Briggs Type Indicator as a tool for leadership development? Apply with caution. *Journal of Leadership & Organizational Studies*, 10, 68–81.

Michael, W. B., & Colson, K. R. (1979). The development and validation of a life experience inventory for the identification of creative electrical engineers. *Educational and Psychological Measurement*, 39, 463–470.

Milgram, R. M., & Hong, E. (1999). Creative out-of-school activities in intellectually gifted adolescents as predictors of their life accomplishments in young adults: A longitudinal study. *Creativity Research Journal*, 12, 77–88.

Miller, D. (1983). The correlates of entrepreneurship in three types of firms. *Management Science*, 29, 770–791.

Millward, L. J., & Freeman, H. (2002). Role expectations as constraints to innovation: The case of female managers. *Creativity Research Journal*, 14, 93–110.

Miron-Spektor, E., Erez, M., & Naveh, E. (2011). The effect of conformist and attentive-to-detail members on team innovation: Reconciling the innovation paradox. *Academy of Management Journal*, 54, 740–760.

Mokyr, J. (1990). *The lever of riches: Technological creativity and economic progress*. New York, NY: Oxford University Press.

Moran, S., Cropley, D. H., & Kaufman, J. C. (Eds.). (2014). *The ethics of creativity*. Basingstoke, UK: Palgrave MacMillan.

Morgan, D. N. (1953). Creativity today: A constructive analytic review of certain philosophical and psychological work. *The Journal of Aesthetics and Art Criticism*, 12, 1–24.

Mostafa, M. (2005). Factors affecting organisational creativity and innovativeness in Egyptian business organisations: An empirical investigation. *Journal of Management Development*, 24, 7–33.

Moustakis, C. E. (1977). *Creative life*. New York, NY: Van Nostrand.

Mueller, J. S., Melwani, S., & Goncalo, J. A. (2012). The bias against creativity: Why people desire but reject creative ideas. *Psychological Science*, 23, 13–17.

Mumford, M. D. (Ed.). (2012). *Handbook of organizational creativity*. London, UK: Academic Press.

Mumford, M. D., Antes, A. L., Caughron, J. J., Connelly, S., & Beeler, C. (2010). Cross-field differences in creative problem-solving skills: A comparison of health, biological, and social sciences. *Creativity Research Journal*, 22, 14–26.

Mumford, M. D., Baughman, W. A., Maher, M. A., Costanza, D. P., & Supinski, E. P. (1997). Process-based measures of creative problem-solving skills: IV. Category combination. *Creativity Research Journal*, 10, 59–71.

Mumford, M. D., Baughman, W. A., Threlfall, K. V., Supinski, E. P., & Costanza, D. P. (1996). Process-based measures of creative problem-solving skills: I. Problem construction. *Creativity Research Journal*, 9, 63–76.

Mumford, M. D., Bedell-Avers, K. E., & Hunter, S. T. (2008). Planning for innovation: A multi-level perspective. In M. D. Mumford, S. T. Hunter, & K. E. Bedell (Eds.), *Innovation in organizations: A multi-level perspective* (pp. 107–154). Oxford, UK: Elsevier.

Mumford, M. D., Hester, K. S., & Robledo, I. C. (2012). Creativity in organizations: importance and approaches. In M. D. Mumford (Ed.), *Handbook of organizational creativity*. London, UK: Academic Press.

Mumford, M. D., & Moertl, P. (2003). Cases of social innovation: lessons from two innovations in the 20th century. *Creativity Research Journal*, 15, 261–266.

Mumford, M. D., Scott, G. M., Gaddis, B., & Strange, J. M. (2002). Leading creative people: Orchestrating expertise and relationships. *The Leadership Quarterly*, 13, 705–750.

Myers-Briggs, I., & McCaulley, M. H. (1992). *Manual: A guide to the development and use of the Myers-Briggs Type Indicator*. Palo Alto, CA: Consulting Psychologists Press.

Nebel, C. (1988). *The dark side of creativity: Blocks, unfinished works and the urge to destroy*. New York, NY: Whitston Publishing Company.

Nussbaum, B. (2013). *Creative intelligence: Harnessing the power to create, connect, and inspire*. New York, NY: HarperCollins.

OECD. (2005). *Oslo Manual: Guidelines for collecting and interpreting innovation data* (3rd ed.). Paris, France: Author.

Oldham, G. R., & Cummings, A. (1996). Employee creativity: Personal and contextual factors at work. *Academy of Management Journal*, 39, 607–634.

Olson, M. (1982). *The rise and decline of nations*. New Haven, CT: Yale University Press.

Oman, S. K., Tumer, I. Y., Wood, K., & Seepersad, C. (2013). A comparison of creativity and innovation metrics and sample validation through in-class design projects. *Research in Engineering Design*, 24, 65–92.

O'Shea, D., & Buckley, F. (2007). Towards an integrative model of creativity and innovation in organisations: A psychological perspective. *The Irish Journal of Psychology*, 28, 101–128.

Park, J., & Jang, K. (2005). Analysis of the actual scientific inquiries of physicists. Retrieved September 17, 2014, from www.arxiv.org/abs/physics/0506191

Parker, S. K., Williams, H. M., & Turner, N. (2006). Modeling the antecedents of proactive behavior at work. *Journal of Applied Psychology*, 91, 636–652.

Paulus, P. B. (1999). Group creativity. In M. A. Runco & S. R. Pritzker (Eds.), *Encyclopedia of creativity* (pp. 779–784). San Diego, CA: Academic Press.

Paulus, P. B. (2002). Different ponds for different fish: A contrasting perspective on team innovation. *Applied Psychology: An International Review*, 51, 394–399.

Paulus, P. B., & Nijstad, B. A. (2003). *Group creativity: Innovation through collaboration*. New York, NY: Oxford University Press.

Perkins, D. N. (1981). *The mind's best work*. Cambridge, MA: Harvard University Press.

Petersen, S. (1989). *Motivation von Laienautoren* [Motivation of hobby authors]. Unpublished master's thesis, University of Hamburg.

Piaget J., & Inhelder, B. (1969). *The psychology of the child*. New York, NY: Basic Books.

Pilzer, P. Z. (1990). *Unlimited wealth: The theory and practice of economic alchemy*. New York, NY: Crown Publishers.

Pink, D. H. (2005). *A whole new mind: Moving from the information age into the conceptual age*. London, UK: Allen & Unwin.

Planck, M. (1948). *Wissenschaftliche Selbstbiographie. Mit einem Bildnis und der von Max von Laue gehaltenen Traueransprache* [Usually referred to in English as "Scientific autobiography and other papers"]. Leipzig, Germany: Johann Ambrosius Barth Verlag.

Plsek, P. E., & Bevan, H. (2003). Organizational culture for innovation self-assessment. IHI Forum 04. Retrieved September 28, 2014, from http://www.directedcreativity.com/pages/SpiderDiagram.pdf

Plucker, J. A. (1999). Is the proof in the pudding? Reanalyses of Torrance's (1958 to present) longitudinal data. *Creativity Research Journal*, 12, 103–114.

Plucker, J. A., & Makel, M. C. (2010). Assessment of creativity. In J. C. Kaufman & R. J. Sternberg (Eds.), *The Cambridge handbook of creativity* (pp. 48–73). New York, NY: Cambridge University Press.

Prindle, E. J. (1906). The art of inventing. *Transactions of the American Institute for Engineering Education*, 25, 519–547.

Proctor, R. M. J., & Burnett, P. C. (2004). Measuring cognitive and dispositional characteristics of creativity in elementary students. *Creativity Research Journal*, 16, 421–429.

Puccio, G. J. (1999). Teams. In M. A. Runco & S. R. Pritzker (Eds.), *Encyclopedia of creativity* (pp. 640–649). San Diego, CA: Academic Press.

Puccio, G. J., & Cabra, J. F. (2010). Organizational creativity: A systems approach. In J. C. Kaufman & R. J. Sternberg (Eds.), *The Cambridge handbook of creativity* (pp. 145–173). New York, NY: Cambridge University Press.

Puccio, G. J., Murdock, M. C., & Mance, M. (2005). Current developments in creative problem solving for organizations: A focus on thinking skills and styles. *Korean Journal of Thinking and Problem Solving*, 15, 43.

Puccio, G. J., Treffinger, D. J., & Talbot, R. J. (1995). Exploratory examination of the relationship between creativity styles and creative products. *Creativity Research Journal*, 8, 152–157.

Raisch, S., Birkinshaw, J., Probst, G., & Tushman, M. L. (2009). Organizational ambidexterity: Balancing exploitation and exploration for sustained performance. *Organization Science*, 20, 685–695.

Rauch, A., Wiklund, J., Lumpkin, G. T., & Frese, M. (2009). Entrepreneurial orientation and business performance: An assessment of past research and suggestions for the future. *Entrepreneurship Theory and Practice*, 33, 761–787.

Read, A. (2000). Determinants of successful organisational innovation: A review of current research. *Journal of Management Practice*, 3, 95–119.

Rechtin, E., & Maier, M. W. (2000). *The art of systems architecting*. Boca Raton, FL: CRC Press.

Reis, S. M., & Renzulli, J. S. (1991). The assessment of creative products in programs for gifted and talented students. *Gifted Child Quarterly*, 35, 128–134.

Reiter-Palmon, R., Illies, M. Y., Cross, L. K., Buboltz, C., & Nimps, T. (2009). Creativity and domain specificity: The effect of task type on multiple indexes of creative problem-solving. *Psychology of Aesthetics, Creativity, and the Arts*, 3, 73–80.

Rhodes, M. (1961). An analysis of creativity. *The Phi Delta Kappan*, 42, 305–310.

Richards, R. (Ed.). (2007). *Everyday creativity and new views of human nature: Psychological, social, and spiritual perspectives*. Washington, DC: American Psychological Association.

Rickards, T. J. (1993). Creativity from a business school perspective: Past, present and future. In S. G. Isaksen, M. C. Murdock, R. L. Firestien, & D. J. Treffinger (Eds.), *Nurturing and developing creativity: The emergence of a discipline* (pp. 155–176). Norwood, NJ: Ablex.

Rietzschel, E. F., Nijstad, B. A., & Stroebe, W. (2010). The selection of creative ideas after individual idea generation: Choosing between creativity and impact. *British Journal of Psychology*, 101, 47–68.

Roberts, E. B. (1988). Managing invention & innovation. *Research Technology Management*, 33, 1–19.

Rogers, C. R. (1961). *On becoming a person*. Boston, MA: Houghton.

Root-Bernstein, R. S. (1989). Productivity and age. In M. A. Runco & S. R. Pritzker (Eds.), *Encyclopedia of creativity* (Vol. 2, pp. 457–463). San Diego, CA: Academic Press.

Root-Bernstein, R. S., Bernstein, M., & Garnier, H. (1993). Identification of scientists making long-term high-impact contributions, with notes on their methods of working. *Creativity Research Journal*, 6, 329–343.

Rosenbusch, N., Brinckmann, J., & Bausch, A. (2011). Is innovation always beneficial? A meta-analysis of the relationship between innovation and performance in SMEs. *Journal of Business Venturing*, 26, 441–457.

Rosenman, M. F. (1988). Serendipity and scientific discovery. *Journal of Creative Behavior*, 22, 132–138.

Ross, L., & Nisbett, R. (1991). *The person and the situation: Perspectives of social psychology*. New York, NY: McGraw Hill.

Rossman, J. (1931). *The psychology of the inventor: A study of the patentee*. Washington, DC: Inventors' Publishing Company.

Rothenberg, A. (1983). Psychopathology and creative cognition: A comparison of hospitalized patients, Nobel laureates and controls. *Archives of General Psychiatry*, 40, 937–942.

Rothman, J. (2014). Creativity creep. Retrieved March 28, 2014, from http://www.newyorker.com/books/joshua-rothman/creativity-creep?utm_source=tnyandutm_campaign=generalsocialandutm_medium=twitterandmbid=social_twitter.

Runco, M. A. (1993). Creative morality: Intentional and unconventional. *Creativity Research Journal*, 6, 17–28.

Runco, M. A. (2003). (Ed.). *Critical creative processes*. Cresskill, NJ: Hampton Press.

Runco, M. A., & Jaeger, G. J. (2012). The standard definition of creativity. *Creativity Research Journal*, 24, 92–96.

Runco, M. A., & Nemiro, J. (2003). Creativity in the moral domain: Integration and implications. *Creativity Research Journal*, 15, 91–105.

Runco, M. A., Plucker, J. A., & Lim, W. (2001). Development and psychometric integrity of a measure of ideational behavior. *Creativity Research Journal*, 13, 393–400.

Ruth, J. E., & Birren, J. E. (1985). Creativity in adulthood and old age: Relations to intelligence, sex and mode of testing. *International Journal of Behavioral Development*, 8, 99–109.

Savransky, S. D. (2000). *Engineering of creativity*. Boca Raton, FL: CRC Press.

Sawyer, R. K. (2006). Educating for innovation. *Thinking Skills and Creativity*, 1, 41–48.

Schein, V. E. (1994). Managerial sex typing: A persistent and pervasive barrier to women's opportunities. In M. J. Davidson & R. J. Burke (Eds.), *Women in management: Current research issues* (pp. 65–84). London, UK: Chapman.

Schermerhorn, J. M. (2012). *Management* (12th ed.). Hoboken, NJ: Wiley.

Schuldberg, D. (2001). Six subclinical spectrum traits in normal creativity. *Creativity Research Journal*, 13, 5–16.

Schwebel, M. (1993). Moral creativity as artistic transformation. *Creativity Research Journal*, 6, 65–81.

Scott, S. G., & Bruce, R. A. (1994). Determinants of innovative behaviour: A path model of individual innovation in the workplace. *Academy of Management Journal*, 37, 580–607.

Scott, T. E. (1999). Knowledge. In M. A. Runco & S. R. Pritzker (Eds.), *Encyclopedia of creativity* (Vol. 2, pp. 119–129). San Diego, CA: Academic Press.

Sekaran, U. (2006). *Research methods for business: A skill building approach.* New York, NY: John Wiley & Sons.

Shaw, M. P. (1989). The Eureka process: A structure for the creative experience in science and engineering. *Creativity Research Journal*, 2, 286–298.

Shelton, R. D. (2001). Developing an internal marketplace for innovation: Balancing creativity and commercialization. *Prism*(1), 15–19.

Siegel, S. M., & Kaemmerer, W. F. (1978). Measuring the perceived support for innovation in organizations. *Journal of Applied Psychology*, 63, 553–562.

Silvia, P. J. (2008). Discernment and creativity: How well can people identify their most creative ideas? *Psychology of Aesthetics, Creativity, and the Arts*, 2, 139–146.

Silvia, P. J., Kaufman, J. C., Reiter-Palmon, R., & Wigert, B. (2011). Cantankerous creativity: Honesty-humility, agreeableness, and the HEXACO structure of creative achievement. *Personality and Individual Differences*, 51, 687–689.

Simon, H. A. (1989). The scientist as a problem solver. In D. Klahr & K. Kotovsky (Eds.), *Complex information processing* (pp. 375–398). Hillsdale, NJ: Erlbaum.

Simonton, D. K. (1994). *Greatness: Who makes history and why?* New York, NY: Guilford.

Simonton, D. K. (1997). Historiometric studies of creative genius. In M. A. Runco (Ed.), *The creativity research handbook* (Vol. 1, pp. 3–28). Creskill, NJ: Hampton Press.

Simonton, D. K. (1998). Masterpieces in music and literature: Historiometric inquires. *Creativity Research Journal*, 11, 103–110.

Simonton, D. K. (1999). *Origins of genius: Darwinian perspectives of creativity.* New York, NY: Oxford University Press.

Simonton, D. K. (2009). Varieties of (scientific) creativity: A hierarchical model of domain-specific disposition, development, and achievement. *Perspectives on Psychological Science*, 4, 441–452.

Smith, W. K. (2009). A dynamic approach to managing contradictions. *Industrial and Organizational Psychology*, 2, 338–343.

Smith, W. K., & Lewis, M. W. (2011). Toward a theory of paradox: A dynamic equilibrium model of organizing. *Academy of Management Review*, 36, 381–403.

Sosa, R., & Gero, J. S. (2003). Design and change: A model of situated creativity. In C. Bento, A. Cardosa & J. S. Gero (Eds.), *Approaches to creativity in artificial intelligence and cognitive science* (pp. 25–34). Acapulco: IJCAI03.

Staw, B. M. (1995). Why no one really wants creativity. In C. Ford & D. Gioia (Eds.), *Creative action in organizations: Ivory towers and real voices* (pp. 161–166). Los Angeles, CA: Sage.

Stenmark, D. (2005). Organisational creativity in context: Learning from a failing attempt to introduce IT support for creativity. *International Journal of Technology and Human Interaction*, 1, 80–98.

Sternberg, R. J. (1985). *Beyond IQ: A triarchic theory of human intelligence.* New York, NY: Cambridge University Press.

Sternberg, R. J. (1998). A balance theory of wisdom. *Review of General Psychology*, 2, 347–365.

Sternberg, R. J. (2003). *Wisdom, intelligence, and creativity synthesized.* New York, NY: Cambridge University Press.
Sternberg, R. J. (2006). The nature of creativity. *Creativity Research Journal,* 18, 87–98.
Sternberg, R. J. (2007). Creativity as a habit. In Tan, A.-G. (Ed.), *Creativity: A handbook for teachers* (pp. 3–26). Singapore: World Scientific Publishing Company.
Sternberg, R. J., Kaufman, J. C., & Pretz, J. E. (2002). *The creativity conundrum: A propulsion model of kinds of creative contributions.* New York, NY: Psychology Press.
Sternberg, R. J., & Lubart, T. I. (1995). *Defying the crowd: Cultivating creativity in a culture of conformity.* New York, NY: Free Press.
Taggar, S., Sulsky, L., & MacDonald, H. (2008). Sub-system configuration: A model of strategy, context, and human resource management alignment. In M. D. Mumford, S. T. Hunter, & K. E. Bedell-Avers (Eds.), *Multi-level issues in creativity and innovation* (pp. 317–376). New York, NY: Elsevier.
Tardif, T. Z., & Sternberg, R. J. (1988). What do we know about creativity? In R. J. Sternberg (Ed.), *The nature of creativity* (pp. 429–440). New York, NY: Cambridge University Press.
Taylor, I. A. (1975). An emerging view of creative actions. In I. A. Taylor & J. W. Getzels (Eds.), *Perspectives in creativity* (pp. 297–325). Chicago, IL: Aldine.
Thanksgiving for Innovation. (2002, September 21). *Economist Technology Quarterly,* 13–14.
Thomson, W. (1889). Electrical units of measurement. In W. Thomson (Ed.), *Nature series: Popular lectures and addresses, Vol. 1: Constitution of matter* (pp. 73–136). London, UK: MacMillan and Co.
Tierney, P., & Farmer, S. M. (2011). Creative self-efficacy development and creative performance over time. *Journal of Applied Psychology,* 96, 277–293.
Torrance, E. P. (1963). *Education and the creative potential.* Minneapolis, MN: University of Minnesota Press.
Torrance, E. P. (2007). *Torrance Test of Creative Thinking: Norms and technical manual.* Bensenville, IL: Scholastic Testing Services.
Treffinger, D. J. (1985). Review of Torrance Tests of Creative Thinking. In J. V. Mitchell (Ed.), *Ninth mental measurements yearbook* (pp. 1632–1634). Lincoln, NE: University of Nebraska Press.
Treffinger, D. J. (1995). Creative problem solving: Overview and educational implications. *Educational Psychology Review,* 7, 301–312.
Urban, K. K. & Jellen, H. G. (2010). *Manual for Test for Creative Thinking: Drawing Production (TCT-DP).* Frankfurt, Germany: Pearson.
Van de Ven, A. H. (1986). Central problems in the management of innovation. *Management Science,* 32, 590–607.
Van de Ven, A. H., Poole, M. S., & Angle, H. L. (2000). *Research on the management of innovation.* Oxford, UK: Oxford University Press.
VanGundy, A. B. (1984). *Managing group creativity: A modular approach to problem solving.* New York, NY: American Management Association.
Veryzer, R. W. (1998). Discontinuous innovation and the new product development process. *Journal of Product Innovation Management,* 15, 304–321.

Vincent, L. H., Bharadwaj, S. G., & Challagalla, G. N. (2004). Does innovation mediate firm performance? A meta-analysis of determinants and consequences of organizational innovation. Unpublished working paper. Georgia Institute of Technology.

Vosburg, S. K. (1998). Mood and the quantity and quality of ideas. *Creativity Research Journal*, 11, 315–324.

Walberg, H. J., & Stariha, W. E. (1992). Productive human capital: Learning, creativity and eminence. *Creativity Research Journal*, 5, 323–340.

Walczyk, J. J., Runco, M. A., Tripp, S. M., & Smith, C. E. (2008). The creativity of lying: Divergent thinking and ideational correlates of the resolution of social dilemmas. *Creativity Research Journal*, 20, 328–342.

Walk, C. L. (1996). *Management and leadership. MBTI applications: A decade of research on the Myers-Briggs Type Indicator*. Palo Alto, CA: Consulting Psychology Press.

Wallach, M. A., & Kogan, N. (1965). *Modes of thinking in young children*. New York, NY: Holt, Rinehart and Winston.

Wallas, G. (1926). *The art of thought*. New York, NY: Harcourt Brace.

Walton, A. P. (2003). The impact of interpersonal factors on creativity. *International Journal of Entrepreneurial Behavior & Research*, 9, 146–162.

Ward, T. B. (2004). Cognition, creativity, and entrepreneurship. *Journal of Business Venturing*, 19, 173–188.

Ward, T. B., & Kolomyts, Y. (2010). Cognition and creativity. In J. C. Kaufman & R. J. Sternberg (Eds.), *The Cambridge handbook of creativity* (pp. 74–90). New York, NY: Cambridge University Press.

West, M. A. (2002). Sparkling fountains or stagnant ponds: An integrative model of creativity and innovation implementation in work groups. *Applied Psychology*, 51, 355–387.

West, M. A., & Rickards, T. (1999). Innovation. In M. A. Runco & S. R. Pritzker (Eds.), *Encyclopedia of creativity* (pp. 45–55). San Diego, CA: Academic Press.

West, S., Hoff, E., & Carlsson, I. (2013). Playing at work: Professionals' perceptions of the functions of play on organizational creativity. *International Journal of Creativity and Problem-Solving*, 23, 5–23.

Westby, E. L., & Dawson, V. L. (1995). Creativity: Asset or burden in the classroom? *Creativity Research Journal*, 8, 1–10.

Williams, C. C. (2007). The nature of entrepreneurship in the informal sector: Evidence from England. *Journal of Enterprising Communities, People and Places in the Global Economy*, 1, 27–37.

Woodman, R. W., Sawyer, J. E., & Griffin, R. W. (1993). Toward a theory of organizational creativity. *Academy of Management Review*, 18, 293–321.

Wortman, C. B., Loftus, E. F., & Marchall, M. E. (1985). *Psychology* (2nd ed.). New York, NY: Alfred A. Knopf.

Yamin, S., Gunasekaran, A., & Mavondo, F. T. (1999). Innovation index and its implications on organisational performance: A study of Australian manufacturing companies. *International Journal of Technology Management*, 17, 495–503.

Yue, X. D., Bender, M., & Cheung, C. K. (2011). Who are the best known national and foreign creators: A comparative study among undergraduates in China and Germany. *Journal of Creative Behavior*, 45, 23–37.

Zhou, J., & Shalley, C. E. (2008). Expanding the scope and impact of organizational creativity research. In J. Zhou & C. E. Shalley (Eds.), *Handbook of organizational creativity* (pp. 347–368). New York, NY: Erlbaum.

Zuckerman, M. (1969). Theoretical formulations. In J. Zubek (Ed.), *Sensory deprivation: Fifteen years of research* (pp. 407–432). New York, NY: Appleton-Century-Crofts.

INDEX